LATIN LOVER
THE PASSIONATE SOUTH

Rudolph Valentino (Ullstein Bilderdienst)

ISBN 88-8158-049-7

LATIN LOVER
THE PASSIONATE SOUTH

Edited by

Giannino Malossi

Graphic Designer

Italo Lupi

With contributions by

Giuliano Accordi

Franco La Cecla

Loredana Leconte

Giannino Malossi

Alberto Panaro

Lorenzo Pellizzari

Laura Piccinini

Norma Rangeri

Maurizio Rebuzzini

Carlo Romano

Luigi Settembrini

Antony Shugaar

Giorgio Triani

CHARTA

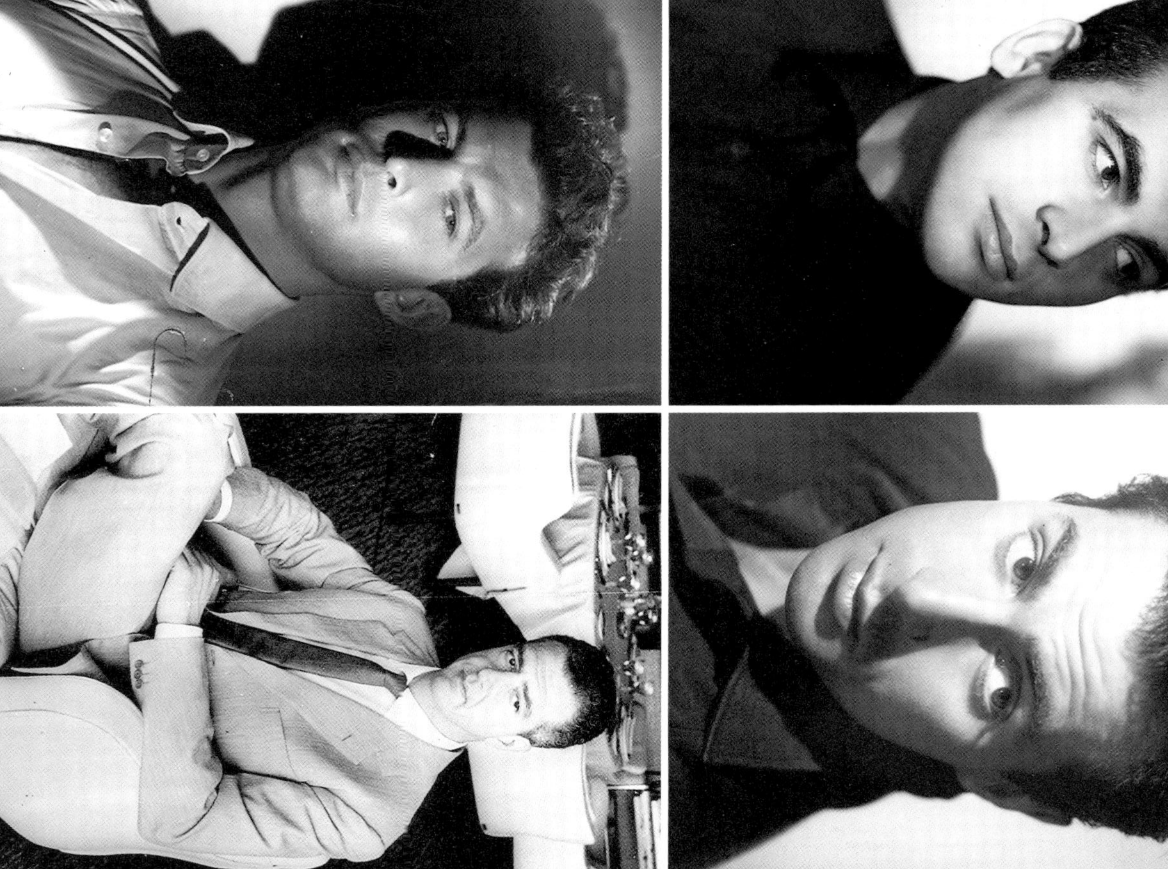

Erno Crisa (Archivio Frassa)

Maurizio Arena (Publifoto)

▼ *Rossano Brazzi (Ullstein Bilderdienst)*

Baby Pignatari (Farabolafoto)

Antonio Cifariello (Archivio Frassa)

Vittorio Gassman (Publifoto)

Amedeo Nazzari (Farabolafoto)

Marcello Mastroianni (Publifoto)

Don Jaime de Mora y Aragon (Ullstein Bilderdienst)

Mario Lanza (Hulton Deutsch Collection)

Walter Chiari (Farabolafoto)

Porfirio Rubirosa (Farabolafoto)

▼ Rudolph Valentino (Kobal Collection)

LATIN LOVER
THE PASSIONATE SOUTH

An exhibition, a book
and a special event
produced by Pitti Immagine,
with the contribution of Ente Moda
Italia and the Ministero
del Commercio con l'Estero

11th January–15th February 1996
Florence, Stazione Leopolda

Project Director of the Exhibition
Luigi Settembrini

Art Direction
Italo Lupi

Artistic Coordinator
Gherardo Frassa

Research
Frassa Associati
Annmaree Kealy
Alberto Panaro
Gisella Canali

Video Production
Show Biz Srl Milano
Texts
Alberto Panaro
Direction
Daniela Frassoni
Montage
Fabrizia Vitaletti
Executive Producer
Ranuccio Sodi
Thanks to
Cineteca del Friuli, Gemona
Civica Raccolta delle Stampe A. Bertarelli,
Castello Sforzesco, Milan
Casa Editrice Universo, author of the
drawing Walter Molino
Gemma Testa, Agenzia Armando Testa,
Turin

Public Relations
Sibilla della Gherardesca

Press Office
Cristina Brigidini

Production Secretary
Anna Pazzagli

Pitti Immagine thanks
Samuele Mazza
for his help in planning the project

Project and Editor of the book
Giannino Malossi

Art Direction
Italo Lupi

Layout
Silvia Garofoli Kihlgren

Documentation
Alberto Panaro

Photographic Research
Giannino Malossi
Annmaree Kealy

Production Assistant
Annmaree Kealy

Special thanks to
Archivio Brandini-Sanguinetti, Rome
Biblioteca Comunale, Milan
Cineteca Comunale, Bologna
Dino Jarak, Milan
Farabolafoto, Milan
Giancolombo, Milan
Giornalfoto, Milan
Sandro Girella, Milan
Grazia Neri, Milan
Hulton Deutsch Collection, London
Kobal Collection, London
Musée Granet, Aix-en-Provence
Museo Nazionale del Cinema, Turin
Ruth Orkin Archive, New York
Publifoto, Milan
Ullstein Bilderdienst, Berlin

and also
Sybille Bolmann, Romano Frassa,
Antony Shugaar, Santi Urso
*and for the special creative
contribution*
Roberto Rosati

Press Office Charta
Silvia Palombi Arte & Mostre, Milan

Design Coordination
Gabriele Nason

Editorial Coordination
Emanuela Belloni

Editing
Anna Albano, Emanuela Di Lallo

Technical Project
Amilcare Pizzi Arti grafiche, Cinisello
Balsamo, Milan

Translated from the Italian by
F.B. Lutz, S. White and A. Victor,
for Scriptum Srl, Rome

Cover: Rudolph Valentino in Blood and Sand, *1922 (Kobal Collection)*

Camille, *1921*, *with Alla Nazimova* *(Kobal Collection)*

Tamara Lees and Leonardo Cortese, Canzoni di Primavera *(Spring Songs) by Mario Costa, 1951 (Archivio Brandini-Sanguinetti)*

Pitti Immagine organizes fairs in the textile and clothing sector, events that many people consider to be amongst the most important and influential in the world. This book and the interesting exhibition at Stazione Leopolda, which, to coincide with the Pitti Uomo Fashion Show, will display this and other material on the same theme, are the most recent Pitti Immagine cultural products.
Industry, commerce and culture, therefore. Or rather: industry and commerce also seen as cultural phenomena. For at least ten years we have been offering—in addition to our exhibitions—many different initiatives that have contributed towards focusing not merely on the commercial aspects of fashion, for a general public not only consisting of experts and specialists. It is not solely a Pitti Immagine discovery that fashion is part of the cultural background belonging to both groups and individuals, that it influences and is influenced by other creative languages, and by changes in lifestyle and social relations. It is becoming increasingly evident that the production, distribution and consumption of fashion products is closely interwoven with our need for self-expression. And the longstanding textile and clothing industry is light-years ahead in this field, thanks to excellent communication in everything that concerns it.
Pitti Immagine must be given credit for promptly recognizing great changes and for having displayed them in that well-established ritual

known as the trade fair. We have produced exhibitions, events, publications, researches, conferences, shows and—via all this—we have added a new dimension to traditional trade fairs.
These initiatives have made a vital contribution to the success of Pitti events, because experts in this sector have gleaned useful and up-to-date information and hints that have helped them hold their own in an increasingly mature, demanding and complex market.
Finally, a last word on the theme of the book and the exhibition.
Dealing with the subject of the Latin lover today represents something of a provocation, even though, in the rather problematic scenario of relations between the sexes at the end of this millennium, seduction lends itself to considerations that are far from marginal. But it is above all a further chapter in the enquiry into the popular and universal image of Italy and Italians which we have already dealt with in the past. This is interesting because it seems to include some elements which later find their way into Italian fashions and make them an international success.
In fact, from this point of view, the provocation has been useful and the various people who have been "provoked" to write texts for this book have also made it intelligent.

Mario Boselli
President of Pitti Immagine

CONTENTS

A Sainted Devil, 1924, *with Helen d'Algy (Kobal Collection)*

latin lover [*pr.ingl.* /ˈlætinˈlʌvə/] *loc.sost.m.invar.* amante di temperamento focoso ma romantico, come, soprattutto nei paesi nordeuropei, si ritiene che siano gli uomini dei paesi latini; conquistatore, seduttore ¶ Loc. ingl.; propr. 'amante (*lover*) latino (*latin*)'.

Latin lover: passionate, but romantic, lover; it is believed, above all in Northern European countries, that they are men from Latin countries; heartbreaker, seducer.

Heading from: Il grande dizionario, *Garzanti, Milano 1987*

INTRODUCTION
THE BANALITY OF THE LATIN LOVER

Giannino Malossi

This book could be considered a monument (a Trajan's Column?) to one of the most obvious male icons: that irresistible seducer, the Latin lover of film, pop songs and gossip columns.

In this age it is licit to suspect cultural analysis of national/popular legends of being revisionist and an attempt to revive it. We have tried not to slide into cheap indulgence for imagery which in its superficial joviality defines the limits of subordination in the roles and relationships between the sexes. Every Latin lover thinks that sooner or later his prey will say the words that epitomize Rudolph Valentino's career: "I am not afraid when I'm in your arms, Ahmed, my desert love, my sheik."[1]

But what at best we may define as the anachronism of the Latin lover does not prevent us from dispensing with rhetoric in an examination of this model of male categorization so common in the media that it has become a cliché through which Italians and non-Italians perceive one another. Lack of attention to the superficial aspects of behaviour and lack of research into popular Italian culture is one of the biggest obstacles in the path of renewing Italy's common national identity, and indeed goes some way towards explaining its listless identity within the context of global Pop culture. On the other hand, do not bother to read on if you are driven by a "politically correctness," of the sort that inspires the ever-present warnings you read about in tourist guides for the English and Americans: here we shall range freely from tango dancers to louts. Moral standpoints, like ideological standpoints, are not useful research tools. What rankles in the Latin lover is not so much his tendency towards sexual harassment, but the total lack of perception of other possible roles, as he continues to remain the same while everything around him changes. It is not his longing look which is offensive, it is his outlook. As for us, we have known for some time, with Adorno, that "there is no longer beauty or consolation except in the gaze falling on horror, withstanding it, and in unalleviated consciousness of negativity holding fast the possibility of what is better."[2]

The figure of the Latin lover does not surprise, it is nothing new, it has been with us for at least the last seventy years. If anything it should surprise us that it continues to exist, that it continues to "play a part in society." Raul Vaneigem's words fit the situation perfectly: "To the extent that the role becomes one with a stereotype,

Rudolph Valentino in A Sainted Devil, *1924 (Ullstein Bilderdienst)*

[1] *Lady Diana (Agnes Ayers) and Ahmed (Rodolfo Valentino) in The Sheik, Paramount, 1921.*

[2] *Theodor W. Adorno, Minima Moralia, London 1954, p. 25.*

it tends to become fixed, to take on the static nature of its model. It has neither present, past nor future, because it is a pose and, so to speak, a pause in time."[3]

It is easy to deconstruct the superficial image, clearly manipulated for the use and consumption of an easy-to-sell subcultural stereotype. In many photographs now consigned to the archives — in Brazzi's gaze and Maurizio Arena's affectation — we see the transparency; those of high-class playboys, the Rubirosas, Pignataris, and especially Jaime de Mora y Aragon, come complete with a good pinch of self-irony.

Less obvious is the corresponding change in behaviour patterns and in everyday life and a view of "maleness" which has a tendency to be fulfilled more or less awkwardly. Any discussion of the Latin lover must necessarily include a discussion of the male "gender" and this in turn is intertwined with that of identity and of entertainment in an age when relationships between people are mediated by images.

Rudolph Valentino and Wilma Banky in The Sheik, *1921*

"Why did you bring me here?" "Aren't you woman enough to know?"[4]

For his part the Latin lover, bent upon the standard conquest, is already a "gender" model: the role he chooses to play is that in which there is no other virility besides his own, and this throws light on the totalitarian tendency that is part of the identity of the Latin seducer: Mussolini, Peron and our third-rate Peron[5] are obvious examples. We cannot turn to him for clarification or critical awareness: he is the real man, the man that breaks records and so sets the norm.

But his most overwhelming proof is tautological. The Latin lover exists and survives the years, given his persistence in Italian popular culture and its products. Like the housewife awarded the prize of spending a day with the hero of picture stories in Fellini's film *Lo Sceicco Bianco* (The White Sheik), the Latin lover models his existence on the gossip columns: another case of the medium being identified with the message.

After all, the heroic and legendary feats of the Latin lover, generally accomplished against a backdrop of picturesque countryside idealized for centuries in romantic culture constitute the only real male epic in the Latin imagination. Some conquered the ocean

[3] Raul Vaneigem, Trattato di saper vivere ad uso delle giovani generazioni, Florence 1973, p. 124.

[4] From Lo Sceicco (The Sheik), Paramount, 1921.

[5] This is how the honourable Bossi described Silvio Berlusconi in a recent statement to the press.

waves and mysterious continents, others conquered the West, a symbol of every frontier, while others still conquered other men's sisters, girlfriends and wives. There is something prodigious about all this, yet a certain ambiguity remains. While it is true that the average Italian male is very happy to fantasize about being the world's greatest lover, and at the first opportunity will play at seducing "foreign" women, we may at least suspect that this dream continues to have a corollary in a desire for adventure in diversity, the submission of the "civilized" woman (another totalitarian concept) to the wild man, mistaken for the erotic romance which many commentators have pinpointed as the substance behind Rudolph Valentino's success with the American female public in the Twenties. Does this thrill remain today in the embarrassed delight of some American girls who, walking along an Italian street, are the object of an unexpected yet scandalous compliment, and in the message Madonna wore emblazoned across her chest, that "Italians do it Better?" Does the average Italian man's dream of conquest have a corollary in the unavowable desire to be conquered which stirs the depths of an eternally weak female sex?

Valeria Fabrizi and Ciccio Ingrassia in a scene from Veneri al sole *(Venuses in the Sun) by Mario Girolami, 1964 (Farabolafoto)*

Giancarlo Giannini in Mimì Metallurgico *(Archivio Brandini-Sanguinetti)*

In short, what is it that makes Italian men so different, so appealing? Did Valentino's films begin the cult of the seductive Italian demi-god, or was it this Italian immigrant, the handsome and sensitive tango dancer, who provided the pretext for the entertainment industry to construct a mass market product, using its own strength of persuasion to immortalize it? Aside from the gaunt travellers and decadent dandies à la von Gloedel, whose ultimate fate we rightly feel diverges from the mainstream of the male Italian approach to the art of love, nobody found Italians so sexy before Rudolph Valentino's films made millions. In his wake Italians considered themselves to be great lovers, and went to great lengths to

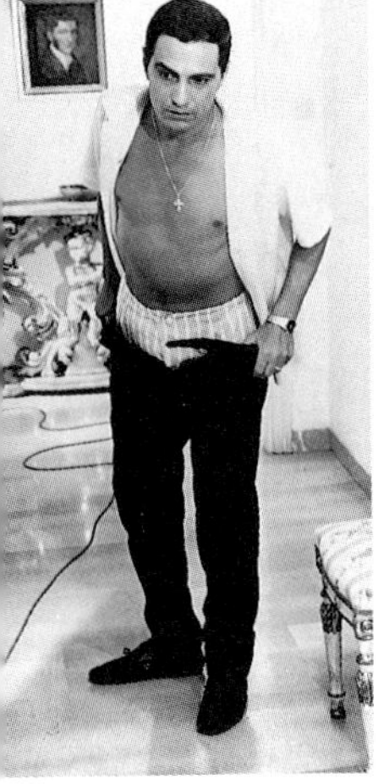

Nino Manfredi (Archivio Brandini-Sanguinetti)

prove it to the whole world, generally for free. Since the Fifties the Latin lover such as Brazzi, pre-dating and over-arching fashion, has been the sole expression of mass Italian culture to interact with the Pop culture that has spread across the globe, the only genuine success of Made in Italy creativity that was not based on labour cost differentials: an example once and for all of a spontaneous mass marketing strategy. A fossil remains of a pose of seduction indifferent to the transition to the modern (right from the start it was anti-modern, from when Rudolph Valentino dressed up as a Gaucho, a Sheik, a Young Rajah, a fugitive from the modern age, ill-adapted to urban social life), the Latin lover has arrived in the post-modern age as if to say: "Well now, where was I..." It is no coincidence that the favourite hunting grounds of these "Romeos" are the non-places created by freedom of movement: night clubs, beaches, squares voided of their original social significance and transformed into sit-com sets. The preferred time of his activities — and the predictable outcome — is the summer, or so it seems from the more or less indignant reportage of the prestigious foreign weekly whose turn it is to report on the phenomenon. This year it was the *Sunday Times*, with its feature on four attractive female journalists sent out into the world to study the state of the art of the pick-up, which was subsequently taken up by all the Italian dailies.

In media terms the Latin lover leaps from the screen and bursts onto the stage of Italian holiday culture: as the female tourists holidaying in Italy well know, Italian males become the stars of a show based on the interaction of the spectacular image of seduction and its execution, which takes shape in a set of rituals codifying identity, gestures and language, which in turn rejuvenate and consolidate the stereotype and its media appeal. Perhaps the true nature of the Latin lover is as an advertising aid. The Latin lover sells, no matter whether the product is a film, a holiday spot or a whole country. Much like the Mulino Bianco, which after an Italian advertising campaign created a surge of tourist interest in the fake mill in Tuscany where the famous advertisements were shot, the Latin lover is a consumer icon that has turned real. He is a theme park character, like Mickey or Minnie Mouse in Disneyland. Meeting an Italian "would-be Casanova" is one of those cherished optional extras for women booking a trip to a country of postcard views that has turned into a postcard of a country.

NON PIÙ ANDRAI FARFALLONE?

A COMPARATIVE APPROACH TO THE ANTHROPOLOGY OF THE SEDUCER

Franco La Cecla

" ...Each woman has her own particular charm: a cheerful smile, a mischievous gaze, a lusting eye, a bowed head, a licentious spirit, a soft breathiness, a deep presentiment, a prophetic melancholy, an earthly nostalgia, vague emotions, fluttering eyelashes, questioning lips, a mysterious forehead, charmimg curls, veiling eyebrows, a heavenly haughtiness, an earthly modesty, an angelic purity, a secret blush, an agile gait, light movements, a languid pose, desirous dreams, an incomprehensible sigh, a slim figure, soft curves, dancing breasts, a deep cough, a small foot, a light hand..."

Translated from the Italian. Søren Kierkegaard, *Diario di un seduttore* (Diary of a Seducer), 1843, Italian translation Attilio Veraldi, Milan 1994, p. 147.

" ...he who is not able to outwit a young girl so that she loses sight of everything he does not want her to see, he who does not succeed in taking possession of a young girl's mind so that she will concede all he desires, is and will remain a bungler."

Søren Kierkegaard, *op. cit.*, p. 84.

"Intercourse and discourse, copula and copulation, are subclasses of the dominant fact of communication. They arise from the life-need of the ego to reach out and comprehend, in the two vital senses of 'understanding' and 'containment' another human being. Sex is a profoundly semantic act."

George Steiner, *After Babel*, London 1975, p. 38.

An honest anthropological work on the Latin lover should entail a comparative approach to the problem: in other words, it should consider whether other cultures possess characters, a personality or a constellation similar to that of the Latin lover.

All in all, from a comparative, synchronic approach, it should be evident that the Latin lover is not only a relic of the Fifties, but a constellation that is present in other cultures and epochs in different personalities which, however, bear a family resemblance. In this respect one can approach the Latin lover with a certain seriousness, without treating this poor beach figure too badly.

A few days ago some Latin lovers from Rimini declared on TV that nothing was the same as it used to be and that now all you find on the Rimini beaches are Russians and they are a bit on the short side at that, whereas "then," in the "golden age," there were Scandinavians who were all tall.

Of course it is difficult to take the Latin lover seriously, he himself gives us a helping hand to avoid doing so. But the Latin lover is a reincarnation, the revival of that forerunner, the truly eternal Don Juan, the ultimate seducer.

It seems that the story of Don Juan is one of the few that has lasted as a western mythologem, together with and perhaps only equalled by the Faust story.

Don Juan and Faust are two pillars of the western collective imagination and we may say that, in a way, we are all born, from Seville to Novosibirsk, with genes that are imprinted with the constellation of Faust and that of Don Juan.

These two "characters" respond to an extreme temptation, that of taking seriously the desire for the infinite (or for an infinite present) that exists in the thirst for power on the one hand and the thirst for regeneration on the other.

Faust and Don Juan are brothers, they can swap costumes, and above all they are very aware of the limits of human experience and this does not go down well. That is why they make a pact with the devil or prefer to be dragged off to hell rather than abjure their calling to be lovers beyond the limits and men who never age (but isn't that the same thing?).

Certainly "our Latin lover" is far less damned, far more of a dandy without the faded glory of dandyism, he is a remake of an archetype glazed with provincial sentimentalism.

Our Latin lover is a man who always goes back to his village and recounts his love affairs.

We boys who met up every evening in the Piazzetta di Terrasini, in the Sicily of the Fifties, always asked our seniors, who had just come back from holidays away from home, military service or service in the navy: "So what did you get up to?"

It was the all too familiar world of the provinces, which was an "oral" world where conquests were recounted and there was an audience to tell them to.

The real Latin lover knows how much he needs this, to what extent conquests are made to be recounted. There are even modes of discourse regarding the conquest that influence actual practice.

The Latin lover "observes himself" while he is making a conquest, and savours in advance the details he will be able to recount later. For this reason the Latin lover constellation is a constellation made up of anecdotes, it is fragmentary and brilliant, it is full of innuendo, it wants to show off to an audience that continues to ask "and then?"

The Latin lover creates a story based on himself and his feats, a story he tells his three friends in the bar or a story for the Copenhagen public. Let us not be scandalized, Kierkegaard in his *Diary of a Seducer* is a real Latin lover, even if he calls himself a "seducer." He is a Latin lover because he makes us enjoy every single stage of his conquest. His work is brilliant because it is the real crystallization of a gaze turned upon himself while he is talking about himself, where what is denounced is not the aesthetic approach to life, but his narrative approach. But then it is a question of seeing what is meant by "is denounced" — perhaps this narrative quality detaches the philosopher from the seducer, and does it not make him twice as responsible?

THE TRICKSTER

But let us return to the comparative approach. If I were to do my job honestly I should consider other Latin lovers, in other cultures and latitudes. And of course there are others, there are hundreds of others, both in legend and in reality. Different cultures from ours are not morally any "purer." Only a stupid politically correct view would make us think so. Men and women in all cultures can be good husbands and wives, passionate lovers or simply "ambiguous" lovers, like Don Juan.

The trickster who likes to disguise himself, wile his way in, seduce and flee is also found in the Coyote of the American Indian myths or any other scheming ladykiller, like Gaman, the heroic founder of the Burma Sea nomads.

In the legend, he gives an identity to these nomadic fishermen, by marrying the king's daughter, but running away with her sister. Furthermore, the constellation of the trickster finds a correspondent in Dionysus's wiliness, in Hermes' sneaky ways, and Mercury's or Harlequin's lightness.

The Latin lover is the reincarnation of an approach which negates the tragic in the man-woman relationship.

"Is it not irony perhaps which prevents the passionate tendency of the game from going back to being serious?"

Translated from the Italian. Vladimir Jankelevitch, *L'avventura, la noia, la serietà* (The Adventure, Boredom, Seriousness), Paris 1963, Italian translation C.A. Bonadies, Genoa 1991, p. 31.

Neither is the Latin lover an exclusively male character. There are many femmes fatales from the Sirens to Lilith. The fact is that the constellation of the Latin lover responds to the ambiguity of man-woman relationships, to their indirect complementarity, and is for this reason often (though not always) deceptive. Don Juan, Casanova, Peter Camenzind, Evgeny Oneghin and Porfirio Rubirosa found themselves in a state of "confusion" and they "made use of this." The confusion is the fact that men and women think they want the same thing when they imagine a possible relationship, but this is not the case, or, on the contrary, they think they have conflicting objectives and instead they are forced to realize that they coincide.

"No man or woman but has felt, during a lifetime, the strong subtle barriers which sexual identity imposes in communication. At the heart of intimacy, there above all perhaps, differences of linguistic reflex intervene. The semantic contour, the total of expressive means used by men and women differ. The view they take of the output and consumption of words is not the same. As it passes through verb tenses, time is bent into distinctive shapes and fictions." George Steiner, *op. cit.*, p. 41.

The Latin lover, seducer and femme fatale, are the artists and victims of misunderstanding and of the most basic misunderstanding, that between two different genders, between men and women.

One of the few people who have interpreted the myth of the eternal seducer in this key recently is Marina Warner, in a text that is part of a collection of writings on *Don Giovanni* (Jonathan Miller, *The Book of Don Giovanni*, London 1990). Marina Warner finds another forerunner of Don Giovanni in Valmont in *Dangerous Connections*, and she follows his development through all the various film versions up to the present. She notes that many things have changed, she notes that it is the type of archetypal relationship that has changed. In the more modern versions of the story a woman (the marchioness) who is a rival, a seducer, a maternal and, finally, a femme fatale figure is increasingly set against the male seducer. This time Don Giovanni does not lose out to the "Commendatore" but to the Woman herself: it is he who has not understood that the game is becoming tragic and that he is the victim, no longer of a principle external to the relationship, which is real or social Damnation, but of the Other. The Latin lover comes off badly when faced with a Woman who has become more astute, more aware and feminist than he is in manipulating the relationship. The Latin lover is punished, he loses, but it is not the priest, the devil or old age that gets the better of him, it is the very Woman he has been attempting to sweep off her feet. Valmont dies in a duel, the Latin lover fails, he gets nowhere, he receives a rebuff that has nothing to do with a "battle" any more, he falls into the ditch (Valmont in one of the most recent film versions fights the fatal duel in a kind of trench) into the trap in which the Woman causes him to fall.

Marina Warner says all this very cleverly, while in the same text politically correct readings of the story of Don Juan take a moral stance. How can you use a moralizing tone to Don Juan? How can you use a moralizing tone to Faust? Only by forgetting that figures like this are figures in a relationship. Don Giovanni embodies the theme of confusion. Don Giovanni does not "deceive" women any more than a husband deceives his wife (or vice versa) when he says to her "I want only you." Don Giovanni does not want to "lay women," he wants to create a world of confusion in the official relations between men and women which permits him to encounter women in an instantaneous affair. Does he deceive them? Must he be punished for this? Yes, but his punishment is his glorification, in other words, a reconfirmation of his "exceptional nature," of his being an exception, out of the ordinary and therefore truly charming and a seducer. Certainly Don Giovanni, Kierkegaard and Julio Iglesias deceive women, they ensnare them in a sea of words, muscles, cars or promises.

"No impatience, no avidity, all will be enjoyed in good time. She has been chosen: she will end up by being attained." Søren Kierkegaard, *op cit.*, p. 30.

And the women are victims, they are victims of the confusion into which they have been lured, they are victims of exceptional seduction. The seducer is a real "shit."

"Now it is all over, and I ask not to see her any more. When a girl has given everything, she is finished, she has lost everything; because whereas innocence is negative in a man, in a woman it is the essence of life."
ibidem, p. 164.

THE MISUNDERSTANDING

But just a minute! This is the seducer's story. Though he tells himself this version, are we always sure that this is the woman's version too? In his account the seducer tells us that he behaved really badly at the end, because that way his victory can be declared. But if you reread the diary of a seducer you ask yourself, in actual fact, if he made it all up and it is "much ado about nothing." Perhaps she had already decided before all the wily manoeuvres.
In other words, the fact is that Don Juan or the Latin lover can be understood in the relationship, through the way in which the idea of the "basic" man-woman relationship has changed and is changing.
Let us go back to the question of ambiguity. The Latin lover of the moment's seduction technique is based on the misunderstanding between man and woman. The Latin lover knows or thinks he knows how to use this misunderstanding.

"Our relationships are not based on a delicate and true understanding nor on mutual attraction, they are based on the repulsions of incomprehension."

Søren Kierkegaard, *ibidem*, p. 66.

Half way through his advances, he makes her think that he wants something from her and he encourages her to feel that it is the same thing that she wants. The seducer is a mechanic of ambiguity, an artist of the indirect proposition. He uses words, a lot of words, because he knows that language is by nature ambiguous.

"Whatever the underlying causes, the resultant task of translation is constant and unfulfilled. Men and women communicate through

never-ending modulation. Like breathing, the technique is unconscious; like breathing, also, it is subject to abstraction and homicidal breakdown. Under stress of hatred, of boredom, of sudden panic, great gaps open. It is as if a man and a woman then heard each other for the first time and knew, with sickening conviction, that they share no common language, that their previous understanding had been based on a trivial pidgin which had left the heart of meaning untouched, abruptly the wires are down and the nervous pulse under the skin is laid bare in mutual incomprehension."

George Steiner, *op. cit.*, p. 44.

In this way the Latin lover stages a play of misunderstanding, the misunderstanding which lies at the basis of the man-woman relationship. This is the same misunderstanding that causes Romeo and Juliet's mistimed suicides, it is the misunderstanding that in Racine's play causes Tito to love Berenice, and Berenice to love Tito, but they part for ever because "they did not understand each other."

The seducer is an actor in a tragedy which takes place in the public eye, often in every "serious relationship between a man and a woman." The seducer, and the Latin lover even more so, "simulates deception," he takes the misunderstanding upon himself to pretend (to himself and his friends in the bar) that he has come out of "this affair" better off.

Today the Latin lover is becoming extinct because the misunderstanding is much greater than before. It could be said that until some time ago the man-woman game, the game of seduction and rebuff, the game of the ambiguity of two desires passed off as being similar but that were in fact different, was based on a tacit agreement — the rules of the game — in which it was accepted that there was a misunderstanding and that it might be useful and sometimes amusing "to play the game." Today this agreement has been swept away by the demand for "Communication" with a capital C, the demand that everything you need to know to understand each other should be said openly. "Communication" has cancelled out the centuries-old awareness that men and women speak different languages, have different desires, get pleasure from different things, and has created an even greater "Misunderstanding," the belief that there is no ambiguity to be taken into account, no misunderstanding on which to base seduction and an attempt to live together, at least for a while.

No one better than Harvey Sachs and his friends who founded conversational analysis was aware of the change when it was occurring. His *Laughing in the Pursuit of Intimacy* is a masterpiece that makes us understand to what extent "seduction" is "interactive" (ah! ah! how amusing to think that to save conversation you can use a term that derives from the man-machine interface!).

An expert from Harvey Sachs's circle, Deborah Tannen (*That's not What I Meant, How Conversational Style Makes or Breaks Relationships,* New York 1986) has described the transformation in courting practices and the decline in the "practice" of courting on both sides. Courting presupposes a common culture of misunderstanding, a tolerance and a game of understanding and not understanding, a capacity to transform courting space into courting time.

"However she must not feel at all obliged to me, since she needs to be free; only in freedom is there love, only in freedom is there the eternal pleasure of time passing. Though I impose myself upon her in such a way that, almost by natural necessity, she has to fall into my arms, I attempt nevertheless to lead her there in such a way that she gravitates towards me; and yet at the same time it is important that she does not fall like a heavy body, but like a spirit that gravitates around another spirit. Though she must be mine, yet this must not be something that is not beautiful, in other words, she must not weigh on me like a burden. She must not be a harassment, from the physical point of view, nor a commitment from the moral point of view, only the game of freedom must reign between us, she must be so light that I can lift her with my arms."

Søren Kierkegaard, *op. cit.*, p. 76.

LIGHTNESS

There are suitable times, places and ways, there is an intelligence of seduction. The seducer applies himself to something that makes him become intelligent. The seducer knows (knew) that most of the things to be learnt "girls know instinctively" (*All Girls Know It* was the title of a British film from the Seventies).

“Though later I shall become old, I shall never forget that everything is over for a man only when he has become too old to learn anything from a young girl.” Søren Kierkegaard, *ibidem*, p. 104.

Places are perhaps more important than times and ways. For its permanent residents every self-respecting city, village or district has a place or several places that are “pick-up” spots. Some time back I and a group of female friends of mine, historians and feminists, thought of writing a collective work on how males and females pick each other up. By agreement with Lucetta Scaraffia and Anna Foa, it was to have been called *Rimorchio rimosso* (Sublimated Pick-up), but then nothing came of it because the publishers had scruples. But right from the beginning it was clear from the stories and cases reported that the pick-up venue is of prime importance and that it differs for men and women. There are bars, cafés, libraries, discos, wine bars, party offices, churches and parish halls, escalators and underground stations (for the most skilful).

A delightful story told of a successful gentleman who had understood that it is easier to pick up girls in the underground if you happen to be holding a dog or a cat. Another told of the advantages of taking a baby for a walk. However, the pick-up scenario is always one of those things you only teach a new arrival after she/he has been there for a while, though it is essential for survival in a new town.

Every nation and every culture — here we come back to the honest comparative approach — reveals its hidden depths and we can begin to understand them only when we begin to understand how the first advances between men and women work, when they are permitted to take place and what gestures, words, and moves create the difference between an acceptable pick-up and harassment.

All this is a formalized structure, a frame of reference, and like all systems it is fragile, ecologically fragile. There is an ecology of how you make eye contact that is fundamental.

The Latin lover, the seducer or femme fatale “look” or rather cast glances. The glance is "cast" and therefore it has a target like the arrow in Zen archery. Knowing how to cast a glance in a split second, knowing how to look away, knowing how to make eye contact without smiling, yet making the other person feel that a response is expected, all this becomes confusing as soon as you cross a border, leave a city, or move to another district. What an effort!

"Seducing a girl means for most people simply seducing a girl, and that is all; and yet there is a whole science hidden behind this thought." Søren Kierkegaard, *ibidem*, p. 79.

There are countries where if you make eye contact with people they panic and they respond with a smile, a castrating smile that eliminates all tension. There are countries where eye contact is the main game, it is even more important than the climax the game is supposed to lead to. But even here, if you read the funny manual *Sex and Dating, The Official Politically Correct Guide*, by Henry Beard and Christopher Cerf, New York 1994, you will find out how dangerous it can be to look at people. Eye contact may be taken to be annoying, aggressive, and lead to a battle of the sexes in the courtroom and at the psychiatrist's.

But let us consider for a minute the fact that fans have gone out of fashion and the consequences of this. In Mediterranean countries the fan was for centuries the *maleta*, the cape, the red cloth women used to avoid eye contact with men. There is a kind of bullfight that can only be fought with instruments, just as there is a kind of courting that cannot do without instruments, on both sides.

Until a while ago the Latin lover's accessory was the cravat. In a comparative approach I would not be able to explain how it originated and became popular. I remember that David Niven always wore a silk cravat (perfectly complemented by a silk smoking jacket). It is almost as though the Latin lover were a bit afraid of draughts in the places where he was paying court. It is almost as if he abhorred the mundane tie, the pleb accessory of those who think there are more remunerative jobs than seducing women. Domenico Modugno's man in evening dress, in the song

L'uomo in frac, must also have worn a cravat, which he probably took off before jumping into the Tiber (by the way that man really existed and lived at the time of the *viveur*, the seducer who paid for being exceptional in person, who showed that the true seducer seduces because this allows him to go "to extremes" — Kierkegaard had understood this very well, "zu Grunde gehen").
But the cravat distinguishes the Latin lover from other categories of seducer. A playboy would never wear a cravat. Precisely for the same reason that the Latin lover possesses the alert awareness and detached power of observation that the playboy may lack. The Latin lover is an expert in falling in love.

THE MIRROR

"How beautiful to be in love and how interesting to know how to be in love."

Søren Kierkegaard, *ibidem*, p. 48.

Let us go back to the question of the discourse of seduction, in which the first real target of the account is oneself. The Latin lover "knows" better than anyone else what love does to people and to himself. He knows it so well that he takes precautions because:
"I am in love, very true, but not in the usual way; I must therefore be very careful because there may be dangerous consequences, and one is only in love like this once in one's life. However, the god of love is blind, if one is prudent one can deceive him. Art, compared to emotion, is being as perceptive as possible, knowing what impression you are making on and what impression you are receiving from every girl. In that way you can also be in love differently with each of them. Loving only one is not enough, loving them all is superficial (the playboy? my note). Knowing oneself and loving as many of them as possible, allowing one's soul to hide within itself all the powers of love so that each receives her due, while consciousness embraces all: this is pleasure, this is living."
Søren Kierkegaard, *ibidem*, p. 77.

The Latin lover is the son of an examination of conscience, the son of a state of consciousness as a permanent objective. Casanova is a master of this. His lucidity consists in the art of recounting his and others' states of mind, in "describing" a passion that is thoroughly examined, analyzed, staged, remembered and re-experienced at the moment in which it is remembered. Passion for Casanova is a feeling that is savoured coolly. It is not that he does not feel, is not involved, does not fall in love, the fact is that he finds all this "interesting," the world of the emotions and innermost feelings is the laboratory for his detached research. Casanova is "cool" not because he is "frigid," but because passion has to be savoured first in the preliminaries and later in the memory and the analysis of the memory. Casanova, Don Juan or the seducer are for this reason "lords of confusion," because they know seduction is an indirect logic, a "strategy." If strategy means a battle manoeuvre, they too, in a way, are doing "battle" with women. There is conflict, no doubt of that, and there are also the victims of this conflict, but there is also the game of conflict, which may be the game of seduction. Deborah Tannen documents a new stage, (in *Talking from Nine to Five, Women and Men in the Workplace: Language, Sex and Power,* New York 1995) that in which "You don't understand" has become an accusation rather than a fact on which to begin to base a relationship (and seduction). In his brilliant book *Gender and Sex,* snubbed by Italian publishers, Ivan Illich reminds us that we have lost the whole art of the man-woman relationship that was based on the acceptance of the misunderstanding as the starting point, of the man-woman difference, of the difficulty in relating to each other, as a fact. This art meant that there were certain ways of making advances and retreating, ways of seducing and rebuffing, in which the rules of the game were clear (and hence those of the conflict and the ways of dealing with it). There is such a narrow gap today between making advances and harassment that next to nothing remains of the poor Latin lover, not even his wig. But few people realize that the battle of the sexes has not flared up, but that the relationship has become impoverished.

THE ADVENTURE

"The future is a je ne sais quoi." Vladimir Jankelevitch, *op. cit.*, p. 11.

The Latin lover is also to be reconsidered the reincarnation of another constellation, that of adventure. He represents someone who not only recounts, but has "adventures." And it is because of the "adventurous" nature of his feats that the Latin lover, like every seducer, lives in the "*je ne sais quoi* of the future."

This element too is found in a large number of cultures, myths, fairytales and stories. The adventurous man is the hero, the trickster, the young drifter, the pilgrim turned vagrant, the hippie or simply someone who at a certain moment "detaches" a "story" from the repetitive and coherent time of a life. The adventurous person is she/he who happens, at a certain point, to live his/her life as an encounter, as chance circumstances, as chance encounters.

Georg Simmel taught us before Vladimir Jankelevitch that the adventure is a mode of time.

"It is true that the form of the adventure, in its broadest sense, consists in escaping from the linked chain of life." Translated from the Italian.
Georg Simmel, *Saggi di Cultura Filosofica* (Essays on Philosophical Culture), 1923, Italian translation M. Monaldi, Parma 1985, p. 21.

The time defined by the adventure is a time outside time, it is the time of a story that has a beginning and an end. The person who has an adventure knows that something has begun, that this is a parenthesis in the constant flow of time. His adventure takes place within this parenthesis. Will circumstances be in his favour? The adventure mode is, according to Simmel and Jankelevitch, acting "as if" everything was conspiring in our favour, drifting with the circumstances, surfing life, riding on the crest of the wave. From this point of view, the person who has the adventure, according to Simmel, has the "self-confidence of a sleepwalker."

"In the adventure we proceed quite differently: we stake everything on the variability of chances, on fate and on approximation; we burn our bridges behind us and we venture into the fog as if the circumstances were not important."
Georg Simmel, *ibidem*, p. 21.

The person who "has the adventure" goes to meet fate, he plays with fate in such a way that circumstances may be favourable to him. Here it is a question of luck, of "the gods' favour," it is an event associated with uncertainty, actually, it is defined by uncertainty. The prince of Ligne says of Casanova, “He doesn’t believe in anything, except that which is less worthy of faith than anything else,” luck, favourable circumstances.

The romantic adventure is holding your breath, you are waiting for fate and for the Other; there is the gift that the Other may decide to make of her/himself, but there is also the “grace” that all this may find a way of occuring.

“The woman waits for the adventure, whereas the man seeks adventure, the woman abandons herself to fate, the man challenges it.” Georg Simmel, *op. cit.*, p. 31.

Jankelevitch claims that from this point of view men and women are different, because:

But both are at the mercy of fate, both are afraid that everything may go wrong, that they will be disappointed, that appointments will not be kept, that an unforgivable distraction will keep the lover away. There is an essential tension in a romantic adventure, tension created by something that may perhaps happen, but that is not inevitable. In this sense a romantic adventure challenges inevitable death and old age. Simmel says that old age is marked by the end of romantic adventures. Those who can no longer have a romantic adventure are old, in the sense that:

“It is an enclave in the whole of life, its beginning and end have no point of contact with the unitary current of experience.”

Georg Simmel, *ibidem*, p. 23.

The human soul’s capacity to “suspend” experience to have a love affair is a very strange one. We withdraw from the flux of life when we live in a parenthesis which gives us a feeling of regeneration and of the end, as if, in reality, the sense of the beginning and the end were excluded from the “normal rhythm of things.” In this sense the adventure and the romantic adventure *par excellence* render us protagonists, it is “our story,” or “our stories.” It is not what makes the official “biography” of a man or woman, but it is that which constitutes the capacity to “have stories.”

The seducer too is of the same mind as regards challenging fate and the lightness required of the adventurer.

"Cursed fate! I never cursed you when you showed yourself and now: I curse you because you don't show yourself!... Like a Hindu dancing girl who dances in honour of the god, I have devoted myself to your service; light, with few garments, agile, disarmed, I renounce everything."
Søren Kierkegaard, *op. cit.*, p. 41.

In this light, agile garment the male or female adventurer moves furtively on tiptoe. In actual fact, what they represent and the romantic adventure represents is the reappearance of the experience of life as *monde flottante*. The floating world is a Japanese concept (from 16th-century theatre and literature), taken up again by the director Ozu in his *Stories of Floating Grasses*. It is the idea that life is as fleeting and instantaneous as haiku, that it is manifested in a stretch of river which is seen for a second and an instant later has changed, because all the water that constituted it has flowed away.
This world, which is the world of beauty *par excellence*, is a world closely associated with its appearing and immediately disappearing. The love affair is a similar experience, "a fleeting experience, just as the general stretching towards the light is associated with the fortuitous and immediately vanishing glow" (Jankelevitch).
But this appearing and disappearing has a regenerative quality. For this reason the Latin lover is someone who is a placemarker for the space of regeneration, because, though in a rather ridiculous and egoistic way, he occupies the constellation of the beginning.

"Absorbed in dizzy imminence or straining towards frenetic urgency, the romantic adventure tends to regenerate a second life within life, a fervid and intense life, a life lived to the full which is a kind of exemplary compendium of real life: this erotic parenthesis is sometimes a kind of work of art, a bizarre episode inserted into existence, a becoming with feverish and timorous rhythms by virtue of which the stagnant time of the daily continuum undergoes a temporary acceleration: 'lively,' 'fantastic,' 'whim' or 'joke,' the romantic adventure is a little life within the big life, wedged into the big, boring, colourless, gloomy life of our everyday existence, the romantic adventure therefore is like a romantic oasis in which men, following the high temperature of passion, feel that they exist for

the first time: leaving behind them their ghostly life for delicious illicitness, they finally know the passionate condensation of a real becoming. But it happens that the little intense life, included in the big, serious and formless life, becomes a substitute for the latter, takes its place, invades and occupies the whole destination; these interlocking lives tragically compete with one another. The big, serious life and the little, intense life are to one another as daytime truth is to night time truth; both are contradictory yet both are equally true, and all in all incomparable. Is not the choice made between them rather like a bet?"

Vladimir Jankelevitch, *op. cit.*, p. 33.

In this sense the romantic adventure confronts men and women with the insoluble problem of how to live their whole life as an adventure and the impossibility that this may happen.
The Latin lover, the adventurer, the smart gipsy who causes a woman bored by her bourgeois husband to rediscover love, the seducer who "represents in young girls' eyes" a love that is free from false glitter and external commitments — if all this did not exist it would have to be invented and woe betide societies who lose this figure and expel it from their collective imagination. But this is an ambiguous figure, it has the ambiguity necessary for things to take on the controversial contours they possess. Once again Jankelevitch puts this very well.

"The man impassioned by the exciting uncertainty of the adventure, by the exciting risk of the future is in the passionate situation of those frenetic lovers who cannot live together or apart: if they are together they fight, they cannot bear the other's presence; apart they become sad and yearn again for their intricate symbiosis. They adore each other and detest each other by turn. It is said that they do not know what they want. In actual fact they would know well what they want, but what they want is impossible, unrealizable and superhuman; it is not the desire itself that is contradictory, it is the things desired that contradict each other.
In seeking a romantic adventure, the shy man wants and does not want at the same time, he wants what he does not want and does not want what he wants, he wants on the basis of a mixture of wanting and not wanting; in a way he wants by virtue of a wanting

and not wanting which is quite similar to love-hate. Will he dare? Wanting without wanting yet wanting: is it not like this? The 'evasive' will of the man who is tempted, reticent, attracted by his own conflict and by his inner resources. Man is dying to do what he fears most. Passionate curiosity and delicious horror, the temptation to have a romantic adventure is not unlike dizziness."
Vladimir Jankelevitch, *op. cit.*, p. 12.

But if this is what the romantic adventure is like it is not very different from the misunderstanding. In a way, our whole excursus on the Latin lover talks of him as someone who lives the misunderstanding between men and women, but even more so the lover's or beloved's essential misunderstanding of himself or herself. The misunderstanding lies in not being able to understand or guide the romantic adventure. The Latin lover too is a victim, the sacrificial victim of the misunderstanding in love.
He needs a white suit, as we see in Ray Bradbury's fine short story. The five chicanos friends who want to turn themselves magically into love objects have to go around with their alter-ego immaculately dressed in a creamy white suit. They are transformed by this sacrificial guise. They realize that it was their desire to change, their smiling attitude to life, rather than the suit, that has transformed them. But that is another story.

Don Jaime de Mora y Aragon in Naples with Melina Mercouri in Il Giudizio Universale, 1961 (Publifoto)

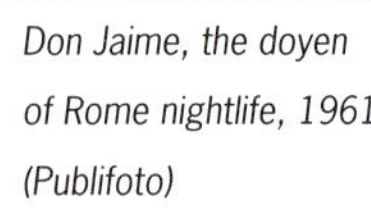

Don Jaime, the doyen of Rome nightlife, 1961 (Publifoto)

The Rome debut of Don Jaime de Mora y Aragon as singer and pianist in a nightclub, 1961 (Publifoto)

Don Jaime with his guitar (Publifoto)

Yoga exercises? No, Don Jaime de Mora y Aragon relaxing with a glass of whisky at a party for music publisher Will Meisel, Berlin, 1961 (Publifoto)

Don Jaime de Mora y Aragon in East Berlin, 1961 (Publifoto) ▶

Don Jaime with his car in Madrid (Publifoto)

Don Jaime and his tw dogs (Publifoto)

Don Jaime de Mora y Aragon (Farabolafoto)

ANARCHY HURT THE LATIN LOVER

FANTASY, DECLINE AND ETERNAL FASCINATION OF THE CASANOVA

Carlo Romano

Latin lover: we should begin with a definition that does not actually exist. Although we are hard put to define a "lover," we presume to know exactly what a Latin lover is. We can even trot out a few names. Through the years, the gossip magazines have persuaded us that Latin lovers — or at least the "originals" — were Rossano Brazzi and Porfirio Rubirosa, and possibly Mastroianni, Louis Jourdan, Alain Delon, Walter Chiari, and a few others. Rudolph Valentino began it all. However, the fact that the lives of these men bore little or no resemblance to each other, makes our task all the more difficult.

Rubirosa coming out of a bend during the Sebring race (Publifoto)

As intense as any Greek tragedy, Porfirio Rubirosa's life has nothing in common with that cool, amorous character, with devastating manners, that Brazzi played on-screen. Off-screen, however, he exhibited in the press a wife who was not at all pretty, despite the fact that he received the attentions customarily reserved for a "heart-throb" from many female admirers. Like many screen idols, starting with Valentino, he was wrongly suspected of being homosexual. Brazzi also found himself implicated in arms trafficking, for which he was tried and acquitted, but in this affair he came across as an extremely middle-class businessman rather than a romantic adventurer.

Rubirosa and Zsa Zsa Gabor arriving in New York, 1954 (Farabolafoto)

Porfirio Rubirosa's life was like a compass gone crazy. He married the beautiful daughter of Santo Domingo's dictator General Trujillo, who was so jealous that she shot him (more than once, it seems). Rubirosa had no choice but to divorce her as soon as possible. The general, who obviously knew his daughter well, did not hold it against him; on the contrary, he appointed him foreign minister plenipotentiary. Afterwards, Rubirosa married Doris Duke, the heir-

Rubirosa with his wife Odile Rodin and the Cuban Consul's wife at a charity dinner, New York, 1958 (Ullstein Bilderdienst)

ess of an enormously wealthy family of American tobacco merchants, and then the famous Barbara Hutton who, he confided to a friend: "Sleeps all day and is too tired to get up at night." Rubirosa, on the other hand, lived as if there were no tomorrow. The marriage ended when Hutton spread the word that more than one of her husbands was a gigolo. Rubi, as he was known to his friends, finally hooked up with a third-rate actress named Odile Rodin. He was killed, one morning, when his Ferrari ran into a tree in the Bois de Boulogne.

Whether they play the part on the silver screen or the fashionable stage of the beau monde, the one thing all so-called Latin lovers have in common is a mother tongue deriving from the language spoken by the ancient Romans. It must nevertheless be borne in mind — in order not to illude ourselves that ethnolinguistic criteria constitute an absolute value — that English-speaking actors like Tyrone Power and Robert Taylor are also eligible for the Latin lover category because of the roles they interpreted. Furthermore, in Hollywood it happened that a handsome hunk who spoke German was billed as Ricardo Cortez, to exploit the Rudolph Valentino myth.

Rubirosa with his lawn mower (Publifoto)

"The renowned playboy Porfirio Rubirosa, former Consul of Santo Domingo, was killed this morning while driving his Ferrari..." (Publifoto)

To further complicate matters, these extremely different personalities were flanked by someone who gave a paradoxical twist to the uncertain profession (or vocation) of the Latin lover by deliberately making the seducer something akin to a Dadaist jest: Don Jaime de Mora y Aragon.

The whole of Marbella went into mourning when Don Jaime died this summer. He had risen to the rank of Chief of Protocol in the municipality, but was remembered more as a Casanova than an official. If the town was in his debt, it was for the publicity he gave the fashionable resort. He himself was a real publicity hound, notorious for his debts and extravagant living, who occasionally made a profession of it (starring in Italian TV commercials, for example). When his sister was betrothed to the King of Belgium, Don Jaime threatened to attend the wedding ceremony riding on an elephant. Pressure was exerted on the Spanish Government and they had his passport temporarily confiscated, thus avoiding further embarrassment. But Don Jaime was not beaten that easily, and dedicated an irreverent cha-cha-cha to his royal brother-in-law, which blared out mockingly from all the juke boxes. Luxury hotels and beautiful women (including Anita Ekberg) were his staple diet. As he merely accompanied the ladies (he was prepared to marry at least two of them) Don Jaime never paid hotel bills, doing his utmost to make life one big party. "I am the only de Mora who has understood life," he was heard to declare. There were members of his family who fervently hoped that he would become a saint at some point.

Baby Pignatari, Viareggio, 1959 (Farabolafoto)

It is only natural to see Don Jaime as the nth manifestation of Don Juanism, particularly with regard to the Kierkegaardian interpretation of the Don Juan myth as sensualistic and singular genius ("I would like them to engrave 'that singular man' on my tomb" Kierkegaard wrote in his diary).

Linda Christian with Baby Pignatari in Rome, 1957 (Farabolafoto)

However, the period involved — the Sixties and the Seventies — necessitates further reflection at a historical level. Events that are commonly referred to by indicating the year 1968 and the influence they had on morals in general, did irreparable damage to a certain type of seducer, so much so that sexuality — after the initial stand taken for free love — seemed to become a social obligation. The Latin lovers still featured in the gossip magazines were Beppe Piroddi and Gigi Rizzi. They possessed a style that was shamelessly young, disreputable and devil-may-care, and decidedly less formal and refined than that of the classic Casanova. It was a style anticipated by a group of sybarites

Baby Pignatari and Jackie Lane caught unawares in a Rome nightspot, 1959 (Farabolafoto)

Baby Pignatari and Rosanna Schiaffino, Rome, 1959 (Farabolafoto)

who in the Fifties flocked to Capri in the wake of Roman prince Dado Ruspoli, where they pathetically aped the vegetarian bohemianism that flourished in Ascona at the beginning of the century, which was also practised by certain early literary patrons of the Isle. It was basically a snobbish cult that was not for the common people, although they did see the funny side of it; the leading figures were ridiculed in two of Totò's films: *Totò a colori* (Totò in colour) and *Totò imperatore di Capri* (Totò Emperor of Capri). In the latter, there is a scene in which Galeazzo Benti introduces a rake dressed up in a sailor suit, informing those present that he is Pupetto Turacciolo — which sounds very much like Caracciolo, the name of a family of Neapolitan princes — "who has revived the Mithraistic cult of sun worship on the island." Rizzi and Piroddi simply lived the life of the young and, therefore, had no use for masks. Gigi Rizzi's fling with Brigitte Bardot was perfectly in keeping with the trend of spontaneous and unbridled passion that the actress was partially responsible for establishing. In 1956, when Bardot drew back the sheet and revealed her voluptuous curves in *Et Dieu crea la femme* (And God Created Woman) moralists and priests of every type condemned her behaviour as indecent and created all kinds of problems for young people. It was not what Bardot revealed that caused such a scandal, but the artless way in which she displayed the sensuality of a mature woman with a childish pout. The publication of *Lolita* by Nabokov also seems quite deliberate in the context of the period. People were becoming disenchanted with sex, as it was belatedly made to conform with modern attitudes.

The public figure created by Don Jaime de Mora y Aragon evoked a natural sympathy that allowed him to stay in tune with the times. What Don Jaime actually did was to ridicule the seductive technique — that which makes a man the right man at a particular moment — of an influential, but ill-defined, social animal. He did to the image of the classic Don Juan practically the same thing that avant-garde movements attempted to do to art, achieving in one fell swoop what they had enacted in stages — association, evolution, dissolution — using the manifesto to spread their message like wildfire and producing works that were already a declaration of intent. As far as the Latin lover was concerned, Don Jaime simply had to be himself. Art and love, if this is how we are going to describe the art of seduction, are not the same thing. The lover operates alone when making a conquest. He then has to make an effort to keep his promises (or at least convince his partner that he intends to keep them) if, of course, he has actually made any. When it comes down to it, however, he does not have to do anything different with the means at his — and everybody else's — disposal, to that which ordinary people ordinarily do. The message communicated by art, when (and if) it is received by the public, arrives by a tortuous route. The fact that it is a "message" also means that it is often exhausted by art historians, enthusiasts and fellow artists, before it gets to people. On the contrary, the Don Juan who makes a splash in the rag sheets, or makes it in the movies or on TV, becomes a model for all, as far as his style, dress and little peculiarities are concerned.

Piacentini dancing the twist with Dahlia Lavi, Rome, 1963 (Farabolafoto)

Mondo Cane, the famous documentary by Gualtiero Jacopetti, begins with the unveiling of a monument to Rudolph Valentino in Castellaneta, his home town in Apulia. After framing the official speaker, the camera pans over a number of men who appear to think that they not only embody the physical attributes, but also the sexual prowess, of the local boy made good (moreover, the images that follow are of Rossano Brazzi surrounded by a crowd of hysterical fans in New York). It was also the generally-held opinion in Italy that Northern European and American women found Italian men quite irresistible, a reputation gained on the strength of the passion and warmth they put into their lovemaking; whereas their Anglo-Saxon counterparts were considered somewhat cold and drunkards into the bargain. This opinion was apparently shared by the large number of popular personalities (not only movie stars, but also individuals like Roman Prince Vittorio Massimo who married Dawn Addams) who actually had brief flings or lasting relation-

Roman aristocrats vacationing on Capri pose for the American monthly *Holiday*, 1955 (photo by Slim Aarons)

ships with foreign actresses, and in fact sometimes married them! It was a social climate that, after Federico Fellini's famous film, became known as the "dolce vita" (sweet life). Gualtiero Jacopetti, in fact, was one of its leading exponents — or at least that was how he was portrayed in the newspapers.

Journalist, former editor of *Cronache*, and director of a Rizzoli newsreel, Jacopetti kept company with a lovely English actress called Belinda Lee, who died prematurely in Los Angeles while Jacopetti was scouting for locations for *La donna nel mondo*. A few years previously, in 1954 to be precise, the documentarist had stood trial for having conspired with a woman of high society — whose name he did not wish to reveal — to pay a young gipsy girl to take part in an orgy. To describe such an act as "degenerate" — even though the word has long lost the scientific respectability it acquired through Lombroso and Nordau — is putting it mildly. When Jacopetti started shooting his documentaries, he had still not been able to clean up the hellish reputation that he had acquired with that episode. The films received a certain amount of publicity in the press, but it was generally thought that many of the most revolting scenes had been faked. The commentaries were characterized by a derisive tone, which also left him

Totò during the shooting of L'Imperatore di Capri *(The Emperor of Capri) (Farabolafoto)*

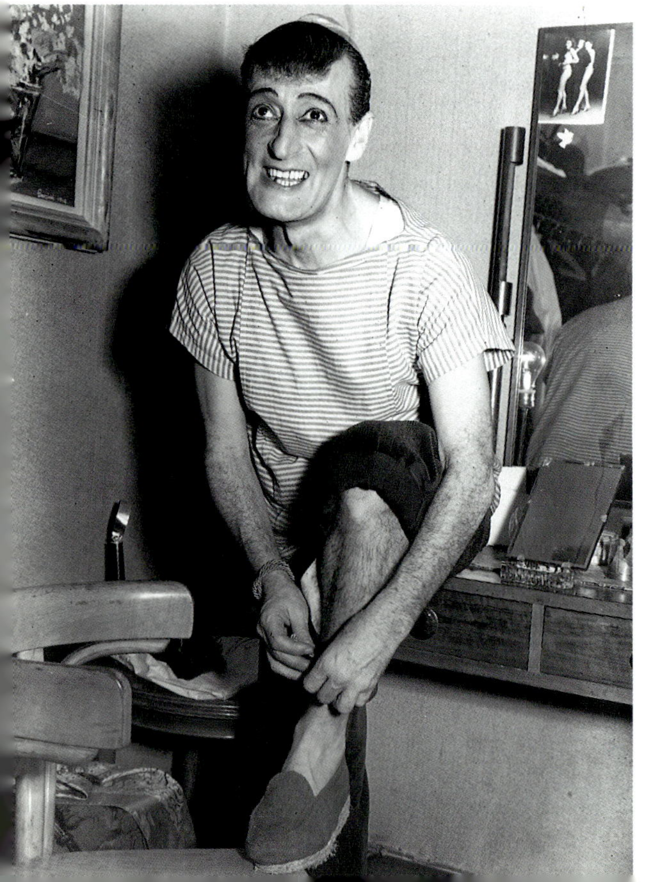

wide open to accusations of racism. Judged to be "fascist," Jacopetti's films were panned by the critics. For documentaries, however, they were a great success with audiences. When you think about it, these films (Jacopetti's documentaries started a trend) were also used to generate and spread a particular kind of sensibility at least in Italy (a Catholic Italy, it must be pointed out, where people who decided on a civil wedding were accused of "living in sin" by finger-pointing parish priests and bishops), partly induced by the widespread application of psychoanalytical models, that at the end of the Sixties manifested itself in the young in an anarchic and sexual form. Which makes you think.

Many anarchic and socialist ideals were reawakened by the events of those years and, after a cool initial response, political parties with a communist bias succeeded in bringing grist to their mill by setting themselves up as the sole authentic representatives of the youth movement. In reality, the traditional idealistic elements assimilated by the movement were brought to it by obscure minority groups (one or two of which shone thanks to the presence of some prominent intellectuals) whose political activity was directly opposed to that of the parties in question. With regard to the turmoil caused by the adoption of uninhibited social and sexual behaviour, there is still a great deal of confusion concerning points of reference, ideologies, and surviving testimonies. The possibility of attributing this turmoil to someone in particular, in spite of the overwhelming amount of cultural evidence to the contrary — and the anarchic left-wing tradition of free love — is not necessarily a foregone conclusion. For some time, writers such as Ennio Flaiano and Luciano Bianciardi had been lampooning the dominant behavioural trends, including (or perhaps it would be better to say "above all") those that distinguished the intelligentsia who patronized the former Italian Communist Party. We nevertheless remain within the sphere of anarchy fired by long-standing left-wing traditions, at least as far as Bianciardi is concerned. The man who left these traditions behind but remained fairly close to Bianciardi in spirit, was Jacques Laurent (who under the pseudonym Cecil Saint Laurent wrote *Caroline Chérie*, the character made famous in movies by Martine Carol) who insisted on describing himself, and his "hussar" friends, as rightist, which gave added bite to his mockery of the circle dominated by Sartre and the "committed" intellectuals — but was rewarded by his being accused, inevitably, of "fascism." Spain's most popular writer, Camilo José Cela (Nobel laureate 1989) was for some years responsible for literary censorship under the Franco regime, with which he always had close ties. Notwithstanding this, his books (not infrequently censored for their irreverence and pornographic content) ruthlessly exposed public morals, government officials, priests, and the family. Cela had himself photographed with a blonde bombshell as soon as he was nominated for the Nobel prize and, in fact, liked to play the Casanova. This is how he is portrayed in a book written by his son (also called Camilo José). The so-called Beat Generation authors constituted the strongest bohemian link with the Sixties movements, whose cause they often espoused. Unlike his friends, Jack Kerouac never missed an opportunity to display his patriotism. In those same years, the classic works of D.H. Lawrence and Henry Miller that were published before the Second World War, came out in paperback. The unexpurgated version of *Lady Chatterley's Lover* by Lawrence was first published in England as recently as 1959, and pornography charges brought for the hundredth time. Those courageous publishers who finally brought out unexpurgated editions of the great classics of erotic and freethinking literature (like the works of Pauvert with overtones of de Sade) were the victims of trials and sequestrations. A refined and surreal form of eroticism was constantly featured in the French magazine *Planète*, published in the Sixties. An ambitious publica-

Belinda Lee and Gualtiero Jacopetti at the Cannes Film Festival, 1960 (Hulton Deutsch Collection)

tion, it nevertheless had a very large circulation, was printed in a whole variety of languages, and offered readers the opportunity to collect a series of volumes (including an anthology of erotic literature). The magazine was edited by Louis Pawels who came from the spiritualist circles associated with Gurdjieff, and went on to become one of the most prominent "neoliberalist" journalists in Europe in the Eighties. Soft porno magazines with a large circulation (in 1955 Hugh Hefner founded *Playboy* and ten years later Bob Guccione brought out *Penthouse*, which were followed by various magazines such as *Playmen* and *Lui*) had to fight a hard battle against the old fogeys of the day, and seemed to assume a radical position. However, this battle was also waged energetically by politicians and journalists from all parties, far more so in fact than it was by those with communist sympathies, who were inevitably cautious and querulous, and scorned problems they frowned on as "middle-class." An Italian weekly called *ABC*, which hooked readers with naked, or semi-naked women (a practice that was not even disdained by a conservative magazine with the explicit name of *Il Borghese*), ousted the strait-laced *Domenica del Corriere* from people's homes and waiting rooms, and took up the struggle for freedom. It may have been a radical publication but it was definitely non-communist, and proud of it. It is easy to see why public opinion, in all political groups, started to feel the need to eliminate, amongst other things, the remaining hypocritical barriers that prevented the portrayal of sex and related public behaviour.

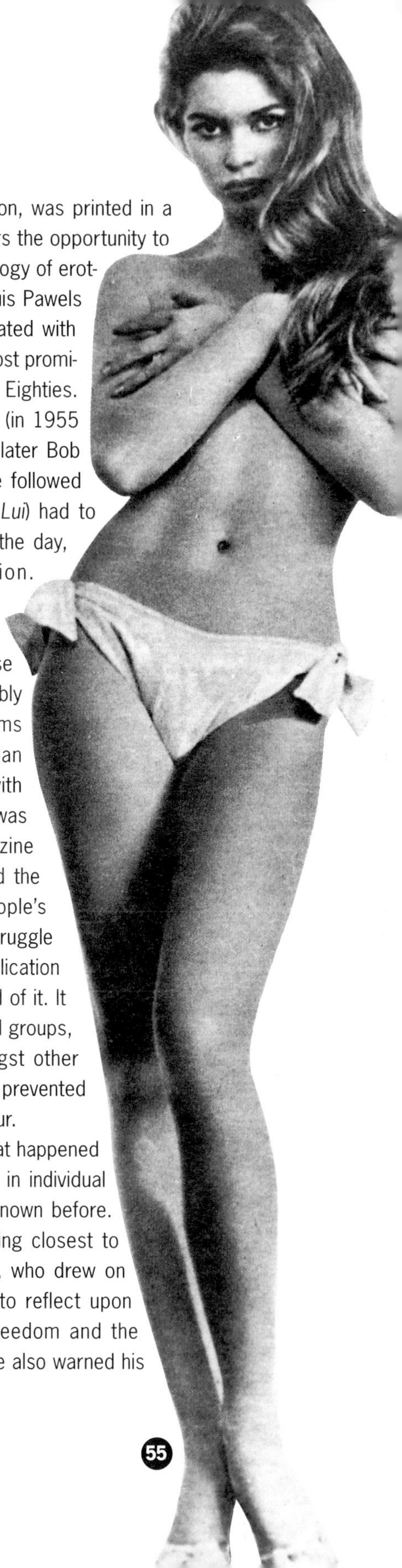

Brigitte Bardot
(Farabolafoto)

From an economic point of view, everything that happened during those years was linked to an increase in individual spending, the like of which had never been known before. The philospher indicated by the press as being closest to the demands of youth was Herbert Marcuse, who drew on Marxism, psychoanalysis and Existentialism to reflect upon the insidious authoritarianism of political freedom and the superficial nature of sexual permissiveness. He also warned his

Beppe Piroddi and Odile Rodin at a party held at the Number One nightspot in Rome, 1968 (Farabolafoto)

readers against believing that the end of lack was the beginning of real living. Later, this valid philosphical observation on mankind was transformed by others into a kind of anti-consumerist moralism that completely lost sight of humanity. When the initial fervour began to wane, coinciding, more or less, with the economic downswing, ideas that had been circulating in blithe confusion automatically structured themselves into groups which became prey to political, feminist, homosexual, terrorist, and neo-religious, dogmatism. Although the figure of Don Jaime de Mora y Aragon had initially aroused sympathy, he had now fallen into disrepute and was scorned as a Casanova. Newspapers and magazines that had turned Don Jaime, and his like, into a legend, became more circumspect. It was not that the popular press and smut magazines had abandoned their scoops on crowned heads, wealthy marriages, and the secret trysts of the stars. They had simply become aware of an anachronism: it was no longer the time to reserve a form of treatment, practically akin to worship, for the protagonists of society life. In a society that set great store by respectability, the Don Juan staked everything on being able to enjoy money and sexuality without feeling guilty. It was he who realized the ordinary man's desires. And the ordinary man was just starting to feel good when feminist fanatics, seeing him as a born rapist, simply accused him of being male. It became a problem to talk about women in the way that they had always been talked about, and a new and grotesque code of behaviour began to emerge. Woody Allen's movies created a man who was considered weak, in all the conventional ways, and was only sincere in the irony he used to temporarily ward off the blows of female aggression. In the late Seventies —when John Travolta was trying, most probably, to re-create the myth of the Latin lover by playing a character who was apparently in keeping with that particular reality — Alberto Sordi cynically portrayed in his episode of *I nuovi mostri* (The New Monsters) the dated *savoir faire* of the Casanovas of the *dolce vita* (in the film aristocrat Francesco Maria Catalan Del Monte picks up the victim of a hit-and-run driver and tries to get him into one of the hospitals filled to overflowing. He is repeatedly turned away, and finally takes the man back to where he found him. The aristocrat chats to the man while they are riding along in his antiquated Rolls-Royce, using such delightful phrases as: "the old banger comes in useful for picking up pussy").

A study carried out in 1967 by the Institute for Research on Poverty at the University of Wisconsin — conducted by Robert Haveman and Irwin Garfinkel — established that the most suitable model for overcoming poverty was the work-family-religion trinity (married couples were more motivated than singles, people with children more than those without, men more than women, whites more than blacks, etc.). At the same time, criticism of the theory of the State as the sole font of law become more pronounced and real economic freedom was once again emphasized.

Experts like Robert Nozick, to cite the most famous, went as far as to recommend drastically reducing the body of law, embracing an idea of society that was very close to anarchy. Although politicians who were neoliberalist sympathizers established a dialogue with these extremists, they tended to act on the results of studies such as the one effected by the University of Wisconsin. The liberalism of Western politicians ended at conventional middle-class values and they opposed everything, such as drugs, thought by the gullible masses to undermine those values. The "transformation of all values" signified a pause. Once again, the youth movement gloried in anarchism by using the infantile and extreme provocation of punk; however, the period that had begun with the Sixties was coming to an end — if it had not already been hit on the head by terrorism and feminism.

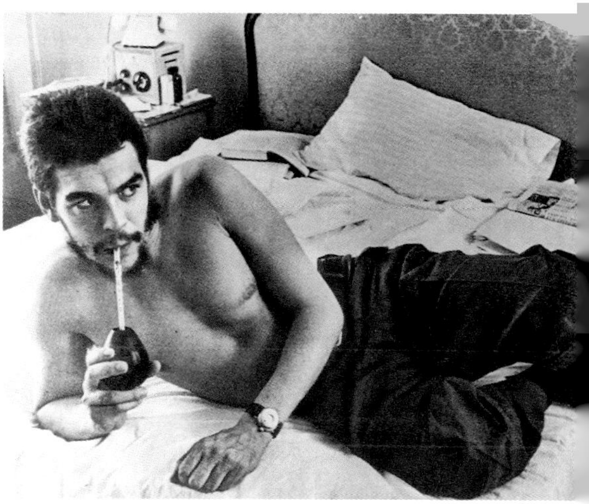

Ernesto Che Guevara when he was president of the Cuban National Bank (Farabolafoto)

All this did not happen without a few things leaving their mark. The stereotypes that had existed in the not-too-distant past were regarded with irony and cynicism, rather than nostalgia. People cited examples. It was "postmodern" to name names. Even Julio Iglesias, former Spanish soccer player turned international singing star, seemed more like an example of the Latin lover rather than a survivor of the species. Every attitude assumed by the individual served to create a particular, yet transient, quality that was considered to give one the edge in relating to the world. One was prepared, in fact, to adopt any attitude as long as it was advantageous, and the only thing experienced at a visceral level were "professional" aims. The combination of liberty and moralism seemed to give birth to a type of social climber, who gained greater expertise from the years during which moralism was attacked. Whatever the studies carried out by the theorists to establish the ethics on which the new liberalism was founded, this social animal, rapidly labelled as a "yuppie" (young urban professional), was said to draw

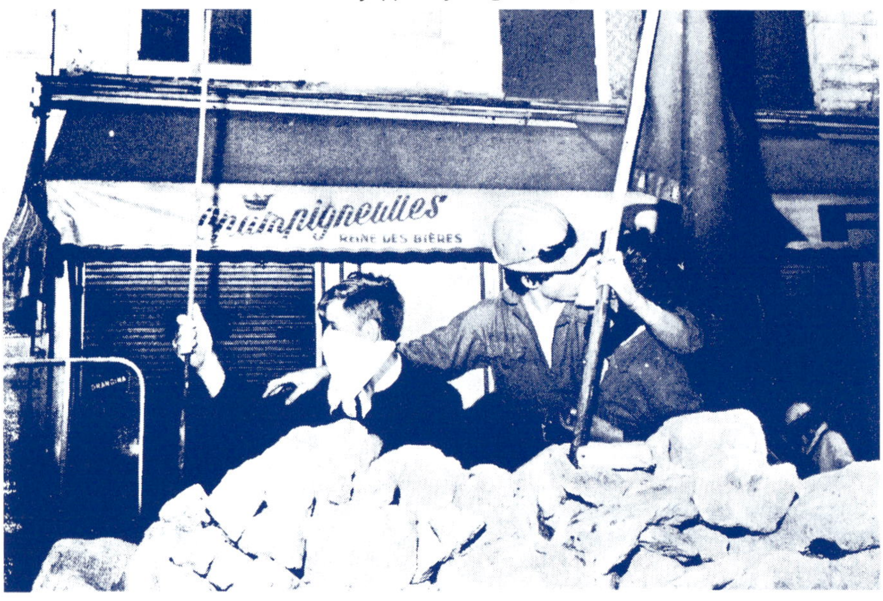

Paris, May 1968 (Archivio Critico)

sustenance from such fonts of knowledge as *The Art of War*, by Sun Tzu, and other Oriental writings, which equipped him with the necessary coldness to make it in the business world.

Scene from Zabriskie Point *by Michelangelo Antonioni, 1969 (Grazia Neri)*

All things considered, the demise of the Latin lover, in the way in which he was perceived until the Sixties, should perhaps be interpreted according to such concepts as "secularization," borrowed from religious sociology. However, the process that led to his making an exit appears to be far more radical than the effect that such an important international gathering as the Second Vatican Council had on Catholics (and not only them). At first, the Latin lover as a cult figure appeared to embody a secularized form of religion and a pagan hero. Later the victim of a good debunking, he nevertheless survived as a classic figure, dreamboat and, let's say it, shamanist vision — to continue in the above vein. In an age

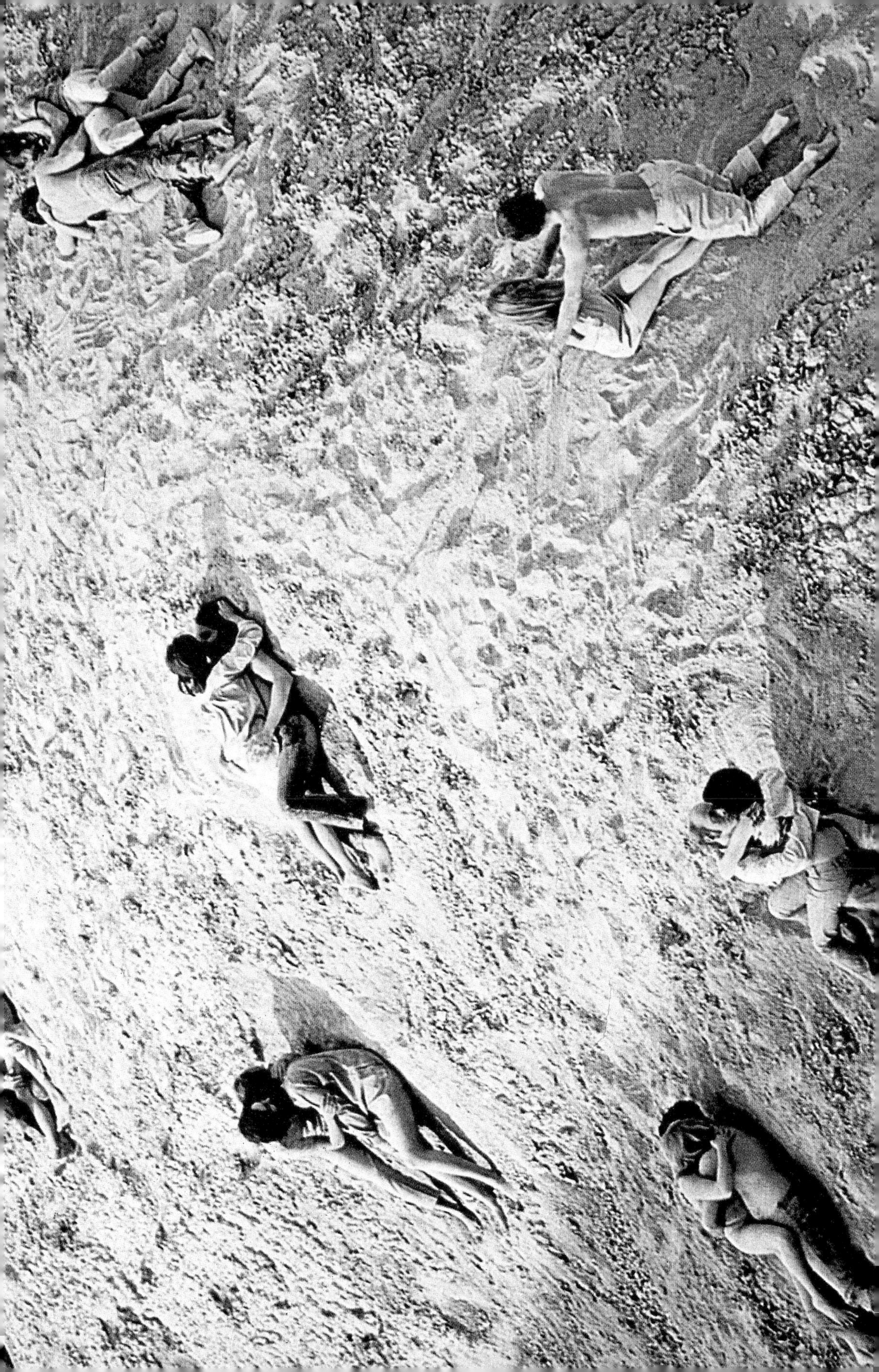

in which the image revolution that began with the cinema is being sustained by the invention of ever-more sophisticated illusionistic machines (virtual reality), the Latin lover could be one of the most racy types to conjure up (imagine if this revolution was to extend to all the senses!). Except for the fact that there is no "typical" Latin lover. Their personalities and lives have always differed, as we have seen. Therefore, the fantasy varies. There remain certain distinguishing features which, however, are by no means common to all: the cravat; the open-necked shirt (very popular) and the polo shirt (one of Rubirosa's favourites), all worn with a certain aplomb that was exploited to the full (or so it was said) by Italian tailors (when couture tailoring was synonymous, above all, with Florence and Rome), before they sold out to international style.

In Italy in the Fifties, a refined Milanese lady left her wealthy husband to follow a romantic dream: her love for one of the bandits behind the notorious "Via Osoppo Robbery." She was to end up as a cashier in a coffee bar. In the Nineties, countless teeny-boppers (and also grown women) went crazy over Pietro Maso, a young Venetian who murdered his parents in order to inherit their wealth. Maso appeared cold and unfeeling at the trial. He sported a cravat, and evidently liked the idea of being a "lady-killer." While in prison he was inundated with letters from female admirers. Although the two cases are juxtaposed, there is obviously no relationship between them: the second could have occurred before the first, and vice versa. We are comparing passion and coldness, rather than eras. All we see is the criminal nature of the passions of this century that is now drawing to a close. The free democracy of the West manifests all the signs of a state of equilibrium without alternatives. Glizot's old maxim ("Get rich!") is echoed as the only antidote to the general malaise. In truth, freedom goes hand in hand with wealth rather than legality. The scenario in which the Latin lover made his conquests has by no means lost its fascination. Nothing has been compromized. The "former" nature of Hegelian-inspired art has not stopped the creation of new works, which has never been more profuse than in the last two hundred years. Up until this point we have concerned ourselves with the "former" nature of the Latin lover, but this does not mean that the phenomenon no longer exists. On the other hand, the so-called "sexual revolutions" have not eliminated from bedside tables those

Underground cartoon from Vivere insieme, il libro delle comuni, *1974 (Archivio Critico)*

books that Rousseau said could only be read if you left one hand free. Videocassettes leave both hands free. From a historical point of view, we can consider the wider horizons of the present or discuss re-emerging trends; but we have to acknowledge that everything changes except the substance of things. The point is that we are examining a particular aspect of decadence that interprets reality at one level, while excluding another: that of cross-fertilizations, interactions, and new models. This does not make it any the less valid, because it is simply one perspective that clarifies what it is meant to clarify. Another thing to ask ourselves would be whether the cause of this decadence has seriously interfered with our capacity to dream of an impossible love, such as the type aroused by personality cults. This is obviously not the case. Furthermore, if we acknowledge a need for self-aggrandizement in the artist, we cannot refuse to recognize this same need in the Latin lover.

In fact, a certain urbanity — characteristic of the bon viveur type as much as the absurd radical chic element — displayed by those who were inclined to flirt with everything on the bubble in society, has succeeded in emerging virtually unscathed by time and by an exacerbated public. Prominent industrialists, professional men, aristocrats (even the heir to the British throne to some degree), and the well-heeled set, belong to this class. An example of the classic Don Juan who managed to avoid social repercussions (but not those of age, as he was already fifty at the end of the Sixties) was Don Jaime's fellow countryman, José Luis de Villalonga. A big name in Spain and friend of Porfirio Rubirosa (they played polo together), he had a certain insolence in common with Don Jaime but possessed a completely different spirit, which made him far less exhibitionist and inclined to dedicate himself to own writing rather than being the talk of the press. When as a young man he tired of his father's expectations, he proceeded to inform him that he was homosexual, he intended to marry the daughter of a Jewish store-keeper, and he was about to join the clandestine Communist Party. All hell did not break loose, as he had hoped, but months later when Villalonga had a short story published in a popular magazine, his father contemptuously referred to him as: "The intellectual!" Villalonga also played in movies (working with Fellini, Louis Malle, Blake Edwards, Henri Verneuil, and many others, making more than thirty films). He wrote a good many novels and published interviews in the press with many of his actor friends. Villalonga himself confided to a journalist that he felt impotent at the end of an affair, saying that he was going to discuss the matter with Prof. Lacan (a Casanova named Pierre Ray, the columnist of the Paris beau monde, also sought help from the well-known psychoanalyst, and embarked on a brilliant career as a novelist after treatment). Villalonga had a horror of extremism. He considered the worst example of this to be Francoism, which he described as "radical mediocrity." As for *gauchisme*, it never left the bistrot, young people only talked about revolution. He described himself as "clear-thinking and liberal-minded."

The type of man of the world and refined gentleman that existed in Villalonga still has an appeal deriving from intelligence and class, which is not easy to emulate. It is difficult to find his equivalent today. The cards have been jumbled up. Popular fashion has long since contaminated that of the upper classes (the same thing has happened in the area of food), and this is just one of the many examples. Taste seems to have become more uniform than in the past. Certain poses, however, still manifest themselves unexpectedly, but with conflicting results. The neocommunist leader Fausto Bertinotti (who speaks with a lisp that is thought to be an affectation in Italy) appeared in a programme on television (where he is often featured as a political celebrity) during which he was interviewed by a bevy of females who went into ecstasies over his elegant dress and refined manner. "Yes," Bertinotti replied, as cool as you please, "I prefer a subtle style." Palmiro Togliatti, one of the most influential leaders of the Stalinist International, introduced a style known as middle-class honour. When he spoke of Freud it was to say that his ideas led straight to the whorehouse. Bertinotti is also for the home and family at present. Liberals who do not want to jeopardize the family institution argue that it is an expression of privacy and, therefore, of individualism. If it were up to Bertinotti, however, the communists would go beyond the constricting limits of middle-class individualism by favouring homosexual couples to obtain for them the same legal status as the family (which would be like officialdom meddling in friendship) and the possibility of adopting children. We are evidently witnessing the results of a wrongly-handled "sexual issue." Not so much by Bertinotti, as the spectre of political opinion that seeks to combine the usual strategies for gaining power with "realpolitik." Utopia seems almost sensible and "realistic" in comparison, if only as an expression of those problems that generate a need for its creation. If we take advantage of the flexibility of words and interpret "utopia" as dream and myth (when words are substituted for one another, which often happens, their meanings are often clarified), we find ourselves in the domain where the Latin lover lives on determinedly. Let us pretend that it is located on that planet featured in the short story by Borges, where life consists of everything that is merely imagined on Earth. Not even there can we hope to realize our dreams to the full, just as we will not find a map of Utopia in the atlas. He who desires to emulate the Latin lover cannot hope to find a guide, even if it were Casanova himself, to living a life of passion, without scruples. There is also the fact that Utopia (as Karl Kraus said of psychoanalysis) may well be the ill it claims to cure.

THE PASSIONATE SOUTH

HOLIDAY FUN

Luigi Settembrini

Although the myth of the Latin lover is fairly recent, it already has a great past: a past that reached its apogee in the Sixties. Just twenty years ago the Latin lover was the most authentic example of male virility in the Mediterranean and the standard-bearer of the national tourist industry — especially at fashionable coastal resorts. Not only, he had also risen to the rank of hero, lending his name to the well-known cult of romantic sentimentalism "with a view." Despite his illustrious forebears (Zeus, Don Juan, Casanova), the Latin lover is, at least as far as definition and vocation are concerned, a product of the cultural market of fairly recent times; a product whose supply was actually created by the demand. Therefore, he is the anthropological-individual-masculine result of female and social evolution over the last couple of centuries; in fact, he is more of a complement to, rather than the protagonist of, that particular period of history. Something (I'm sorry, *someone*) that obliges us to speak about women, instead of the Latin lover and the men who modelled themselves on him.

However, there are very few Latin lovers left. They are a species that risks becoming extinct, like the panda, the Greenland whale and the Bengal tiger, without even the smallest WWF to campaign for their survival. On the contrary, the Latin lover has thousands of dismissive, contemptuous detractors: veteran feminists who want him abolished; pontificators; pure spirits; progressive intellectuals (bona fide and political), and repentant male chauvinist pigs who are suckers for punishment. Would it therefore appear out of context, unfounded and deliberately provocative, to take an interest in the Latin lover at this point in time and to make him responsible for something positive, like a promise of happiness for future relationships between men and women? We don't think so. Promises, especially those made by lovers, are expressions of hopes and dreams, rather than principles. This promise is also a little old-fashioned; therefore, no one will want to know unless it is kept. All things considered, the Sixties appear more innovative, happy and colourful, in direct comparison with the difficult Forties and Fifties, the terrorist climate of the Seventies, and the vulgar Eighties without ideals. This could partly explain why that superficial world known as fashion, which always has its ear to the ground, is re-launching the Sixties look. Returning to the past is as typical of fashion as it is of certain types of baroque putti (cherubs) who

Jupiter and Thetis *by Jean Auguste Dominique Ingres, 1811. Musée Granet, Aix-en-Provence (photo by Bernard Terlay)*

Rossano Brazzi and June Allison, 1957 (Ullstein Bilderdienst)

wing their way forward, while casually and charmingly looking over their shoulder. Flying, like Cupid's arrow, to the promise he will make, the Latin lover, stripped of his typically Italian characteristics and macho attributes by the philosophers, could also embody a concept of love as playful deceipt: that sublime deceipt of which we all dream, which is accepted and consciously pursued by both partners in a game of role- playing, during which guises are cast off and donned at will, aimed more at creating an atmosphere than a steady relationship, let alone starting a family! Who is the Latin lover? What sets him apart from those other men who are lucky enough to be lucky with women? What makes him different from an international playboy or a lady-killer from Boston or Stockholm? It is not necessarily the usual exaggerations (down to the last fraction of an inch) concerning physical attributes and sexual prowess; the intense preoccupation with keeping score, and the obsession with hitting the mark every time — all characteristics to be found in the stud at the local bar. It is not money (although it always helps). Shirts unbuttoned to the navel, gold chains, pendants, flashing smiles, and perennial tans that withstand the small hours, are not typical only of our boy. He is however distinguished, at a psychological or psychopathological level, by his incurable narcissism, lack of restraint, sheer nerve, and unwavering persistence, which have been known to degenerate into arrogance and violence. So, what are the most striking characteristics of the ideal Latin lover? Let us try and enumerate them, as they come to mind. First of all, an intensity of passion or "Mediterranean heat" that can be regulated at will (a chameleon-like sentimental opportunism), combined with a rampant and hyperactive sex life; highly imaginative seduction techniques (the baroque-style conquest); an elaborate eye-contact strategy and instant propositioning that floors the lady in question and knocks out the competition; a certain reckless conduct in the area of public decency (the Latin lover puts all his cards on the table: courting, kissing, loving in the open air); an ostentatious portrayal of love that destroys but, at the same time, exalts the intimacy of a formal love relationship (a romantic who successfully adopts a non-romantic attitude); a ludic and polymorphic sexuality (both infantile characteristics that bring out the maternal instinct in women); a sophisticated elegance and aesthetic sense that are highly individual; quite a good physique, with a tendency to be short and olive-skinned; an excellent all-rounder who pursues sports with a casual determination; a certain amount of courtesy and tact; and, to wind up, a flair for exploiting picture postcard locations, violins, and favourable astrological and weather conditions. Whatever the type (and there are many, all completely different), Latin lovers are essentially among the "unemployed," in that either they have "no fixed occupation" or they hold an "important position" that makes them a big shot with social obligations. They are *flâneurs* who are experts at whiling away the hours, the lucky so-and-sos — a talent that could be passed on to those people who, in present-day society, find themselves having to deal, more and more, with their own solitude rather than office or factory jobs. Even the most fanatic Latin lover never gives the impression that he is in a hurry. At least not "before," while he is weaving the web in which he will catch his prey (if we still want to use words like "web" and "prey" that are exaggerated and inappropriate, because it was the "prey" that created the "hunter," as specified in the introductory paragraph). It is "after" that he shows a little more haste, when it comes to getting rid of the "body," and preparing for the chase again; in fact, preparing for the chase, and the excitement it arouses, is the best thing about this whole story. I believe Casanova admitted to this in his *Memoirs*, although he was slightly bored by everything else. The general traits of the complex figure of the Latin lover reveal behavioural patterns deriving from a widespread, age-old, sentimental and sensual education and a period of history dating from the end of the eighteenth, and the beginning of the nineteenth century. It was then that the myth of the Latin lover was born, with the awakening of romantic sensibility whose exponents soon tired of producing literature along the lines of the "affected Arcadian verse and bucolic scenes"

Rossano Brazzi (Archivio Brandini-Sanguinetti)

John Travolta in Saturday Night Fever, *1977 (Farabolafoto)*

Giuseppe Garibaldi (Farabolafoto)

dear to Schiller, and of theorizing about Nature, Beauty and Tradition; in fact, they went to look for the real thing in that particular part of Southern Europe — the cradle of civilization — which was to become the southern hemisphere of love. When the Grand Tour was all the rage a few years later, it stimulated women to embark on a search that with time became more assiduous and demanding, and extended to the masses: they were conducting a *cherchez l'homme* that was certainly very innocent and strait-laced at first but which, step by step, gradually descended to the edge of the swimming-pool in which Esther Williams, former Olympic swimmer and movie star, performed her aquatic ballets and was attracted solely to Latin lovers. In *Neptune's Daughter* (1951) it was Mexican Ricardo Montalban, who captained Argentina's polo team; in *Fog over the Channel* (1953), the lucky man was Argentinian Fernando Lamas who, at the helm of his yacht, succeeded in doing three things at once: steering, strumming the guitar, and kissing. Any number of Latin lovers went in to movies, and some of them were as lucky as Rossano Brazzi whom the public considered to be the ultimate Latin lover. In the Fifties, he was renowned the world over for the way in which his nostrils quivered as his lips closed on those of the lady of the moment. The search continued even lower down, when the women came south to Italy. They gradually discarded their purist and intellectual attitudes, with all classes acting more openly, and female German tourists finally fell upon the Rimini lifeguards, who are still partially responsible for a successful summer season on the Adriatic Riviera. It was a movement, therefore, that originated in a cold, cultured, wealthy Northern Europe that was already civilized and advanced enough to have made heterosexual relationships in that society more considerate, polite, refined, thoughtful, confused, critical, sad, tired, indifferent, and last but not least, detached. This desperate situation, which still exists today, was to produce the various Hedda Gablers, Lulùs, Lady Chatterleys, and all those other ladies who demanded to be allowed to ride a bike, smoke in public, and cast their vote. The same cultural climate also spawned the blonde "dark" ladies featured in every kind of film in the Forties and the Fifties: the celluloid alter egos of the male hunter and collector of female trophies, whether Latin or an inferior breed. On the other hand, the male universe in those countries was to become conventional, stiff, hesitant, inconclusive, and scared. The men developed a taste for hunting (real animals), clubs, pubs, gardening, making money, and sporting rituals from which women were rigorously barred, until the men finally started to kick with the left foot, and what had been occasional experiences at boarding school became more frequent in adult life, especially if you were an MP. The thrill of love, let alone passion, was becoming an increasingly rare experience in the lives of those emancipated Northern European women. At home they may have been suffragettes, Red Cross nurses who carried a torch for Florence Nightingale, heads of reformatories, and cigar smokers, but on their trips in search of warmth, beauty and history — the cultural background necessary for their still vague expectations — they inevitably allowed themselves to be guided by romantic sentimentalism acquired from all the novels they had read, the paintings they had viewed, and the travellers' tales they had heard tell. This cultural background permitted them to meet up with idealistic figures and behaviour, and unfamiliar practices that were comprehensible because they had already been brought into perspective. They were certainly exotic, but it was a "tame" exoticism that was neither extreme nor dangerous, but confined to the precise and reassuring geographical limits of Western civilization. Beyond, *erunt leones*: veiled concubines in crowded harems; little girls whose feet were doubled back and bound from the tenderest age, and white slave trade. The general female condition was one of unmitigated slavery, which no one made any attempt to justify by supplying the poor wretches with a carpet beater, washing machine, or fitted kitchen. Far from being a tourist attraction, venturing into such places required an ethnological expedition of the type that was later to be carried out by Ruth Benedict, Margaret Mead, and the like. It is only today, in this multicultural, interracial

Cover photo of Rudolph Valentino in The Sheik *in* Motion Picture Magazine, *February 1921 (Archivio Cineteca Comunale, Bologna)*

era of global tourism, that such things are no longer the territory of specialists but available to everyone, laying who knows what foundations for future theories about "Amazonian, Indonesian or Australian Aboriginal lovers." Therefore, the myth of the Latin lover had already been planted in the minds of the women from the cold northern hemisphere. Completely unbeknown to the interested parties (who were only budding Latin lovers then), it was still locked inside them, simply waiting for the right moment to emerge in the progenitors of the dusky young men in singlets, bronzed lifeguards, fawning waiters, singing gondoliers, and fiery toreadors — who are the classic image of the breed. Try and imagine what happened when these two worlds first met: the bewilderment, surprise, awkwardness, curiosity, respect, fear, and excitement, that must have been tremendous on both sides. Let us forget for a moment the more intellectual aspects of this culture clash, and consider how traumatic it must have been for these women, who even greeted their mothers with a polite handshake, when they came into contact with men who had been, hugged, caressed, covered with kisses and patted and slapped on the bottom, by their mothers, grandmothers, sisters, aunts and their female friends, ever since they were bambinos. Men with an exceptional talent for mime and gesture, which came in very useful when there were no idioms or words in common, and enabled them to quickly move on to the "manual" aspect of things (a weak handshake, or something more vigorous, like wandering hands that were everywhere). These Latin lovers had become all too familiar with invasions over the centuries, possessed an instinctive flair for improvising deals, and were blessed by a religion that pardoned their sins when confessed; therefore, they very quickly adapted and elaborated extremely refined strategies to meet the needs of the fair sex. They actually succeeded in making these women more aware of their own needs, which they also developed, creating and manipulating female behaviour patterns to suit their own purpose. This unfailingly leads to regrettable misunderstandings: not only with regard to the Latin lover's awareness of his social and historical role (leading everyone to believe that he belongs to a race of magnificent lovers who have been God's gift to women since the days of Romulus and Remus); but also at a psychological level, with regard to personal conduct, when he assumes things that should never be taken for granted in matters of the heart ("But I thought she was willing...") or he is persistent, as mentioned above, to the point of becoming vulgar or coming on too strong, which sometimes results in a visit to the local police station. But on the whole most coarse and violent manifestations of male chauvinism are kept under control. They are moderated and refined by criteria that must be respected to secure and develop the market, to meet expectations; in other words, by the "DOC" (controlled denomination of origin) sentimentalism and passion that are inevitably acted out against a backdrop of spectacular sunsets, ancient ruins, and Capri rock formations. The "novice" Latin lover, simply because he is and simply because that is what he does, is able to

Marcello Mastroianni and Anita Ekberg in La dolce vita *(The Sweet Life), 1960 (Farabolafoto)*

learn and teach at the same time. He changes, perfects his technique, and deftly manipulates the red and green lights of his own and other people's instincts. But he is still a male chauvinist pig underneath it all. Especially at home, because mamma, grandma, and wifey, are all there to iron his shirts and prepare his *tagliatelle*, leaving him perfectly free to indulge in his refined games and gratuitously display his charms, and those of his native land. Naturally, there are the Latin lovers who stand out from the crowd, the most famous of whom are worshipped by the gossip columns, and whose sensitivity, elegance, attributes, titles, education, way with words, and worldliness, permit them to embark on memorable conquests. Unlike your average Latin lover, the big guys have important jobs and impressive careers; in fact, they never have a minute to spare — unless it is to make advances to some gorgeous creature. Who are they? Apart from those whose names have appeared thousands of times in any tabloid worthy of the name, maybe Paris, and, in chronological order, Ulysses, Mark Antony, Garibaldi, Puccini, Mussolini, Salvatore Giuliano, Che Guevara, Fellini-Mastroianni, Aristotle Onassis, Gianni Agnelli (who is really too nasty to be a Latin lover, or so it is said), Dominguin, Placido Domingo, Julio Iglesias, Fiorello (Italian television idol), and Zorro... dammit! And what if there were a tiny fascist flame smouldering in the heart of the Latin lover? As we said earlier, the Sixties marked the apogee of the Latin lover myth, and also the beginning of its decline. Economic development flourished in Southern Europe and the cultural gap between the two worlds slowly began to narrow. The tourist flow was marked by a slight counter trend: the first few Latin lovers who ventured as far as the Northern European capitals to "play away from home," received a nasty shock — which taught them a great deal — when they came into contact with the way of life of the female tourists they had been accustomed to picking up in bikinis on the beaches at home. The ladies who had so enjoyed their company in the delightful summer haunts of the Mediterranean, during their week in a *pension* with all meals included, gave those poor Latin fish out of water a very cool welcome! Student uprisings, cultural revolutions, and free love, finally arrived to brazenly shake everything to its foundations. As was to be expected, a veritable earthquake was started by the straight-talking, vitriolic, emergent feminist movement, which condemned far more private and timid sentiments than those displayed by the Latin lover. The rest is history, today, when everything is "post-something." A number of themes, trends and personalities that are re-emerging in movies, advertising and glossy magazines, seem at first glance to be neo-male chauvinist, but are, in fact, post-feminist. While it is impossible to go back to the "pre-," the "post-" has only just begun. What if that sophisticated game of "I-know-that-you-know-that-I-know" in which every Latin lover gives his best performance, were also a fundamental element in the complex, language of casual, but not superfical, love affairs between the two sexes? Or three... or however many there are today, and will be in the future?

A FEW HELPFUL NOTES:

What has been mistaken for a manifestation of the most primitive form of male chauvinist sexism, or passed off by its propagators as the **genius loci,** and sexual suprematism of the Latin and Mediterranean races, turns out to be a product and synthesis of the evolution of modern western society, the cultural exchanges between its different components (tourism), and the emancipation of women in the northern hemisphere.

Women of the North: social and cultural domination mistaken for subordination. Or social and cultural domination (looking down) mistaken also for sexual and affective subordination (running after).

Until the end of the Sixties. Afterwards **(post-feminism),** we have a sophisticated game of role playing, in which the man played at being the hunter and the woman was the prey. But only for those two weeks in Rimini, "all-in," after which she went back to being an executive in Hamburg and he returned to pen-pushing in Gallarate.
These roles can also be exchanged.

Latin lover = Liberating violation of unique and forbidden feelings in the chaos of southern Italian "love trafficking."

Passion as a "commodity-refuge" of the post-modern era.

The **"weak"** reasoning (presumed) of the Latin male brings him close to the traditional sentimentalism (presumed) of women.

At the start of the phenomenon: inflated ideals are set against others. Sometimes **she marries him:** but that doesn't interest us because it is only logical, predictable, and normal, that the magic disappears immediately. The only thing that can be analyzed is the phenomenology of disappointment: why does he criticize her for not being able to make *tagliatelle* like his mamma? (See

Rossano Brazzi and Anna Magnani in Vulcano *(Volcano), (Archivio Brandini-Sanguinetti)*

Gœthe.

the poem by Eduardo De Filippo in his *Cantata dei giorni pari* – Cantata of Even Days, which begins: *"O ragù che me piace a'mme o faceva sulo mammà"* – I only like my mother's meat sauce..., and ends with this protest *"Chist'è carne c'a pummarola!"* – This is just meat and tomatoes!).

Perspectives: from the suffragette movement, the "virile" prototype of feminism, to the post-feminist cult/right of being "different"; from the early twentieth century "penis envy" of Freud to the third-sex, androgynous look launched by Dolce & Gabbana today.

Lord Byron.

Romantic references: Romeo and Juliet (Verona), Othello and Desdemona (Venice).

Don Juan = Don Juan Tenorio (Tirso de Molina *El burlador de Sevilla*, 1630; Molière, Mérimée, Dumas, Balzac, Flaubert, De Musset, Byron, etc. Plus Kierkegaard, Mozart, Strauss, Purcell, Gluck, etc.).
Giacomo Casanova (1725-1798) writer, philosopher, violinist, cabbalist, gambler, diplomat, and spy (*Memorie* – Memoirs, 1791–1798).

Goethe, Stendhal, Byron, Alfieri.

Places: Portofino, Capri, Sorrento, Positano, Amalfi, Naples, Florence, Venice, Rome, and Rimini, in Italy alone.

Couples:
Rossellini and Ingrid
Dominguin and Lucia Bosè
Walter Chiari and Ava Gardner
Mastroianni and Catherine Deneuve
BB and Gigi Rizzi
Fernando Lamas and Lana Turner. The film they made together in 1953, *The Merry Widow*, was launched as the movie with three "Ls": Lana, Lamas, and Love.
Aristotle Onassis and Jacqueline Kennedy
Banderas and Kathleen Turner
Banderas and Tom Hanks (*Philadelphia*).

Alfieri.

The words of Italian Lover (Cassano-Pallavicini) deserve to be quoted in full:

Ho imparato
che un bacio
tu lo chiami
un kiss
ti voglio dare tanti kiss
kiss...kiss...kiss...kiss
come fan qui
kiss...kiss...kiss...kiss
in Italy:
yes...yes...yes...yes
Dimmi di sì
voglio parlar
solo coi kiss.
Io sono Italian lover
love...love...love...love...love
vuol dire amor.

(I've heard that you call a
bacio a kiss
I want to give you so many
kisses
kiss...kiss...kiss...kiss
as they do here
kiss...kiss...kiss...kiss
in Italy:
yes...yes...yes...yes...
Say yes
I want to talk only
with kisses.
I am an Italian lover:
love...love...love...love
it means l'amour).

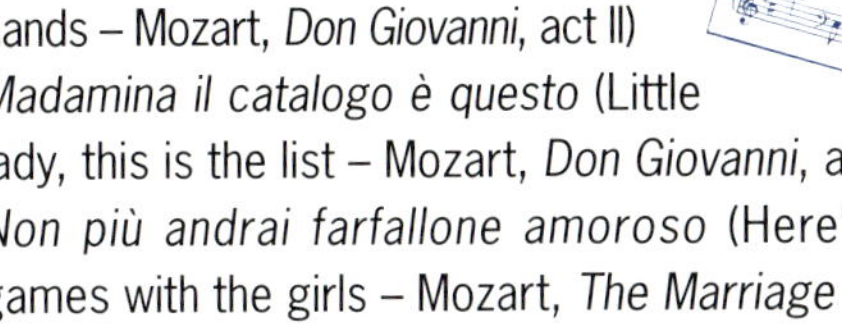

Songs and arias:
Pagan Love Song (R. Novarro)
Arrivederci Roma (R. Rascel)
Souvenir d'Italie (...)
I Found My Love in Portofino (F. Buscaglione)
Una rotonda sul mare (F. Bongusto)
Tre settimane da raccontare (F. Bongusto)
Là ci darem la mano (There we'll take hands – Mozart, *Don Giovanni*, act II)
Madamina il catalogo è questo (Little lady, this is the list – Mozart, *Don Giovanni*, act I)
Non più andrai farfallone amoroso (Here's an end to your games with the girls – Mozart, *The Marriage of Figaro*, act II).

Films:
Blood and Sand (1922) by Fred Niblo, with Rudolph Valentino and Nita Naldi
Blood and Sand (1941) by Rouben Mamoulian, with Tyrone Power and Rita Hayworth
Three Coins in the Fountain (1954) by Jean Negulesco, with Rossano Brazzi and Jean Peters
La ragazza del Palio (1957) by Luigi Zampa, with Vittorio Gassman and Diana Dors
Stromboli (1949) by Roberto Rossellini, with Ingrid Bergman
Il sorpasso (1962) by Dino Risi, with Vittorio Gassman and Jean Louis Trintignant
I vitelloni (1953) by Federico Fellini, starring Alberto Sordi
La dolce vita (1960) by Federico Fellini, with Marcello Mastroianni and Anita Ekberg
Otto e mezzo (1963) by Federico Fellini, with Marcello Mastroianni and Sandra Milo
Brevi amori a Palma di Majorca (1959) by Giorgio Bianchi, with Alberto Sordi and Belinda Lee
Souvenir d'Italie (1954) by Antonio Pietrangeli, with Gabriele Ferzetti, Vittorio De Sica, and Inge Schoener
Le ragazze di Sanfrediano (1954) by Valerio Zurlini, with Antonio Cifariello and Corinne Calvert
Il principe fusto (1960) by Maurizio Arena, starring Maurizio Arena and Michelle Girardon

Publicity photo of Rudolph Valentino (Grazia Neri)

Rudolph Valentino
(Kobal Collection)

Rudolph Valentino wearing a singlet, which caused a scandal in those times, in Blood and Sand, *1922 (Kobal Collection)*

LATIN CHARM

INVENTING RUDOLPH VALENTINO

Loredana Leconte

Of the many stories that surround Rudolph Valentino's life and death with a halo of mysterious exoticism, there were one or two — little does it matter whether true or false — whose declared objective was not to promote but to explode the myth of his charisma.

The Latin lover *par excellence*, "every husband's rival" (this was one of the nicknames coined by film magazines of the time) did not arouse unconditional worship in everyone. More than one man took solace in the gossip that the super handsome Rudy was in fact bald, as bald as a coot, and that he had to cover his skull with an assortment of expensive hair pieces. Demoted from the pedestal of the perfect lover by a man often referred to simply as "that young, spineless dandy" (read homosexual), American males tried to get even by resorting to low blows, attacking Valentino for his "physical" attributes, the very features that bring any star public acclaim. A more creditable rumour concerned Valentino's hallmark killer glance; it was, the rumour ran, serious short-sightedness that made his eyes twinkle secretively, as they seemed to plumb the depths of the soul and entrance his female admirers from the screen and in real life. Seven million women, that is to say every American woman who regularly went to the cinema, regardless of age and social class, considered this elegant Italian dancer to be one of the brightest of Hollywood's stars.

Cobra, *1925, with Nita Naldi (Kobal Collection)*

Psychologists and hack reporters went to work with a will to discover what lay behind this collective enthusiasm, that was ultimately to culminate in mass hysteria (Valentino's death led to the mass suicide of despairing fans). They thought they had come up with an answer: American males, it seemed, were poorly versed in the techniques of love.

Although an assiduous worker and an indomitable accumulator of money, the typical male specimen of the up-and-coming WASP middle classes carried the stigma of being a terrible lover; he was far too busy building commercial empires and business relationships to have time for any sort of tenderness or romantic prowess. A reliable companion, yes, ideal for marriage and children, a home and a sure-fire future. But when it came to fantasy... The result was that American women were ready to fall into the arms of any imaginary lover they could dream up (including one conjured up by the providential Hollywood dream factory). Rudy came to embody an ideal, an archetype that catered to the latent needs of American women (without stopping there: after exploiting the home market, he stylishly went on to conquer the rest of the planet). Love requires dedication and takes time: American husbands allotted their time for work, they were far too busy to play the love-sick fool with their wives. American women, so long expected by society to be submissive, meek and chastely moral, could see new horizons opening up in which they were not always and forever chained to the kitchen. They began to see new freedoms in the area of sexual relations, hitherto strictly regulated by puritan moralism. Women wanted more, they wanted to have some of the freedoms men enjoyed, and they also wanted to carve out a space for themselves. Valentino was an exotic object of desire, oozing a kind of charm that was extraneous to highly competitive American culture. He won fans for qualities normally associated with women: tenderness, a pinch of passivity, a disposition towards pleasure, just like any beautiful woman, according to the canons of the day. He certainly was handsome, classically so. His lineaments were pure, his skin was smooth, his body was flexible and elastic, and he was a man of elegant and measured movement.

Moran of the Lady Letty, *1922, with Dorothy Dalton (Kobal Collection)*

Rodolfo Guglielmi (Rudolph Valentino) was one of countless people who emigrated to the United States to seek their fortune. But unlike most of his fellow Italian countrymen, he reached Staten Island with enough of a nest-egg to set himself up in some small business. At eighteen years of age Guglielmi had left home in Castellaneta to live in Paris before travelling on to New York. He sought escape from the drudgery of everyday life, and had no desire to use his diploma in agricultural studies to buy an orange farm in California. He made ends meet in America as best as he could, without needing to ask his family for help in the worst moments (as he had done when in Paris). He honed his natural talent as a dancer, and made a living in New York night-spots before trying his hand at the movies, after a friend persuaded him to go to Los Angeles.

The new medium of cinema had already become the focus of a

Rudolph Valentino in The Four Horsemen of the Apocalypse, *1921 (Kobal Collection)*

Rudolph Valentino in his favourite role, the bullfighter in Blood and Sand, *1922 (Kobal Collection)*

Blood and Sand, *1922 (Kobal Collection)*

A Sainted Devil, *1924 (Kobal Collection)*

A Sainted Devil, *1924 (Kobal Collection)*

collective mania that brought millions of people into cinemas, dazzled by the oneiric and luminescent visions floating in the darkness. The phantoms moving on the screen were, almost unintentionally, transformed into a business that symbolized the booming American economy. In a market characterized by rapid expansion and a lack of rules, Wall Street backed Hollywood productions, which provided the greatest possible return on investment. The film industry created the only metropolis founded this century, practically from nothing, in the Californian desert. Films made in New York and Hollywood offered the public enjoyment and entertainment, aroused fantasy and desire, and at the same time proposed models of behaviour to create a way of life that fitted in with the needs of emerging New World culture. People went to the movies for the entertainment, but they also expected the screen to have some kind of didactic function.

Different ethnic groups living in the same town, different social classes with more than one common point of contact — American society was rapidly becoming increasingly mixed and new arrivals had to take their place in the system, whether they were urbanized Irish peasants, Russian immigrants fleeing pogroms, or parvenus who raced up the rungs of the social ladder without having quite assimilated the behaviour patterns of the new class to which they either aspired or belonged. The fundamental commodity of education and the most important aspects of family or morality were best presented in a popular form. The cinema carried out its duty, offering a range of behavioural situations which gleefully combined extravagant stories with a kind of basic user's manual to life. The "uses" were often quite bizarre.

Our man Rodolfo, born to a French mother in Apulia, Italy, arrived in the midst of this continually evolving background. His was a kind of beauty that did not fit with the parameters Hollywood applied to its leading men. They had to make the heroine fall in love with them, yes, but they did not deviate from the perceived characteristics of middle-class whites. For this reason another erotic male myth of silent American cinema, Sessue Hayakawa, was condemned to playing villains or else to star in stories exclusively conceived for Japanese actors. For women, such as Ann May Wong, the role

The Sheik, *1921*
(Kobal Collection)

of vamp very easily slipped into that of prostitute.

Rodolfo di Valentina, then Rodolpho de Valentina and ultimately Rodolph or Rudolph (as you prefer) Valentino, was first offered small roles in minor movies, in which he was typecast in the rather gloomy and unctuous roles of seducer or self-styled seducer; his dancing skills were used negatively, as a facet of his disquieting sex appeal. In an early film opposite Dorothy Gish he is directly compared to a "healthy" American boy, only to be snubbed by the leading lady, who goes off with his jovial blond rival. Soon enough an attempt was made to slough off this negative typecasting by dressing the dark Rudy up as an insipid "boy-next-door" character, complete with long, thick Scottish socks: the result could only be risible.

What Valentino needed was the expert eye of a woman like June Mathis, a very well-paid and very powerful screen-writer, to discover his latent appeal and exploit his talents to the full. When casting an Argentinian gaucho for the rather minor role of Julio in her version of Blasco Ibañez's *The Four Horsemen of the Apocalypse*, Mathis was very favourably impressed by the charming young Italian. She decided he was her ideal Julio. Applying all her influence, she persuaded the studio heads of Metro to invest in the new prospect. She was supported in this by the film's director, Rex Ingram, who may have agreed to back her up mainly because he himself was part of Mathis's team. The role of Julio was re-written, making Valentino one of the main characters in *The Four Horsemen of the Apocalypse*, and his tango in the film was to become a milestone in the subtle art of seduction. The blend of sexual and sado-masochistic undertones, of shamelessness and the tangible pleasure with which the actor let himself go in the dance sent a huge electric shock through every woman who saw the film. The ex-gigolo of the New York dance halls became an icon overnight, the icon of a lover who combined the most sentimental features of a man in love with the smouldering dazzle of an exotic adventurer.

From that moment on, Valentino's meteoric rise into the firmament of film was masterminded by the women who were instrumental in his career. Through June Mathis, who began the process, Rudy met and became part of the entourage of Alla Nazimova, a great Russian-born actress, another powerfully ambitious woman who was in many respects ahead of her time. Nobody quite knows how, but before long Valentino was married to one of the protégées of the Nazimova clan, a certain Jean Acker. On the wedding night she shut the door in his face, apparently insensitive to the charm he emanated, charm that was recognized by millions of enraptured fans. Long before divorce proceedings were started Rudy was seen in public with another woman, a great friend of Nazimova's, a girl from Utah who was the stepdaughter of a cosmetics baron, who when very young ran away from her London boarding school to "seek protection" in Russia, where she found "political asylum" with the Imperial Ballet.

Publicity photo of Rudolph Valentino (Grazia Neri)

Winifred O'Shaughnessy, as she was called, loathed the cultural illiteracy she felt prevailed in her native country, the coarseness and vulgarity of the *nouveaux riches.* So strong were her feelings that hardly out of adolescence she cast her heritage aside, making a new life and creating a new personality for herself. Under the new name Natasha Rambova she may have been a fake Russian but she was genuinely an excellent dancer and a very accomplished and talented designer. The Russian revolution struck when she was on tour in America with the Russian Ballet: at a stroke Natasha became a refugee in her own country.

Latin lover Rudolph Valentino at home (Grazia Neri)

After the dance company disbanded she and Theodor Kosloff, later to become an actor in Cecil B. DeMille's exotic blockbusters, made their way to Hollywood, where she found herself in an ideal position to bring her influence to bear behind the scenes on the mechanism that was to establish the rituals and legends of the American collective consciousness. For an intelligent and ambitious woman, a beauty like Natasha, appearances counted for relatively little. What mattered was being able to make a mark on the asphyxiating and parochial culture around her. And where better than Hollywood to touch the hearts and minds of American men and women, so needful of role models? Her love of ambiguity, unbridled exoticism and the enchanting aura of decadence took her to the most intellectual of Hollywood's artistic circles, working first with Mitchell Leisen and DeMille, and then through

Cobra, 1925
(Kobal Collection)

dance joining forces with the powerful Nazimova, who wanted her by her side as a designer and artistic director in some of the most avant-garde productions of the time. This was in an age when set- and costume-designers were hardly ever given any recognition for their work (the first art director, in the late 1910s, to be named in the opening credits of a film was Wilfred Buckland, who worked with DeMille, but it was not until as late as 1948 that costume-designers had their own Oscar).

Natasha Rambova possessed presence and an unorthodox European creative flair which enabled her to put a very strong personal stamp on everything she worked on. After marrying Valentino — who, incidentally, was not yet officially divorced from his first wife and was accused of bigamy — she became the mind behind the man and had a great influence on his career. Nazimova and Rambova wanted more from Valentino, the handsome fellow and talented dancer discovered by June Mathis: they wanted to turn him into a Prince Charming, the perfect ideal lover. Alla Nazimova offered Valentino the romantic lead role of Armand in her Metro production of *Camille*, a floral art deco apotheosis designed by Natasha. Under the guidance of the two women Rudy dispensed with the stronger (and coarser) aspects of his Latin nature. He started using strong shampoos to remove that shiny patina of grease that might prove to be unpleasant, and he began to fight his tendency to put on weight — Rudolph had not been averse to resorting to a corset.

The new regime was hours and hours of sport, rising early at seven in the morning for exercise, horse riding, fencing, hot baths and a strict diet. His natural elegance benefited greatly, and Valentino got closer and closer to the romantic and passionate ideal he sought to embody.

Meanwhile Natasha was designing sets and costumes for a film starring Nazimova directed by Charles Bryant, Nazimova's husband, a version of *Salome* that the Russian woman conceived as a homage to Oscar Wilde, a talented playwright but perhaps more importantly the most fashionable tutelary deity of the homosexual community. The film was shot exclusively by homosexual artistes and technicians, whose decadent and figurative taste failed to arouse any favourable public response. The film was a flop, and it so damaged Nazimova's reputation that in future she was forced to be less extravagant in her acting roles by other directors. The experience also undermined her relationship with the Valentinos.

Monsieur Beaucaire, *1924*
(Kobal Collection)

In 1921 Rudolph signed a contract with Famous Players-Lasky, later Paramount. He landed the lead in *The Sheik* and was an overwhelming success, becoming a star, a huge and distant star in a fabulously bright firmament. From that moment on every woman dreamed of being plucked from the ground on his white steed and carried off to a tent among the dunes... The newspapers went crazy: the star's gaze, as he wore the robes of an Arab, hypnotized the entire nation with his "black, inescapable eyes. A perfume of the Orient... his brows, hidden beneath the smooth continuity of his flesh, give him the expression of a man who belongs to a mysterious caste." (Willis Goldbeck, in *Motion Picture Classic*, 1921).

In every article predicting the stars of the future Rudolph Valentino took top billing, as the Latin (or Italian) lover *par excellence*, little matter if he was dressed as a sheik, a tango dancer or a bullfighter. He far outshone Douglas Fairbanks or any other screen lover who had broken hearts. Valentino provided escape from everyday reality and led his fans into a fairytale world where (almost) everything was possible, into a land where a handsome stranger could possess you and put you on a pedestal as the world's most desirable woman.

One after another Valentino churned out the films that were to

Rudolph Valentino dressed as a Red Indian in a private photo (Kobal Collection)

consolidate the myth. After the bullfighter in *Blood and Sand*, in which he returns in all his finery, glorying in the Spanish vein of mystery which had first made a name for him at the beginning of his career, he starred in *Beyond the Rocks* opposite Gloria Swanson, another screen legend, with whom he dances a passionate tango. Rudy learned a great deal from the English writer Elinor Glyn, author amongst others of the novel from which the film was adapted, the undisputed authority on the passion of love since coining the term "it" to describe "that certain *je ne sais quoi*," the indefinite and indeterminate quality that made the unknown Clara Bow a shining (yet rather short-lived) star. Elinor saw that selfsame quality in Rudolph. She taught him a trick or two (not that he needed it) to turn women's heads further still: when he took Swanson's hand he kissed her palm, not the back of her hand (what shivers must have run up the forearms of his adoring female admirers in those darkened cinemas...).

But *Beyond the Rocks* ran up against the first wave of censorship to hit Hollywood, the Hays Code, drawn up in early 1922, which stated that no kiss could last more than three metres of film. Two versions of the film were distributed, one for the American market and one for abroad. An irate Swanson complained that "Only the Europeans and South Americans will see Swanson and Valentino kissing with true passion. From now on America's thrills will be kept in check by the stopwatch."

Elinor, however, worked to subtly alter Valentino's image. Though censored, he could not be allowed to disappoint his fans. Her answer was to whip up a few statements for him to publish in film magazines. Some of the articles attributed to Valentino are pure, ineffable Glyn: "The most difficult thing is to make oneself loved by the man who sees you every day," and "a man can always be tender with a woman who doesn't matter to him... but he can be cruel only to a woman he loves and has loved." (*Photoplay*, March 1922). A master of the passions (and very highly paid in Hollywood to teach refined, high-society manners), Glyn put these words into his mouth and in the process spread the word of Valentino's conversion to romantic love. The number of letters he received each week shot up to over a thousand.

Bare-chested Rudolph in a gym manual in which he was the instructor and the model
(Grazia Neri)

Rudolph and Natasha appeared to live the archetypal star life: gorgeous cars, magnificent houses, clothes that left fans breathless. Diamonds and sable cloaks helped too. Valentino launched fashions, such as wearing a watch on the wrist rather than keeping it in his waistcoat like mere mortals. His most intimate friends were treated to him showing off the little anklet he wore (like a "slave"), an extremely meaningful gift from the imperturbable Natasha. The couple was photographed as if they were royalty, in profile, like on medals or minted coins: she leans forward, almost eclipsing him.

But Rambova was not satisfied with the direction Rudy's career began to take. As far as she was concerned the heads of production did not give him his dues. They gave Valentino colourless and dull films, and didn't let him (or her) have any say. Lasky was happy to let them complain; he had a watertight contract binding Valentino to Famous Players, with no means of escape. Natasha was not the sort to tolerate what she considered tyranny pure and simple. She stubbornly dug in her heels and managed to persuade Valentino to leave Paramount and turn his back on the movies. The two of them returned to dancing, this time as a couple, criss-crossing the States in an advertising tour for a cosmetics company.

But rather than disappearing into oblivion, as happened to many an actor who deserted his public, Valentino's legend took another turn. Hysterical crowds packed out the shows, they could not get enough of seeing their hero close up. The star had given himself to his adoring public, and his public was delighted. Forced to reconsider by Rudolph and Natasha's tangos, Lasky had no choice but to give in to their demands. Rambova returned in triumph to

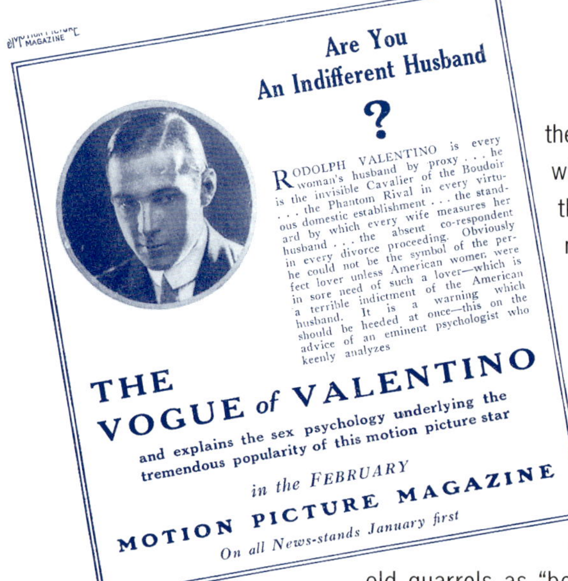

Motion Picture Magazine *dedicates an entire issue to enquiring into Rudolph Valentino's popularity (Archivio Cineteca Comunale, Bologna)*

the studios she had bent to her will, with the power to look after the artistic side of Valentino's next movie, *Monsieur Beaucaire*, second in importance only to Sidney Olcott, the director. Every single newspaper ran the story ("Home Again," *Motion Picture*, 1924), quoting Adolph Zukor, president of Paramount, who saw the old quarrels as "belonging to the past: we are offering Valentino the best possible production, the company is doing everything within its powers, and I am sure that we will all work in harmony, and the movie will be one of the greatest ever made." He meant the words to bring good luck, but with hindsight they couldn't have been wider off the mark. If ever there was a set lacking in harmony it was that of *Monsieur Beaucaire*, a truly pompous production that, Natasha thought, would at last give Valentino a chance to present himself not just as "the perfect lover" so dear to the gutter press, but also as a great actor in a highly artistic film. Natasha's almost maniacal love for historical reconstructions, her wish to spend and spend and spend, and her iron will in getting her own way drove the studio managers mad, but there was nothing they could do about it. The film is the story of a duke at the court of Louis XV who flees to England where he disguises himself as a barber. Valentino gave an excellent performance as an actor and as a swordsman (his training programme had not been in vain!), but he left his fans cold: they did not want to see their idol caked in make up, powdered and bewigged, smothered in ruffles and beauty marks.

It was by no means uncommon to see actors heavily made up in the Twenties, when the cinema had not yet completely evolved a less dramatic and less theatrical approach to make-up, and Valentino often appeared off-screen wearing eye-shadow to heighten his charm. But Rambova did not pay attention to a rule that was to prove fundamental in the cinema: a Twenties film, as much as a film made in the Sixties or Nineties, even if set during the age of the Pharaohs is first and foremost an expression of its time. Although Natasha was very much an exponent of the art deco style when it came to her modern sketches, she made the mistake of moving away from the tastes of the time; she wanted to recreate the eighteenth century as accurately as possible, going right back to Watteau and the traditions of French and English painting. In her hands Valentino, whether as a barber or an eighteenth-century man of court, was no more than a smartly dressed fop, as indeed one would expect from that century of powder and false beauty marks.

Already accused of effeminacy and a lack of masculinity, of being impotent or homosexual long before *Monsieur Beaucaire*, "every husband's rival" was attacked more brutally than ever before. Those who had predicted that the public would not be interested in a ladies-man when *The Four Horsemen of the Apocalypse* was released now redoubled their efforts. This time they had better ammunition. The film was a failure with critics and public alike; it was accused of being too intellectual (it was wonderfully parodied in 1930 in Lubitsch's *Montecarlo*, and then in Donen's *Singin' in the Rain*, starring Gene Kelly, another famous screen dancer and duelling knight in costume).

The studio officially defended the film (much of the over-spending was almost certainly a result of Natasha's penchant for grandeur) and was forced to defend its star as well, as his image was worth millions and millions of dollars. Natasha took the blame for the public flop. From that moment on she was banned from the set. The studio got its revenge, although it continued to draw upon her legacy in *Cobra*, the last film Rudolph was to shoot for Zukor, when they used the huge number of pieces of antique furniture that the Valentinos had bought for vast sums as usual during a previous trip to Spain.

In 1925, after his spell with Paramount, Hollywood's biggest star was made an extremely appealing proposal by United Artists, the studio founded by Griffith, Chaplin, Fairbanks and Pickford. Instead of a watertight contract he was offered extreme freedom and the opportunity to retain a percentage of the profits earned by the finished product. But the new contract had a clause stipulating that Rambova was not to have any authority at any stage of the production process. On the advice of his manager Ullman (the man who had got him out of trouble after his flight from Famous Players, finding him the advertising escape route with the Mineraleva cosmetics company), Valentino agreed to this harsh condition. That was the beginning of the end of the relationship between Rambova and her "slave."

Valentino tried to make things up by buying her a house of uncommon magnificence. But the beautiful woman would have nothing of it. She left him. She tried to carve out a path for herself on her own, directing *What Price Beauty*, a film that has been destroyed and was apparently memorable only for the debut of a very young Myrna Loy. Whether the film was good or bad, we will never know. But Natasha did not completely disappear from sight. She was later to repudiate Hollywood and its ephemeral pomp. She went to live in Spain where she dedicated herself to Egyptology. She became an expert on the subject and married a Spanish aristocrat with whom she was almost shot by the Republicans during the civil war. Her life continued to be as intense as ever.

Valentino's success continued unabated, despite his break with Rambova. His last two films, *The Eagle* and *The Son of the Sheik*, were probably his best. They deliver exactly what his public wanted from him: the embodiment of a secret fantasy that responded to the hidden desires of a society that was far too work-a-day and lacking in romanticism. By setting Valentino's explicitly sexual adventures in distant lands and far-off times Hollywood kept filmgoers from suspecting they were watching something that had a direct bearing on their lives: the discovery of female desire, of carnal violence, of the inverted relationship that was often created between the male object of desire (Valentino) and the female (any of his partners). Entrusting a foreigner with this deviant role altered the terms of the equation. The Latin lover was sufficiently exotic to carry out this function without being "overly" exotic (as was the case with the Japanese Hayakawa).

Even his encounter (after Natasha), which proved to be fatal (sexually speaking), with the disturbing beauty of Pola Negri, incarnation of central European allure, fitted perfectly into the pattern. Together they made another royal couple.

Pola was a truly great actress who became a victim of the huge mincer that Hollywood often became. All that remains of her is a record she made with Valentino in 1924. She had a wonderful voice, that of a great singer, perhaps even better than Marlene Dietrich or Zarah Leander. His voice, on the other hand, is weak (and, sad to say, tuneless too!). The age of the talkies, on the evidence of that recording, would probably have been Valentino's death knell...

Tango dancer Rudolph Valentino in The Four Horsemen of the Apocalypse, *1921 (Kobal Collection)*

After his death Hollywood tried several times without success to find a "new" Valentino. There was even a competition held in Italy (where else could a new Rudy be found if not in the land of the Latin lover?) to find his heir. The competition was won by the young Alberto Rabagliati, who without the fundamental help of a Rambova to put him on a diet, ballooned and faded, though at least he had a singing career to fall back on.

Rudy's shadow has lengthened endlessly in the heavens of the Mecca of the movies. To this day he remains the one and only, the inimitable Latin lover.

I. ALBERTO RABAGLIATI, LATIN LOVER ELECT

Death of a hero: what a tragedy, what luck! However unlikely it may seem, Charlie Chaplin made the following statement in August 1926: "Rudolph Valentino's death is one of the greatest tragedies in the history of the movie industry."[1]

However, Hollywood remained unmoved by this as a tragedy: on the contrary, it was perfect for the posthumous launch of *The Son of the Sheik*. The premature death of the hero was a sure sign that it would be a hit. Ullman, the head of publicity at United Artists, and Klemfuss, the director of the funeral parlour, put their heads together and orchestrated the entire show. For the first time ever the radio had broadcast a live, blow-by-blow account of the peritonitis that had struck him down. As soon as he came round from the ether, Valentino demanded in a peevish tone: "Well, did I behave like a pink powderpuff?" (What other surgical intervention would be necessary to show that he was a "real man"). "The funeral train," as Dos Passos wrote, "arrived in Hollywood on page 23 of *The New York Times*."[2] The newspapers actually received photographs of the procession before it took place. The crowd dutifully allowed themselves to be trampled under the horses hoofs, making it possible to shoot the newsreel: "Rioting at the funeral." And the matinée idol, perfectly laid out and completely oblivious to the screaming women, gave his farewell performance.

Alberto Rabagliati, star of the operetta Paris je t'aime *(Farabolafoto)*

The movie industry saw him as a product that had to be exploited to the full as soon as it was put on the market. They had to find another body with the same characteristics. Or the next best thing.

An Italian in America. For an American, *Latin* meant Mexican, Spanish, Parisian, Italian, Arab (and also included Viennese, Hungarian and Slav touches); in a word, *exotic*. Valentino's homeland appeared on this list, and searching there would guarantee a genuine product. Valentino himself said that it was only in America that he would have been considered handsome; in Italy, he would have passed unnoticed because there were lots of good-looking young men there.

Previous page: Alberto Rabagliati in 1928 when he won an international contest launched by the Fox Film Co to find Rudolph Valentino's successor (Farabolafoto)

So, that same year the Fox Film Co announced a big contest in Italy. They were looking for an actor to become Valentino's successor. Three hundred thousand men applied. A committee composed of Americans travelled the length and breadth of the country to scrutinize young hopefuls. Five hundred were selected. They were summoned to Rome, where they did screen tests that were judged by a jury composed of film directors in Hollywood. Alberto Rabagliati (Milan, 1906) was chosen. In May 1927 he landed in the U.S. to begin his career as a Latin lover. He returned to Italy four years later.

◗ A great deal of trumpet-blowing accompanied the launch of his book entitled *Quattro anni fra le "stelle"* (Four Years Amongst the "Stars"). In the preface, the publisher describes the book as "a serious and precise account of the dazzling Hollywood life, written by someone who has lived it to the full."[3] But today it reads more like the "misadventures of an Italian abroad" — a spirit that prevailed in our film comedies decades later. In America, Rabagliati relates (or rather "confides") to his "dear fans," the skyscrapers are extremely tall ("I was staying on the 22nd floor of the Pennsylvania Hotel, which is literally one of the biggest hotels in New York. It has 45 floors and 2,500 rooms. I did not lean out of the window to watch the people coming and going below, because I had made up my mind that I would only let beautiful women turn my head[4]). And the elevators move at lightning speed ("I then took the elevator, which moved so fast I was unable to count the floors as they went by. I think that someone who wishes to see if they can fly by jumping off a skyscraper would have a much easier time counting the number of floors on the way down"[5]). The new Valentino arrived in America hardly knowing "a word of the language"; but then, "their language is not as pleasant and harmonious as ours."[6] American singers also left something to be desired ("A light tenor sang the latest Broadway hits. That feeble individual, who in Italy would have been shipped off to a private clinic to strengthen his high doh, was given a standing ovation"[7]); every so often, thank the Lord, "I was able to play records on my small gramophone that sent the notes of lovely Italian songs floating across the sea."[8] Even Christmas Day, "a holy day venerated by Italians," is far less beautiful; in fact "we give our children gifts that they naively think baby Jesus has brought," while in America giving presents "is not limited solely to children... gifts are given indiscriminately to relatives, friends, and acquaintances. I think this is a bit too much." When it comes down to it, Americans "lack sentiment."[9]

Ramon Novarro with Greta Garbo in Mata Hari, 1931 (Farabolafoto)

From one tango to another. At the first wild party to which Clara Bow invited him, the young lad appeared dressed as a cowboy, packing a pair of guns. The hostess quickly reminded him of his role as Latin lover.

◗ "You will be my escort for the evening."

"Delighted."

"Ask me to dance often, Albert. I *love* to dance!"

"My pleasure."[10]

When one invites a Latin lover to dance, one is not thinking of a "lively foxtrot" or the "syncopated rhythms" of jazz. One is thinking of a tango, amongst other things. This was made clear by one of two episodes that were crucial in our Latin lover's rise to stardom.

◗ We are in the Montmartre Café on Hollywood Boulevard. One of the "latest orchestras that played languorous tangos" was performing at one of the afternoon tango tea dances that "beautiful actresses who claimed to live on languor"[11] were wild about. The Italian is sitting with Billie Dove, Colleen Moore, Loretta Young, Agnes Ayres (Valentino's former partner), Carmel Myers, Raquel Torres and Estelle Taylor. First, he warms up with Raquel Torres. "After so long, after all those frenetic syncopated dances, during which I performed like a clown, had no style, and my legs went everywhere, the tango finally arrived to liberate me, with its sensual movements that I found utterly relaxing."[12] Next, he sweeps Estelle Taylor off her feet. The actress, who had been devouring him with her eyes, was not too familiar with the steps. It was only natural that she should wind up saying: "You're invited to my house tomorrow. So you can teach me to tango."

The dancer and the boxer. We have arrived at page 153 of Rabagliati's memoirs. Some time has passed since page 21, when he declared with bated breath: "I entered the Hollywood star's apartment." (The same elliptic style favoured by Manzoni in such phrases as "the unfortunate creature replied"). He later tells us how the situation progressed, in equally cryptic terms: "The teacher gave it everything and his pupil made surprising progress."[13] At this point he observes, in all seriousness: "I wondered why her husband had not already been informed."

◗ The Hollywood beauty was married, in fact. As he held her close for the first time, Rabagliati confesses: "I thought I saw Jack's menacing shadow looming over her."[14] Her husband's first name was Jack. His surname was Dempsey. Jack Dempsey, the famous boxing champion. He had read in the *Los Angeles Examiner* that his "other half had found a charming escort in Hollywood, with whom she was seen in all the fashionable places."[15] Poor, aspiring Latin lover! How many male shadows there were hanging over him! The shadow of the boxer "looming" over him as a dancer; the shadow of the husband "threatening" him as a seducer. And hanging over the entire episode, the shadow of the star he had been put under contract to equal: Rudolph Valentino, no less. The Valentino myth, in fact, was born when he danced the tango in the opening shots of *The Four Horsemen*. In the sequel he actually taught the tango, at the Tango Palace in Paris, where he met Marguerite, who went from being his pupil to his sweetheart, and who, to give added spice to the plot, already had a husband.

◗ Valentino was the one who started out as a ballroom gigolo and wound up as a dancer on the screen, replacing the cowboy in the fantasy of American women in the Twenties. He hit the big time "in he-man twofisted broncobusting pokerplaying stockjuggling America" as Dos Passos described it.[16]

◗ Jack Dempsey, the "looming, threatening" champ who disturbed neo-Latin lover Alberto Rabagliati's sleep at night, had actually taught Rudy to box. Valentino set great store by his reputation as a boxer, so that he could challenge anyone who questioned his virility to a few rounds.

Let us recapitulate: Alberto Rabagliati, committed to equalling Valentino, teaches the tango to the wife of the boxer who taught Rudy to fight. Dempsey's wife falls for him. When Rabagliati's "rival in love" made his entrance...

◗ "Estelle begged me to leave" and "unflinchingly faced her husband's anger alone." Things were settled once and for all at the Roosevelt Hotel. "A number of eye-witnesses declared that they saw a woman being dangled from an eleventh-floor window by a man with bulging biceps."[17] Meanwhile, young Alberto (urged by Estelle, of course) had fled to San Francisco.

The Latin lover and other men's wives. Let's deal with the crucial episode. Charles Farrel was the General Manager of Fox Film. He had a wife named Mary Duncan. Mary Duncan, with the "bedroom eyes," is the same Mary Duncan who invited the young Rabagliati, fresh from Italy, to his first smart-set party, which he attended, not in a cowboy suit, but in full evening dress. "As the empty liquor bottles piled up (the alcohol that flowed abundantly — in the face of Prohibition — is the leitmotif running through Rabagliati's anecdotes), Mary Duncan approached me. She reclined on the couch and revealed her fantastic legs. Her exquisitely-formed, erect, white breasts swelled, as she heaved a sigh. 'Albert,' she purred, 'you are a very nice boy.'"[18] The scene ended with a kiss.

◗ Mary Duncan reappears in his life as he continues on the road to success. Her husband — "that big-shot who rules Hollywood" — has taken a liking to him. He summons Rabagliati to his office ("it was an honour merely to be summoned"[19]), asks him if he is making progress with his English, and leads him to understand that his contract is about to be renewed. Although Alberto has only played bit parts so far, the big boss implies that he will soon be partnering a major star like Janet Gaynor.

◗ At this point, Rabagliati comes out with a phrase which, if not elliptic, is certainly lapidary: "My friendship with Mary Duncan is no longer platonic."[20] (Which is the sequel to his previous announcement: "I entered the Hollywood star's apartment." The apartment belonged to Mary Duncan).

◗ In the meantime, a "stranger" advises Alberto to break off the relationship. He doesn't (because Mary Duncan didn't want me to, Rabagliati is quick to point out). When his contract runs out he is summoned by the General Manager. Without beating about the bush, Farrel lets him read an agreement containing some extremely favourable conditions. After which... "he tore it up, right in front of me."

◗ "He said: 'I'm sorry, Mr Rabagliati, but you're through with Fox Film.' He shook hands and dismissed me, adding: 'You're very young and, bit by bit, you'll learn the ways of the world. Start by steering clear of other people's wives, especially when you've been warned. Goodbye.'"[21] The sun went down behind the palms on Malibu beach.

◗ If what Alberto Rabagliati tells us is true, this was the end of the Hollywood career of Valentino's double who was elected Latin lover in a contest and ousted by the competition. How can a Latin lover, especially Valentino's successor, "not insist with other men's wives?" Isn't it his job, his duty even, to lend himself to the fantasies of all women and to place his body at their disposal? He is everybody's. "Other men's women" don't exist, as far as the Latin lover is concerned. On page 161 — the last of his Hollywood "diary" — we find Alberto Rabagliati asking himself, thoughtfully:

"So, what do we do now?"

Yes, what do we do now?

"My darling mother was dying to see me after four years!"

"Goodbye, America!"

Who would have thought it? Or rather, you could have bet your bottom dollar on it. There's a mamma behind every Latin lover.

II. JOHN GILBERT: TALKIES PUT "I LOVE YOU" TO THE TEST

John Gilbert and Eve Von Berne in La Maschera del Diavolo *(Mask of the Devil), 1928 (Farabolafoto)*

More Latin than a Latin. "Hollywood never fails to mercilessly exploit the 'types' who are popular with the public. Therefore, the incredible triumph of Valentino created, from 1920 through 1930, the fad of the Latin lover who, in many cases, was authentic but sometimes only possessed physical qualities that compensated for origins less than exotic. It was the time of that infantile search for Rudy's double; it was the time of Ricardo Cortez, Antonio Moreno, Gilbert Roland... and Ramon Novarro."[22]

◗ And also of John Pringle, better known as John (or Jack) Gilbert who, born in Utah, was not a bit exotic. His physical appearance was described thus: "Tall and dark, with a penetrating, insolent gaze, and dashing moustache that accentuated both his manly pride and refined elegance. He was renowned for his eloquent, ironic smile, with which he was identified."[23] After Valentino, the American actor was able to display sensuality and passion, surpassing the puritan model of the generous-hearted, loyal but cold, sporting type, or at least creating more exciting variations on the theme. Gilbert was also defined as "an Americanized romantic."[24]

◗ Let's return briefly to his physical attributes. "His stylish movements, flashing black eyes, sparkling teeth and his dashing mous-

tache, all helped to counteract a nose that was larger than normal."[25] Don't forget the nose: we'll be coming face to face with it again, soon.

◗ His personality seems to have been even more "Italian" (in the exuberant, extrovert, gipsy-like sense of the word) than that of Valentino. "He drank with the grips, danced with the waitresses, and made love with prostitutes and the movie godesses, without distinction."[26] "He thought that Kant was a baseball champion and pronounced Tolstuà Tolstoy, believing him to be French."[27] "He did not survey Hollywood from top to bottom, but from bottom to top."[28] In any event, Gilbert continued in the Valentino tradition by buying a palatial home, "Falcon Lair," and demanding from the Studios a wild dressing-room built on the lines of an Italian villa.

John Gilbert,
La Bohème, *1926*
(Farabolafoto)

Fire and ice. John (or Jack) Gilbert partnered Greta Garbo in *Flesh and the Devil* (1927), *Anna Karenina* (1927), and *Destiny* (1928). The "marriage" between the two stars was described thus: "His aggressive way of loving created a remarkable contrast to Garbo's unapproachable pallor..., allowing producers to realize the dream that had been shattered by Valentino's death: the combination of icy passion in the new-style vamp with the fiery arrogance of the Latin lover."[29] It was, in fact, love at first sight for Gilbert and Garbo when they shot *Flesh and the Devil.*

◗ Gilbert always identified with his role on- and off-screen. "Whatever part he was playing, he continued to live it in real life. If it was a dashing Cossack officer, Jack hired Russian servants and entertained his guests with music from a thousand balalaikas." "When he read the publicity describing him as the 'Great Lover' sent out by his Studios, he acted accordingly."[30] Gilbert tried to persuade Garbo to marry him by buying a 100,000 dollar yacht named "Temptress," which was to have whisked them off to the South seas. But they never set sail. Garbo possessed a different personality and self-awareness, saying of him: " He has a lively temperament. I mean, he gets excited..., but" (the but is very important) "that's a good thing."[31] She wanted him as her leading man in *Queen Christina* in 1933, even though Gilbert had finished with being the "Great Lover." The reason has to be explored in depth.

The Latin lover's voice. Sound was introduced in film towards the end of the Twenties. Valentino died just in time (it was in 1926 that the first film with recorded music was launched which, as coincidence would have it, was entitled *Don Juan*, while the first "part-talkie" — *The Jazz Singer* — was released in 1927). It is debatable whether the Valentino myth would have stood the test of the new technique, and there are many differing opinions concerning this. There is evidence that he was thinking of giving up acting at that point, and going into film direction or production. Gilbert, however, was dismissed with the following phrase: "He was one of the greatest stars of silent cinema, whose career was cut off in its prime by the talkies because of his 'unphonogenic' voice."[32] People now spoke about being "phonogenic" as well as "photogenic." As to the whys and wherefores attached to Gilbert's final bow, there are again many different explanations.

◗ According to Ben Hecht, "One evening, Jack heard the audience laughing at him while he was sitting in a movie theater watching his first talkie. The shrill voice that accompanied his daring feats, turned him into something of a clown."[33] Although this seems like a perfect explanation, it is difficult to believe that it actually happened this way. Hecht was probably referring to the film *Resurrection*, based on the novel by Tolstoy, made in 1929. MGM suspended distribution because "the actor's thin, high-pitched voice, rendered even more unpleasant by imperfect recording techniques, produced pathetic results. The film was shelved and Gilbert had to take elocution lessons."[34] Speaking of these lessons, Ben Hecht tells us: "He started barging into the moguls' offices, shouting: 'Listen to me. I can recite!' He recited Shakespeare."[35] *Romeo and Juliet* most likely, as the press had now put Gilbert and

John Gilbert and Virginia Bruce in Downstairs, *1932* (Farabolafoto)

Garbo on their list of fairytale lovers.

◗ He was given a second chance. That same year he made *His Glorious Night*. It was "a glorious night" because of his "performance" as a lover, which is perhaps more obvious from the Italian title *Ladro d'amore* (Stolen Love). However... "John's speech started with 'I love you, I love you, I love you.' And the world laughed."[36]

◗ There is another explanation for his being ridiculed. "The words didn't go with his face. When he spoke them on-screen his top lip touched his nose and, for one brief moment, he looked more like a parrot than a lover. It wasn't noticeable in his silent films."[37] We can therefore blame his "beak" (already described as "larger than normal"), which when he said "I love you" seemed to meet his mouth. Now we must ask a delicate question: what effect would sound have had on Valentino's myopic gaze that burned into the "love object," or on his eyelids, one of which was lower — or higher — than the other, which had such a disturbing effect?

◗ Explanation number three. "It was said, and is now generally accepted as a historical fact, that the great Gilbert had a falsetto voice that did not go with his manly physique; a voice that the public obviously became aware of in talking pictures. Jack's voice, although it may not have boomed like the ocean, was in fact quite normal when he spoke. In those days, however, mixing and sound regulating techniques left a lot to be desired. If the microphone was set to record the leading lady's voice, in her favourite key, the hero seemed to be trying to outdo her."[38] We can blame it on the microphone, then.

◗ Explanation number four. King Vidor declared: "Many people believed it was due to the quality or tone of Gilbert's voice. If truth be told, it was the nothing lines he had to deliver which drove him to desperation."[39] The "nothing lines" were, as we have seen, ones like "I love you." Did the great actor go to pieces when he had to say "I love you" for all the world to hear? I have my doubts... seems the only answer to that.

◗ Despite his being a failure, Greta Garbo wanted him as her leading man in *Queen Christina*, in 1933. The film was dubbed by cinema-goers as a "Garbo movie," with no one making any comment about her leading man's performance. Gilbert was the only one who got emotional: "Listen to me speak... It's a real voice, a man's voice."[40] His "real voice" no longer made people laugh, but neither did it make them cry. It was as if he hadn't spoken: a nothing voice to match the nothing dialogue.

The difference between a heart attack and heartbreak. There are also two different stories concerning Gilbert's state of mind before his death. This is Ben Hecht's version: "He frequently appeared in the Studios and gave parties in his dressing-room that was more like an Italian villa. Gilbert showed no signs of depression. He was playing the part of John Gilbert for a small audience of masseurs, fencing and boxing instructors, elocutionists, auctioneers, prostitutes, parasites, and a handful of friends." At a Hollywood party, "he lost his toupée while he was dancing... Amidst jeering laughter, he tried to rescue it from under the dancer's feet. Next morning he was found dead in bed, in his castle on the hill."[41]

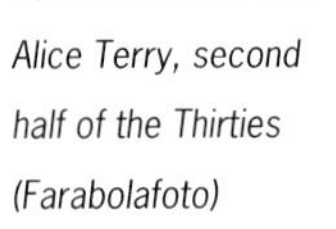

Ramon Novarro with Alice Terry, second half of the Thirties (Farabolafoto)

◗ Here's the second version: "He wound up isolating himself in his fabulous residence (he was still very wealthy), drowning his sorrows in drink..." He died in his home, from a heart attack. Or maybe from a broken heart.[42]

◗ Whatever happened, he passed on in Beverly Hills on 9 January 1936. We know the date of his death, but not his birth date. He was either thirty-nine or forty-one.

III. RAMON NOVARRO, THE MOST BEAUTIFUL BOY IN THE WORLD

Ramon, born in Durango. No one could deny that Ramon Novarro was a real Latin. He was one of the breed North Americans call "latinos"; in other words, he was Mexican. Novarro was born in 1899 in the capital of the State of Durango, located in the *tierras calientes* even though it stood at 2,000 feet! He was called José Ramon Gil Samaniegos, plus another ten names. Mamma

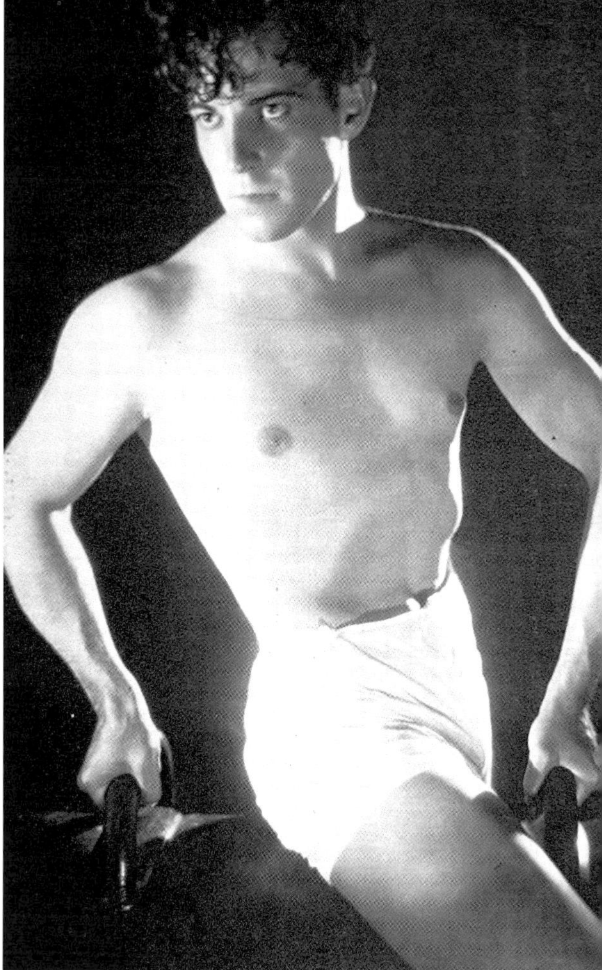

adored him so that she called him "the most beautiful boy in the world." After emigrating to California, he worked as a pianist, a singer, and a dancer. He danced with Mae Murray in *Attila the Hun* — a Mexican playing a Hun, can you imagine!? He also played the Central European "villain," complete with goatee and monocle à la Von Stroheim, in *Prisoner of Zenda* (1922), his first important film directed by Rex Ingram. Again he played a villain, or rather a disturbing, negative type: a role reserved for character actors with Latin looks until Rudolph Valentino became the golden boy.

◗ He had already become the golden boy, in fact. In 1921 Novarro was also given the minor role of a tango dancer in *The Four Horsemen*. It appears that the director Rex Ingram chose him to star in his next film to spite Valentino. He is also said to have declared witheringly: "I can take any extra and make him a star." Rex Ingram was gay, like Ramon Novarro. But that doesn't stop us from finding in the December 1922 edition of *Motion Picture Classic* magazine a close-up of Novarro, expertly modelled with chiaroscuro to render his profile similar to that of a Greek god, accompanied by the information that the majority of the fan mail sent to the magazine was addressed to Ramon. The magazine also informs us that although Valentino had made the Latin type fashionable, Ramon Novarro was stealing the limelight in his absence. It was, in fact, a period in which Valentino was engaged in litigation with his production company and, therefore, was forced to remain idle.

Ramon Novarro (Grazia Neri)

Girls, don't miss him! Ramon Novarro was poised to become the new Latin lover incarnate, notwithstanding his being attractive to both sexes — or maybe precisely because of this. "Girls, don't miss him!", readers of *Photoplay* were urged by one of its columnists in 1923.

◗ He is described as being "dark, stunningly handsome (although his looks are somewhat effeminate) and seductive"[43] and as a "smooth-skinned Apollo whose delicate features are rendered more effeminate by makeup." According to Davide Turconi "he wound up being (more or less openly) a kind of antidote to the brutal arrogance and male chauvinism of his colleagues."[44] They were the years in America when the dancer got his own back on the cowboy. Rex Ingram was to comment: "A good dancer often becomes a good film actor. Why? Because he has poise and elegance."[45] In other words, you had to learn to dance, as well as ride a horse.

◗ Novarro also withstood the test of sound better than most, thanks to his singing voice. *Pagan Love Song*, from the film *Island of the Sun* (1929) sent fans into "a wild frenzy in a way that was only to be equalled by Sinatra."[46] The *Sailor's Song* from *The Broadway Melody* (1930) was also a smash hit. Valentino, on the other hand, left one song to posterity, which one must admit is pretty mushy.

◗ Ramon was a very versatile actor. He participated in the chariot race in *Ben Hur* (1925). In *Mata Hari* (1932) he was the man to whom Greta Garbo whispered hoarsely: "Give me a cigarette."

◗ Director Jacques Feyder describes him as "an upbeat, carefree *charmeur*." "In the Studios he is adored by everyone from the chief technician to the most humble grip. Whether he picks out a tune on the guitar, does a few conjuring tricks or tells a couple of stories, everyone falls under his spell."[47]

Boys, don't miss him! Gianbattista Brambilla hit the nail on the head when he said: "The Studio managers preferred to look the other way when Novarro made a beeline for the electrician with the tightest trousers."[48] Production steered a middle course, doing everything to ensure that photoreporters did not publish any compromising pictures. Gay photographer George Hurrel did some remarkable portraits of Novarro, however.

◗ Ramon Novarro cultivated friendships with a certain exuberance. The release of *Ben Hur* (1925) was therefore an occasion for a nude party, where the guests wore nothing but Roman sandals or a leather band around their heads. When *Tarzan* (1932) hit the movie theatres, they celebrated by wearing only leopardskin wristbands, while "Ramon swung back and forth on a creeper dangling from the balcony, as the guests snatched at his leather thong."[49]

A day in Rome during the Holy Year. Twenty years were to pass before an Italian gossip magazine ran a feature entitled: "Ramon Novarro forgets Hollywood and prays in Rome." There was also a subtitle that read: "The famous screen lover says monastic life is perfect for men."[50] It was the Holy Year of 1950. Novarro stated in the featured interview that he was in Rome to benefit from the Jubilee; in other words, to obtain that Plenary Indulgence that ensures the forgiveness of sins in this life, instead of our having to expiate them in Purgatory. At seven in the morning, our Latin lover (who miraculously sheds six years in the article) attended Mass in the Church of Santa Susanna, near his hotel. Novarro "was granted an audience with the Pope, after which he visited the Sanctuary of the Three Fountains and the monasteries of Santa Prisca and the Trappist Monks. After Rome, he will go to Assisi to visit the places where St. Francis lived; to the Sanctuary of Loreto, and even as far as Turin to pray before the Most Holy Virgin of Succour."

Halloween in Hollywood. It is the Sixties. We are on Laurel Canyon Boulevard, in Hollywood. Novarro has run to fat and gone bald. "He regularly frequented the male prostitutes on the Sunset Strip. One night he picked up a youth with long chestnut-coloured hair. The boy's name was Paul Ferguson. Back home, after having sex, Ramon was happy to show him all the souvenirs he had collected over the years."[51] Backed up by his elder brother, Paul returned to Novarro's house on the night of Halloween, October 1968. The old actor was dead to the world, when the two boys got in by breaking a window and started searching through Novarro's souvenirs, looking for valuables. The actor awoke and started shouting for help. "The Ferguson boys seized Novarro and beat him up. To keep him quiet, Tom grabbed one of the souvenirs at random from the bedside table and rammed it down Novarro's throat." This was how Ramon Novarro met his death in Hollywood, eighteen years after his pilgrimage to the various sanctuaries in Rome. "The Court was very lenient" with his two young killers.

◗ Kenneth Anger wrote: "The memory of Rudy Valentino was very dear to Ramon Novarro who kept in his bedroom, beneath a glass bell, a graphite dahlia, with Valentino's signature in silver. A gift from Rudy."[52]
This was the object that Tom Ferguson had stuffed in the actor's mouth.

IV. ROSSANO BRAZZI, THE ITALIAN WHO COULDN'T SAY NO

The eagle returns... to the nest. "It's not that I lay great store by my reputation as an eternal Casanova, but..."[53] ...but being asked to play Errol Flynn's father (!) was a bit much. Brazzi had most courageously agreed to appear in *Little Women* by Melvin Le Roy: a film in which females literally abounded, but in which Brazzi played an older man, Professor Behr. The actor was aged twenty years by a beard, moustache, white wig and tortoise-shell rimmed spectacles, and "the makeup artist was his only fan."[54] Therefore, Rossano asked the producer to release him from his contract, and returned to Italy in 1949.

Rossano Brazzi in Un certo sorriso *(A Certain Smile), 1958 (Farabolafoto)*

◗ Hollywood is a strange place. Selznick had given him a seven-year contract after having seen his performance in *Aquila Nera* (Black Eagle) by Riccardo Freda (1946), in which he played the part of a "gentleman" outlaw, modelling himself on Valentino (who had played the part in 1925, a year before he died). Hollywood immediately made the Valentino = Latin lover = Italy connection, and Rossano was the umpteenth candidate chosen to wear his crown. The romantic adventure films he had made in the Forties had already earned him a certain reputation as a lady-killer on home ground. For reasons we will never know, Brazzi was offered roles that were an insult as soon as he arrived in the States.

The difficult years. Brazzi's return to Italy was nearly the end of his career. "He was full of himself when he set off for Hollywood, and came back with his tail between his legs. Italians are very unforgiving towards the "prodigal son" who doesn't make it abroad and doesn't return loaded with money."[55] And Brazzi (who spent money like water) came back with a lot of debts — in dollars. In Italy he earned the reputation of being "box-office poison" that is, his films didn't make money.

◗ They were tough years. He played opposite Anna Magnani in

Vulcano (Volcano) (1950), a rival attraction to *Stromboli* that Rossellini was shooting with Ingrid Bergman, made with the sole intention of exploiting the competition between the two actresses. In *Three Coins in the Fountain* (1954), however, he was given a role more in keeping with his former image. Granted he had the opportunity of acting with Ava Gardner and Humphrey Bogart in *The Barefoot Contessa*, but in this film Brazzi was asked to play the husband who, on his wedding night, waves a medical certificate attesting to his impotence under his wife's nose... Between films, he was mainly occupied with avoiding his creditors.

Rossano Brazzi and Jean Peters in Three Coins in the Fountain, *1954 (Farabolafoto)*

Summertime. In 1954, producer Ilya Rupert and director David Lean came to Italy to organize the film version of a Broadway hit. The title was *Summertime* and they were going to shoot it in Venice. Katharine Hepburn had agreed to play the starring role of an American woman who visits Italy, nostalgic for love. She finds it with a Venetian antique dealer who "shouts at her, in a wild fury: 'Don't talk about love, accept it!'"
Summertime: the wonderful affair lasts for a season, the length of a summer vacation. An affair spiced with that perfect mix of landscapes, feelings, sounds and colours, which allows Latin loving to blossom: impassioned words and actions, which are natural and contrived at the same time, are the main ingredients of a cocktail that has the distinct flavour of passion, of genuine Latin love. Rossano Brazzi possesses a physique, a way of expressing himself, and a voice, that make him the perfect Latin lover in this situation.

You must understand that I'm an Italian who can't say no. Hollywood called a second time. "Rossano had to perso-

Rossano Brazzi with Maria Felix in Venice, 1954 (Farabolafoto)

nify the dream and myth of the ultimate Latin lover."[56] He embarked on a highly successful publicity tour of the East Coast of America to launch the film. Naturally, he was compared to Valentino. Brazzi gallantly acknowledged: "There was only one Valentino." Not forgetting to add that "both of us were born in Italy and share a great admiration for women! I adore the female sex, of that there is no doubt. I rarely meet a woman who does not attract me, it is not a question of age."[57] There's more. "I'm always a little in love, I can't help it." This is reaffirmed in all his interviews. "I always fall in love with my leading ladies. You must understand that I'm an Italian who can't say no."[58] Brazzi paid off his debts and bought a penthouse on three floors at Villa Borghese, in Rome, "with a terrace big enough for a plane to land on."[59]

Number one. It was official. Brazzi, "by dint of profession, tendency and acclamation," was "the number one screen lover"[60] in Europe and America. According to the gossip columns, the list of stars with whom he had affairs was endless. It included almost everybody: Liz Taylor, Joan Crawford, Grace Kelly, Olivia de Havilland, Ava Gardner, Katharine Hepburn... Maria Felix confronted Brazzi's wife in the foyer of a hotel, asking her how much she wanted — in money or in jewellery — to give up her husband. Marylin Monroe waited for him half-naked, holding an espresso coffee, and said: "I learned to make Italian coffee because I love you, Roxano."[61] At least, that was his story. Then he would deny it: Marylin and he were just good friends. He did not hesitate to point out that it was the women who fell in love with him. His innate powers of seduction were almost a threat to law and order. "The American and English teenage girls who find it amusing to jump on me is a real worry. However," he added, "too many women at once is never a problem, apart from my clothes being torn and the end of my tie being cut off as a souvenir."[62] Too many women at once are not a problem. It is one woman at a time that the Latin lover finds so hard to take.

Right you are (if you think so). "Brazzi's mouth resembled

[1] Giulio Cesare Castello, Rudy o il fascino latino, in Il divismo, mitologia del cinema, ERI 1957, p. 256.
[2] The few pages of Adagio Dancer by John Dos Passos (who in the Thirties frequented "left-wing" circles) are the finest portrayal of Valentino I know (in The Big Money, 1936; pp. 206-209.
[3] Alberto Rabagliati, Quattro anni fra le "stelle" Aneddoti e impressioni, Giovanni Bolla, Milan 1932.
[4] Idem, p. 12.
[5] Idem, p. 21.
[6] Idem, pp. 16 and 29.
[7] Idem, p. 23.
[8] Idem, p. 30.
[9] Idem, p. 80.
[10] Idem, p. 14.
[11] Idem, p. 150.
[12] Idem, p. 152.
[13] Idem, p. 154.
[14] Idem, p. 152.
[15] Idem, p. 155.
[16] John Dos Passos, Adagio Dancer, in The Big Money, cit.
[17] Alberto Rabagliati Quattro anni fra le "stelle," cit., p. 156.
[18] Idem, p. 26.
[19] Idem, pp. 158-159.
[20] Idem, p. 159.
[21] Idem, pp. 159-161.
[22] Giulio Cesare Castello, I successori di Valentino, in Il divismo..., cit., p. 261.
[23] The description is to be found under "Gilbert" edited by Davide Turconi and Fausto Montesanti for the Enciclopedia dello

spettacolo, v. V, cited on pp. 1286-1287, Rome 1958.
[24] *The definition, given by Filippo Sacchi in Corriere della Sera in 1933, is cited under "Gilbert" in Enciclopedia dello Spettacolo, cit.*
[25] *Giulio Cesare Castello, op. cit., p. 265.*
[26] *Idem, testimony by Ben Hecht, p. 263.*
[27] *Idem, p. 272.*
[28] *Ibidem.*
[29] *Enciclopedia dello Spettacolo, cit.*
[30] *Testimony by King Vidor, in Giulio Cesare Castello, op. cit.*
[31] *Ibidem, p. 268.*
[32] *Enciclopedia dello Spettacolo, cit.*
[33] *Giulio Cesare Castello, op. cit., p. 263.*
[34] *Idem, p. 269.*
[35] *Idem, p. 263.*
[36] *Testimony by Hedda Hopper, in Giulio Cesare Castello, op. cit., p. 269.*
[37] *Ibidem.*
[38] *Idem, p. 270, testimony by Louella O. Parsons.*
[39] *Idem, p. 270, testimony by King Vidor.*
[40] *Idem, p. 262, testimony by Ben Hecht.*
[41] *Idem, p. 264.*
[42] *Giulio Cesare Castello, op. cit., p. 271.*
[43] *Giulio Cesare Castello, op. cit., p. 261.*
[44] *Davide Turconi, under "Novarro" in Enciclopedia dello Spettacolo, v. VII, cit., 1960.*
[45] *Giulio Cesare Castello,*

that of a fish and the pearls of wisdom that fell from his lips were total exaggerations, a heady mix of reality, fantasy, inventiveness and lies." "The way in which he chatted on about things during television shows or press interviews, at parties or dinners for two, was so persuasive, sincere and disarming that he actually believed what he was saying." "He often confused his on-screen love affairs with his little flirtations off-screen. It was difficult to determine whether or not he was imagining it all."[63]
"When listing his conquests," Bolognese actor Rossano Brazzi, "names any woman that comes to mind."[64]

The disadvantage of being handsome. Halfway through the Sixties he began to sing a different song. Statements and anecdotes appeared more and more often in the press, on the same theme: Rossano Brazzi's good looks were bothering him. In *Grand Hotel* magazine a cartoon by Walter Molino depicted Brazzi standing in the street, looking at a poster of Nicola Arigliano, the singer famous for his jug ears and big conk. "Does he want to look like him?" the caption ran. "Rossano Brazzi has said that he is tired of playing the 'Latin lover' and that, from now on, he will use makeup to appear ugly on the screen."[65] "Will he have a facelift?" asked another headline, while a brief article informed us that "tired of playing the *charmeur*, he is thinking of having plastic surgery to ruin his looks, once and for all. If he does, it will certainly be a unique case. Brazzi has been thinking it over for some time, and actually seems on the point of making a decision."[66]

Rossano Brazzi, London, 1958 (Hulton Deutsch Collection)

▸ He never did decide. What happened was that the context changed. The poularity of the Latin lover declined in Hollywood while, at home, there was a boom in mass tourism, beach romances, and the *commedia all'Italiana* (Italian comedy). *Summertime* was no longer set in Venice but Rimini — a stone's throw away, but light years away as far as quality was concerned. Brazzi declared irritatedly: "It's too difficult to work here. Italy is full of Latin lovers."[67] His main rival was Zanza, the Rimini lifeguard who documented all his conquests, displaying a list of names, constantly updated, in the local bar. And to think that in America he had won the Valentino Award for "Best Screen Lover" — after which the Adriatic Riviera had had to present him with the Riccione Award for "bringing international fame to the Latin lover."

I'm selling off everything because I'm stubborn. Headlines like the following appeared one after the other: "Sells off everything and goes back to Hollywood." Subtitle: "I'm going to America because I'm tired of being considered an eternal Latin lover at 52."[68] "Poor Rossano Brazzi is condemned to exile!" "Brazzi declares that being good-looking was the worst thing that could have happened to him."[69] "Rossano Brazzi denies he is on the edge of bankruptcy." "I am not finished. I'm auctioning my house and furniture for 12 million lire because I'm stubborn."[70]

His debts had to be paid off, again. The penthouse on three floors, with a bedroom for his poodles, became a memory. Brazzi went back to receiving journalists at the corner bar, apologizing, in his rich baritone voice, for not inviting them up: the place was being renovated.

Rossano Brazzi giving Anita Ekberg a goodnight kiss, Rome, 1959 (Hulton Deutsch Collection)

Good-looking, to the point of being ugly. Was Rossano Brazzi really good-looking? If so, how good-looking?

◗ "He was short and squat, like a toad, with a large head, bulky physique, and a torso that was out of proportion to his body. He wore shoes with built up heels to make him look taller... Proud of his profile, he always tilted his head upward and stuck out his jaw."

"Brazzi moved with deliberate slowness. He carefully moulded every feeling to match his outer expression. If he had to dance in a film it was necessary, first, to work out a very basic choreography — one-two-three — and second, to point the camera at his blue eyes."[71]

◗ And yet...

"And yet this did not in any way lessen his magnetism... Brazzi had warmth and charm. He was persuasive, gallant, courteous and attractive. The actor exuded sensuality and radiated sincerity to exactly the same degree that he was profoundly insincere. He was romantic sentimentalism personified; but it was the shy, romantic sentimentalism of a little boy..."[72]

We like the "little boy" bit. When Chaplin went to "Falcon Lair" to see Gilbert, he said that the actor was so happy! Like a little boy. Rambova also said that he was like a child... Are all Latin lovers little boys who never grow up?

We'll have to see, because here comes mamma again!

The Latin lover's wife. Lidia Bartolini was Rossano Brazzi's

Op. cit., p. 261.
[46] *Idem, p. 262.*
[47] *Jacques Feyder, cited in Giulio Cesare Castello, Op. cit., p. 262.*
[48] *Gianbattista Brambilla, L'amante latino, in Babilonia, no. 131, March 1995, p. 73.*
[49] *Idem, p. 74.*
[50] *Giorgio Salvioni, A Roma Ramon Novarro prega e dimentica Hollywood, in Gente magazine, no. 45, 9 November 1950, p. 32.*
[51] *Gianbattista Brambilla, op. cit., p. 74.*
[52] *Kenneth Anger, Hollywood Babilonia, Adelphi, 1979, p. 114.*
[53] *Rossano Brazzi, Hollywood mi ha invecchiato. La vita intima dell'ultimo "Latin lover" del cinema, Part 3, in Grand Hotel magazine, no. 864, 1963, p. 19.*
[54] *Hank Kaufman-Gene Lerner, Latin lover, mito e matrimonio, in Hollywood sul Tevere, Sperling e Kupfer, 1982, p. 191.*
[55] *Idem, p. 192.*
[56] *Idem, p. 194.*
[57] *Idem. From an interview with Jesse Zunser in Cue, cited on p. 196.*
[58] *Idem. From an interview with Wanda Hale in the New York Daily News, cited on p. 197.*
[59] *H. Kaufmann, G. Lerner, op. cit., p. 203.*

[60] *Idem. From the interview with Jesse Zunser, p. 196.*
[61] *Roberta Pasero, Rossano Brazzi, il bel tenebroso che voleva un'altra faccia, in Il Giornale, 27 December 1994.*
[62] *Rossano Brazzi, Come mia moglie sistemò una diva innamorata di me. La vita intima dell'ultimo "Latin lover" del cinema, Part 2, in Grand Hotel, no. 863, 1963, p. 25.*
[63] *H. Kaufmann, G. Lerner, op. cit., p. 197.*
[64] *Idem, p. 214.*
[65] *Grand Hotel, no. 937, 1964, p. 33.*
[66] *Grand Hotel, no. 986, 1965, p. 59.*
[67] *Consuelo Priasco, Svende tutto e torna a Hollywood, in Eva Express magazine, no. 46, p. 60.*
[68] *Ibidem.*
[69] *Alberto Pacifici, Povero Rossano Brazzi! Ora è costretto all'esilio, in Eva Express magazine, no. 4, 1970, pp. 10-11.*
[70] *Luca Olivero, Non sono un uomo finito, in Eva Express magazine, no. 16, 1971, pp. 24-25.*
[71] *H. Kaufmann, G. Lerner, op. cit., p. 212.*
[72] *Idem, pp. 212-213.*
[73] *Idem, p. 197.*
[74] *Idem, p. 194.*
[75] *Idem, p. 215.*
[76] *Idem, p. 216.*
[77] *Ibidem.*

wife for forty years. "It seemed that everyone knew about Rossano's continual affairs except Lidia. 'I may be the blindest and most stupid woman on earth,' she used to say, 'but I'm sure my husband wouldn't cheat on me.' She certainly wasn't blind, or stupid." It was more a case of her being "sure that her Rossano would always come back and lay his head on her ample bosom. And he always did."[73] At 9.00 pm., precisely: dinner time.

◗ Lidia weighed about 280 pounds. Brazzi went to America for the presentation of *Summertime*, and the producer had made it clear in the contract that his wife was not, in any circumstances, to accompany him. He commented: "Lidia's presence would have ruined the extremely virile and sensual image he had to communicate to the public."[74]

◗ But Lidia was neither shy, nor submissive. On the contrary, "she showed off her mountain of flesh quite shamelessly, wearing scanty, tight-fitting bathing costumes, and evening gowns that sometimes made it difficult to see if she had a plunging neckline or she was topless."[75]

"It was such a hoot when, in the middle of one of those dinners at home, in Hollywood, or in a crowded *trattoria* like *Angelino* in Rome, Lidia would suddenly lift up a leg, take off her shoe, look maliciously at her husband, and command: "Kiss my foot, Rossano!" "He winked at the guests as he obeyed her, but was obviously annoyed."[76] Therefore, we have also to say of her (particularly of her?): and yet... "...As you got to know that ten-ton-Tessie who seemed like Rossano's mother, she appeared younger, she made you feel younger, until you realized that all that flesh was deceiving. Lidia possessed the grace of a bird taking flight. Dancing with her made you understand that a dancer didn't have to be slim to be light on her feet; in fact, Lidia was as light as a feather."[77] Lidia Bartolini, the fat woman, and the indestructible wife of a destructible Latin lover, floated up to Heaven in 1981. Rossano was to join her thirteen years later. He called himself Edward Ross and made a series of B-movies. Brazzi married again, choosing former model Isle Fischer, for his bride. He finally left Italy, Hollywood, and this Earth on Christmas Eve, 1994.

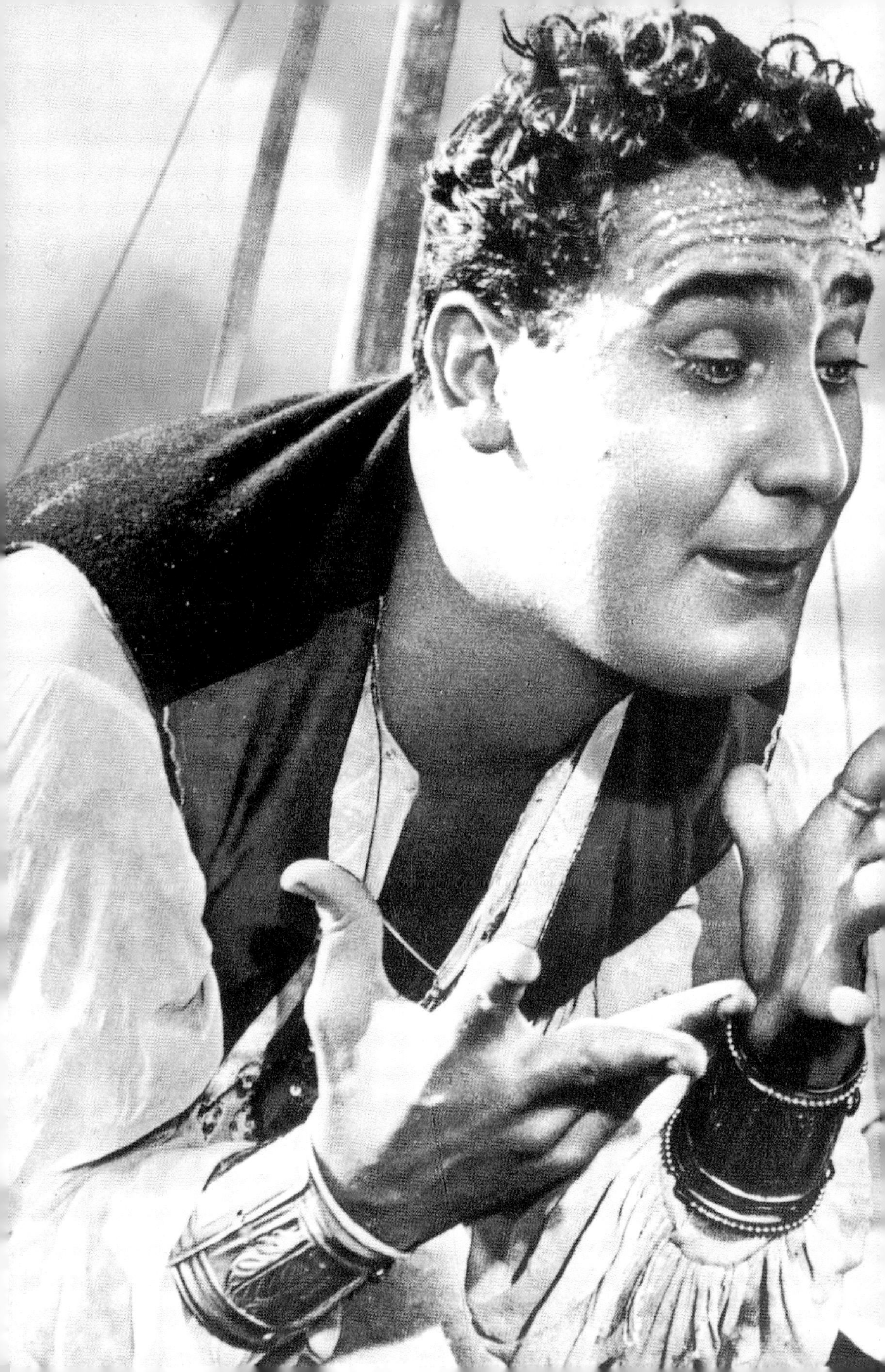

Amedeo Nazzari with Zsa Zsa Gabor, 1959 (Farabolafoto)

Marcello Mastroianni with Pamela Tiffin in Paranoia *(Hulton Deutsch Collection)*

Previous pages: Alberto Sordi and Brunella Bovo in Lo sceicco bianco *(The White Sheik), 1952 (Farabolafoto)*

It was 1950, the Holy Year. Crowds of pilgrims, mostly foreigners, flocked to Rome for the Jubilee. They included females who were obviously devout, but this did not mean they were necessarily unattractive. Thanks to this event, which was intended to be epoch-making and in any case brought a lot of business, the Italians discovered the outside world. Due to the previous regime they had not studied languages for twenty years; they had large accounts to settle with certain foreigners (first and foremost with the Austrians and Germans, from at least two or three wars, but also with their "liberators" the English and the Americans); they had often been extremely ironical about foreign tongues. They had never been xenophobes, but rather xenophiles: you only have to think of the foreign literature — even Hungarian — that had been constantly appreciated, or the American movies, which had held their own even in the blackest periods, or northern European fashions, which dictated the rules even to humble dressmakers.

Alberto Sordi with Jacqueline Pierreux in Il seduttore *(The Seducer), 1954 (Farabolafoto)*

The fact remains that the Holy Year marked the beginning of foreign tourism in Italy. The new Republic, founded on labour (but with a bent for the service sector) and which, according to the constitution, should conserve the environment, opened up its coasts (from Liguria to Romagna and from Latium to Sorrento) to tourism, and not only the beaches, but also the art centres (traditionally Venice, Florence and Rome). Both were to become the ideal settings — out of doors and therefore economic to film — for astute films full of innuendo, like the stories recounted and the conquests boasted about. Let us leave aside the damage to the environment (combined with commercial profit) and concern ourselves with the human aspect. Foreigners, both male and female, were arriving in increasing numbers, it was necessary to "cope" with them in every sense of the word. This was only an initial scenario. And what if, given the favourable conditions, Italy were to become a land of conquest for secret desires (that were sometimes unconfessable, as in the times of Baron von Gloeden), of entertainment and pleasure? This might be the second scenario. A third scenario emerged when Italians thought they could export their potential: no longer as conquered and conqueror, but as conquering conqueror; no longer Latins who tamed barbarians but as *civis romanus* who moved further afield to Gaul or Alemannia, to Pannonia or Daunia.

Previous page: Walter Chiari and Ava Gardner at Paris airport, 1956 (Farabolafoto)

However, if one wants to reconstruct the phenomenon and do-

Ingrid Bergman with Roberto Rossellini (Farabolafoto)

cument it things become confused. And this is all the cinema's fault. The Italian cinema of the Fifties and Sixties, both in its quality films and in its B-movies, was concerned with reality, since neo-realism had not happened in vain. What you saw on the screen, though it may be distorted by political passion or prevailing moralism, by cheap melodrama or grotesque provincialism, was at least based on truth: it "mirrored" real life. In the pre-television and early televison days, cinema was very popular and had a great influence: people "saw themselves" in films, they adopted their fashions and models, ideas and suggestions. It was a two-way relationship. Therefore we have to ask ourselves whether the phenomenon of the Latin lover was original or induced and which "side" of the mirror predominated in this web of fiction and reality. It all started with the handsome hunk, the well-built, athletic male physique shown off to advantage in T-shirts and trousers, or better still, bare-chested (sexy bathing trunks were still to come) in shorts or swimming costume. This outfit, with or without a singlet, was a great leveller. As far as this went there was no distinction between fashionable bathing establishments and popular beaches, public and private swimming pools, and we may include even irrigation canals and pools along the river where the working-class went. The display of the young and not-so-young male body was a provocation, and the would-be Casanova needed his "prey." What better than a "foreigner," she was easier (and easier to get rid of), more uninhibited (because she was ignorant of bad local habits), and hopefully more unsatisfied (since it was said that the northern male soon tired of playing the game of love?).

Nearly everyone thought this. The middle-class youth and those from the slums, as well as the not-so-young with the beginnings of a paunch and receding hair. The "poor but good-looking" boys of Italian cinema thought it on set but also in their private lives — Maurizio Arena, who nearly married a princess and Renato Salvatori, who desperately lived the cinema as though it were a second life, the unfortunate Antonio Cifariello and the lesser-known Enio Girolami, whose family specialized in making films set in coas-

tal resorts. Even the big names of Italian comedy ended up thinking the same way, and took part in a kind of unfair contest, in which the successful businessman beat the lifeguard (until there was proof to the contrary...).
An actor and personality like Alberto Sordi soon thought so too — we hardly have time to savour the phenomenon before it is parodied. He thought himself, handsome, fascinating, athletic and a Don Juan in art as well as in life: but instead he turned out to be rather a whining wimp, with a cocky attitude towards a world he wanted to own. The fact remains that in barely eight years, between 1957 and 1965, Alberto Sordi played the caricature of the Latin lover or a similar character eight times, he made it his *pièce de résistance*. We are taking him as an example because Sordi makes news more than many others, and because he turned a figure that already tended towards the comic into a buffoon.
Sordi began, in quite a conventional way, with *Souvenir d'Italie* (1957), in which a resourceful young man, kept by an older woman, pretends to be a hitch-hiker in order to make advances to a pretty French girl (Isabelle Corey). And continued, predictably, with *Venezia, la luna e tu* (Venice, the Moon and You), 1958, in which a jolly gondolier about to be married gets involved in a complicated relationship with two foreign tourists (Inge Schoeber and Niki Dantine, forerunners of Julia Roberts), and *Racconti d'estate* (Summer Stories), 1958, in which the manager of a fat singer, whom he ends up marrying, falls for the French girl on holiday (Dany Carrell).

Walter Chiari and Moira Orfei in Gli italiani e le donne *(Italian Men and Women), 1962 (Farabolafoto)*

Then things get a little more complicated: in *Il giovane leone* (The Young Lion), 1959, it is the unsatisfied wife of a Cannes bank-teller (Noël Magali) who lets herself be picked up by the Roman boy abroad. Or they become highly complicated: in *Il moralista* (The Moralist), 1959, as soon as the character reaches Germany he is seen to procure girls for nightclubs and be involved in the white slave trade.
We then move on to the Balearic Islands with *Brevi Amori a Palma di Maiorca* (Brief Loves on Majorca), 1959, in which even a humble artisan with a limp tries to seduce an American film star (Belinda Lee), and to distant Sweden, *Il diavolo* (The Devil), 1963, in which a fur coats rep tries it on with all the women, in a vain attempt to add romance to his trip. The series concludes with an explicit title,

Vittorio Gassman and Elizabeth Taylor in Rapsodia *(Rhapsody), 1954 (Farabolafoto)*

Latin lover (an episode from *I tre volti* – The Three Faces, 1965). Here, Sordi, though a good father, is a professional escort rented out by an agency to a rich American passing through Rome (Soraya, the ex-empress) and in this he shows a great sense of duty...

The foreigners in these and many other films were "real." The screen Latin lovers were as advantaged as those in real life. Thanks to coproduction agreements there was a real invasion of northern stars and second-rate actresses at Cinecittà. These included, to mention only a few, May Britt, Abbe Lane, Dawn Addams, Sylva Koscina, Madeleine Fischer, Yvonne Furneaux, Chelo Alonso, Jaqueline Sassard, Margaret Lee, Catherine Spaak, Ira Fürstenberg, and — dancers or princesses, models or respectable middle-class girls — they came from all the four corners of the earth. Taken as individuals they were all unique; often they were not very good but they were self-confident; some of them were only passing through but others settled down; as on the beaches, there was a wide choice of beauty and charm.

Ugo Tognazzi and Rhonda Fleming in La moglie americana *(The American Wife),*

Their male partners were more awkward. Sordi, as we have seen, was just about believable (but he was liked because so many men, unfortunately, identified with his cynicism and insolence). The same applies to other comic actors or actors verging on comedy: to Walter Chiari, Ugo Tognazzi, Vittorio Gassman and even Marcello Mastroianni.

All four of them had real affairs with foreigners, and mostly actresses, professional engagements and involvements abroad (Gassman even played the Latin lover in Hollywood at the time of *Sombrero*, 1953, and *Rapsodia* – Rhapsody, 1954), and yet their Don Juanism leaves something to be desired. They are always a bit over the top, always somewhat inferior to the real "handsome hunk," despite their behaviour, their poses and exhibitionism. They offer a revised and correct, or rather corrupt, version of the Latin lover, that of the Italian on holiday (or in town) on the look-out for easy amusement and possibly a quick fling.

One episode from *I mostri* (The Monsters), 1963, entitled *Latin lovers*, which involves two *mostri sacri* (sacred cows), Tognazzi and Gassman, serves as an example. On the usual beach, Dino Risi's favourite scenario, two men are busy picking up the beauty of the moment: in actual fact they are indifferent to her, since they are really attracted to each other... Is this the decline of the Latin lover or the revelation of another side of his personality, as old as the myth of Rudolph Valentino, who was better known as "powder puff"?

This is only an inference. The fact is that you are born and die a Latin lover. On 18 October 1995, when Franco Fabrizi died — he was neither brilliant nor particularly entertaining, but a great character actor — one immediately remembered him in the guise of the Latin lover, an image he had had to live with, ever since — as Wanda Osiris's chorus boy — Federico Fellini had chosen him to play the *vitellone* (loafer) on a beach that was supposed to be Rimini but was in fact the Tyrrhenian. Yes, because one of our beaches is as good as another, just as one woman is as good as another, and a fictitious life is as good as a real life for the Latin lover.

Alberto Sordi in Il commissario, *1962 (Farabolafoto)*

Giuliano Accordi

"Dai fiò, dai fiò, dai fiordi della Norvegia,
è scè, è scè, è scesa la vichinga,
cercà, cercà, cercava un po' di sole
e invece ha trovato l'amor..."

(From the fiords of Norway/ came the Scandinavian girl/ she was looking for a bit of sun/ and instead she found love...)

This brief quotation captures in a few lines the image of a period that went down in history in a glow of carefree affluence. The Flippers sang this song at the beginning of the Sixties and the sound was still rather restrained and pre-electronic, compared to the beat rhythms that were to come. This was the bright season of the boom; there is no historical essay, statistic or account that has not stressed the importance of the processes taking place: industrial changes, expanding consumerism, and improved quality of life. Signs of prosperity were also to be found in such trivial things, as the deafening juke-boxes on beaches that were now accessible to the masses, the *rotonde sul mare* (beach dance floors) — made famous by Fred Bongusto's hit *La Rotonda sul mare* — foreign tourism, and the summer affairs featuring in songs, films and the press. This is the climate in which popular songs brought to the fore the image of the Latin lover, which complemented that of the Scandinavian girl and embodied the myth of Italian seduction.

I am a Latin lover. Light music has always been based on aspects of seduction and used models that outlive even the most radical social changes. Therefore the point here is to underline the features of that particular variation which, from a certain period onwards, produced a cliché modelled on the male capacity to seduce.

◗ This subject may be approached in various ways. A song from 1961, significantly entitled *Italian Lover* supplies a self-satisfied eulogy of this figure.

Singer Robertino debuts at the Sanremo Song Festival (Farabolafoto)

"Ti voglio dare tanti
kiss kiss kiss kiss
come fan qui
kiss kiss kiss kiss
in Italy:
yes yes yes yes
dimmi di sì:
voglio parlar
solo coi kiss.
Io sono Italian lover:
love love love love"

Johnny Dorelli cover (drawing by G. Crepax)

(I want to give you so many kisses/ kiss kiss kiss kiss/ as they do here/ kiss kiss kiss kiss/ in Italy:/ yes yes yes yes/ say yes:/ I want to talk only with kisses/ I am an Italian lover:/ love love love love)

Kramer-Garinei-Giovannini's swing-style song suggests similar ways of making advances to female tourists:

"O baby kiss me,
please kiss me!
Tu non capisci o non vuoi capir!
Besame mucho, mucho!
Non capisci ancor
e allor ti dico:
Embrasse moi!
Ma tu continui nel non capir!
Sei di New York... Madrid... Paris?
O baby, kiss me, kiss me, kiss me"

(O baby kiss me,/ please kiss me!/ You don't understand/ or don't want to understand!/ Besame mucho, mucho!/ You still don't understand/ and so I say/ Embrasse moi!/ But you continue not to understand!/ Are you from New York... Madrid... Paris?/ O baby, kiss me, kiss me, kiss me)

A close statistical examination of the song lyrics frequently shows that the captured "prey" accepts these advances, if they are made in the conventional way and are "ethically" correct, as can also be seen from the films. The conquest then becomes an amusing game for both, though it is destined to be short-lived. Yet again the Kramer-Garinei-Giovannini trio give us an example of this.

"Merci beaucoup... thank you... grazie tanto,
ch'è suppergiù come un esperanto.

Fred Bongusto, 1964 (Farabolafoto)

Lei si allontana e le fo: Pardon,
se crede le posso far da ciceron
Merci beaucoup, mi rispose ancora,
e non so più quel che accadde allora,
però a Villa Borghese la sera a tu per tu
fui io che dissi a lei: merci beaucoup"

(Merci beaucoup... thank you... grazie tanto,/ which is more or less like esperanto./ She moves away and I say: Pardon,/ if you like I can be your guide/ Merci beaucoup, she answered again,/ and I don't remember what happened then,/ but in the evening when we were alone in Villa Borghese/ it was I who said: Merci beaucoup)

Chromosomes or something else? Is it only the magnet of a presumed genetic virility, deposited in the chromosomes of the Italian male that irresistibly and fatally attracts French, Anglo-Saxon and Scandinavian Venuses through certain seduction techniques? Or is it a question of a more general fascination exerted by factors such as the climate or environment on the alleged cold and self-controlled northern temperament? The sunny Mediterranean has also fascinated people of the calibre of Goethe, Byron and Nietzsche. However, they were attracted by a cultural archetype, which was capable of suggesting answers to philosophical or aesthetic questions, whereas in our case, a tourist setting may be enough to mirror an emotion.

Fatal scenarios. In the Fifties there were a considerable number of films based on the typical situation of an international love affair against an Italian backdrop. The most attractive and colourful settings accompanied the vicissitudes of princesses, heiresses, actresses and modern student globe-trotters (as in *Souvenir d'Italie*, 1953) or other more anonymous figures, who wrestled with champions of the species played by Rossano Brazzi, Alberto Sordi, Maurizio Arena and Ugo Tognazzi (plus a large array of imitators) in the field of conquest.

◗ The cinema and pop music synergy, together with the further development of television, was a decisive factor (not to mention tourist agency promotional campaigns and local commercial interests). The soundtracks of mambos, calypsos, cha-cha-chas and slow dances accompany the scenes of films with evocative titles such as *Napoli terra d'amore* (Naples Land of Love), 1956, *Appuntamento a Ischia* (Appointment on Ischia), 1960, *Fontana di Trevi* (Trevi Fountain), 1960, as well as many others, including the famous *Arrivederci Roma*, 1957. But the most significant film of all was *Tempo d'estate* (Summertime), 1954. The idyllic love affair between the Venetian antique dealer (Rossano Brazzi) and the American tourist (Katharine Hepburn) was a rich source of inspiration for many songs of the period.

◗ There may be a great range of geographical settings. But the fixed pattern of the "brief encounter" remains, often when it is already viewed with nostalgia. Some songs that may now be considered classics are examples of this.

(Under the sweet spell of morning/ the sea brought you to me./ I close my eyes/ and I see you again close to me at Portofino./ I remember a corner of sky/ where I was waiting for you,/ I remember your beloved face/ and your kissable mouth./ I found my love in Portofino,/ I'll never forget those kisses./ My life is no longer sad,/ in Portofino I found my love)

"Nel dolce incanto del mattino
il mare ti ha portato a me.
Socchiudo gli occhi e a me vicino
a Portofino rivedo te.
Ricordo un angolo di cielo
dove ti stavo ad aspettar,
ricordo il volto tanto amato
e la tua bocca da baciar.
I found my love in Portofino,
quei baci più non scorderò.
Non è più triste il mio cammino,
a Portofino I found my love"

Fred Buscaglione (Farabolafoto)

There couldn't be a more explicit confession than this one by Fred Buscaglione set against the backdrop of the Riviera. Here the sentimental aspect takes over from the more typical *tombeur de femmes* image of the Latin lover. The English phrases inserted in the Italian lyrics indicate not only an elementary stage of language learning, but above all an emotional symbiosis between the two partners. The setting of the Riviera was destined to recur even in songs by singer-song-writer Umberto Bindi, who belonged to a group of song-writers at the beginning of the Sixties who were considered less conventional and less bound to popular stereotypes ("Ti vorrei veder con me/ sous le ciel de la Riviera...") (I'd like to see you with me/ sous le ciel of the Riviera).

List of Songs

CREOLA
by Ripp (1926)

TANGO DELLE CAPINERE
by Bixio-Cherubini (1928)

CAMINITO
by Vanner-De Filiberto (1928)

LA CUCARACHA
by Galdieri-Savino (1934)

UNA NOTTE A MADERA
by Marf-Mascheroni (1938)

SERENATA DI DON GIOVANNI
by Bixio-Cherubini (1930s)

LA PALOMA
by Yradier-Rastelli (1940s)

CARAMBA
by Rastelli-Panzeri-Kramer (1940s)

SPAGNA CALAMITA
by Mundus-Filibello (1940s)

IL BACIO DI UNA BELLA BRASILIANA
by Trinacria-Giacobetti (1940s)

CHIQUITA BONITA
by Cofiner (1940s)

HO UNA BELLA IN OGNI PORTO
by Kramer-Garinei-Giovannini (1950s)

MERCI BEAUCOUP
by Kramer-Garinei-Giovannini (1954)

In *La lunga estate di Taormina* (The Long Taormina Summer) the references to the geographical setting have been virtually absorbed by the dynamics of a feeling of nostalgia for an experience that turned out to be "un sogno che non tornerà mai più" (a dream that will never return). Here too we find snatches of basic English ("I love you" or "kiss me bambina") which are a sign that the relationship was more than a brief fling.

Arrivederci Roma. But there is classic and classic. The ingredients of the setting may sometimes be a decisive factor, so much so that the love story seems to be dependent on the spectacular tourist attractions. The forums and excavations, Via Margutta and Trinità dei Monti, wine from the Castelli and *fettuccine* on the table... And last but not least, the Trevi Fountain and the ritual of throwing in a coin in the hope of returning. The tourist protagonist takes her leave with the following expressions:

"Arrivederci Roma...
non so scordarti più...
Porto in Inghilterra i tuoi tramonti,
Porto a Londra Trinità dei Monti,
porto nel mio cuore i giuramenti
e gli I love you!"

(Arrivederci Roma.../ I can't forget you.../ I'm taking your sunsets to England/ I'm taking Trinità dei Monti to London,/ I'm carrying in my heart our promises/ and I love yous!)

This love affair which renders parting so painful may be said to involve the whole city. Furthermore, the song has a complex structure, in which at least three planes of the plot alternate. First a "voice off" in the third person, which begins in Roman dialect and goes on to mix Italian and dialect; then the point of view of "him" and of "her," who both speak in the first person. In this way the male character is also brought in.

"Si rivede a spasso in carrozzella
e ripensa a quella ciumachella
ch'era tanto bella e che gli ha detto sempre 'no!'
E qui, proprio qui l'ho baciata...

(He sees himself riding around in the carriage/ and thinks of that girl/ who was

so lovely and always said "no!"/ And here, right here I kissed her.../ Here she in a lost voice/ said "It's over, I'm going back!")

Lei qui con la voce smarrita
m'ha detto 'È finita, ritorno lassù!'"

It passes from a seemingly neutral account in the third person to the explicit and direct emotional involvement of the male character. During the song the changes of viewpoint and the passages from outside to inside the psychology of the characters, take place continuously and fluidly.

The languages of leave-taking. Here we are far-removed from any display of virility. The male character becomes increasingly involved in sincere feelings and in syrupy nostalgia and regrets, which render him emotionally vulnerable.

◗ The last part of the cited *Merci beaucoup* almost acts as a counterbalance to the first, in which the protagonist brazenly accosts the tourist.

Marisa Allasio and the tenor Mario Lanza, 1957 (Ullstein Bilderdienst)

(Merci beaucoup... I loved you/ and you loved me too./ The train is already far away... I'll never see you again/ but my heart says again: Merci beaucoup...)

"Merci beaucoup... t'ho voluto bene
ed anche tu m'hai voluto bene.
È lontano già il treno... Non ti vedrò mai più
ma il cuor ti dice ancor: Merci beaucoup..."

Ritroviamoci (Let's meet again), implores the singer, Joe Sentieri, with a sob in his voice, in the song of the same title, as the beautiful foreigner is about to leave. The song begins with farewell phrases in three different languages ("goodbye darling, je t'aime, auf wiedersehen..."), accompanied by the sound effects of doors banging and trains clanking.

◗ The moment of parting is the climax of goodbyes and declarations of affection, which displays all the knowledge of the foreign language acquired during the affair: "My wonderful bambina! Mio solo amor/ a braccia aperte verrò correndo da te./ My funny piccolina/ I love you so". (My wonderful bambina! My only love/ I'll come running to you with open arms./ My funny little one/ I love you so.) And also: "Liebelei, liebelei/ nato con l'estate/ nell'autunno finirai./ Breve amor/ liebelei/ coi i primi freddi te ne vai..." (Liebelei, liebelei/ born in summer/ in autumn it will be over./ Brief love/ liebelei/ as soon as it gets cold you'll leave....)

For the first time in modern history Italians had the chance to learn

LA LUNGA ESTATE DI TAORMINA
by Amurri-Ferrio (1950s)

MY WONDERFUL BAMBINA
by Calabrese-Calvi (1950s)

O BABY KISS ME
by Kramer-Garinei-Giovannini (1950s)

TIPITIPITIPSO
by Gietz-Feltz-Pinchi (1954)

ARRIVEDERCI ROMA
by Rascel-Garinei-Giovannini (1957)

MESSICO
by Vinci-Panzeri-Lopez (1957)

GIORGIO DEL LAGO MAGGIORE
by Burkhardt-Tschudi-Panzeri (1958)

BUONASERA SIGNORINA
by Louis-Prima (1957)

LOVE IN PORTOFINO
by Chiosso-Buscaglione (1958)

TIPI DA SPIAGGIA
by Ferrio-Amurri (1959)

RITROVIAMOCI
by Rossi-Calabrese (1959)

RIVIERA
by Testa-Moustaki-Bindi (1960)

LIEBELEI
by Bauer-Screeball (1960)

ITALIAN LOVER
by Cassano-Pallavicini (1962)

languages in a very different context from that of the subordinate emigrant out of his depth. Not for nothing did middle school syllabuses began to include the study of a foreign language...

Valentino at the song contest. There is a considerable difference between the sentimental Latin lover in these songs who goes back to those "romantic" places to mourn or relive the memory of the affair, and that image with its ardent and sometimes amoral tones transmitted in the Twenties, at the beginning of the myth, by the film archetype Rudolph Valentino. There is a vast gap between silent cinema and pop music, both in the quality of the medium, and in specific content. Silent films tended towards an almost enigmatic emphasis of the images. The human figures use expressions that are overladen with pathos and they move with exaggerated gestures through alienating atmospheres and disturbing shadows. Valentino's sex appeal and aura of passion, emanating from his gaze and his dancing, stand out against a background that shows off to advantage his emotional force, impetuosity and screen presence. From the Fifties onwards, when the figure of the Latin lover established itself in our music, it was in a very changed context. This was the era of song festivals, of the television song contests "Canzonissima," "Cantagiro" and "Disco per l'estate." The production of a vast quantity of records led to an unusual consumption of increasingly uniform songs with standard "light" and reassuring messages.

"Tienqo lo sanque caliente..." In Italy too, during the Valentino years, in other words the Twenties, and later in the Thirties, pop songs had begun to include sinful figures in the shape, for example, of gigolos or "nocturnal" creatures of the variety clubs, so-called "vipers," "fireflies" or equivalents. The corresponding rhythms were the tango, rumba and other dances imported from Latin America. "Ardent" seduction had mainly exotic features in such songs as *Creola, Argentinita, Il tango delle capinere, Caminito...*

◗ The same rhythms and themes reappeared in the post-war period, in a climate of renewed ardour. But they arrived as an echo of the roaring Twenties, when the myth first emerged. They are often slavish imitations of foreign songs and were added to our own musical production, until they became a parody ("Caramba, io songo spagnolo/ e tiengo lo sangue caliente").

Little Tony (Farabolafoto)

Broad chests and broken hearts. Thus the male figure of the lover arrived in Italy in the Fifties and Sixties with a physiognomy increasingly purged of all remaining sinful fascination. The Latin lover had only two possibilities of expression: either Fellini's *vitellone* (loafer), which was to become the *fusto* (handsome hunk) and "tipo da spiaggia" (beach boy), or the sentimental romantic languishing in the memories of his love affairs. The former is explicitly described in the lyrics of this song from 1959.

(There's a good-looker/ oh oh oh oh,/ a super handsome hunk/ oh oh oh oh,/ broad of chest/ oh oh oh oh,/ oh how they like him/ oh oh oh oh,/ what beach/ boys!)

He is in his way the heir of a "good-looker" of around ten years earlier, who proclaimed, in a song by Kramer-Garinei Giovannini:

"C'è un bellimbusto
oh oh oh oh
di superfusto
oh oh oh oh,
gonfia il torace
oh oh oh oh,
oh quanto piace
oh oh oh oh,
che tipi...
(repeated seven times)
da spiaggia!"

"Ho una bella in ogni porto
che sta sempre ad aspettar
ed italianamente mi conforto,
sono "made in Italy!"

(I've got a girl in every port/ always waiting for me/ and Italianly I comfort myself,/ I'm "Made in Italy!")

At the other extreme, parting may cause pain and nostalgia, as in the story of the English girl and the young Venetian baker, who, in *Gondolì gondolà,* 1962, a typical Sanremo product, fell in love at first sight: "lei gli sorride/ lui fa l'occhietto/ e tutt'a un tratto/ nasce l'amor" (she smiles at him/ he winks at her/ and suddenly/ it's love). The traditional Venetian steamboat is leaving to take the tourist to the station. The farewell scene is typically heart-breaking.

"Vola colomba, il sole indora
il vaporetto che se ne va...
Gondola gondola gondolì
gondola gondolà

(Fly dove, the sun is gilding/ the steamboat as it departs.../ Gondola

GONDOLÌ GONDOLÀ by Carosone-Nisa (1962)

IL CICERONE by Vianello (1963)

MALAGA by Buongusto-Mancini (1963)

LA VICHINGA (1964)

CIAOI CIAO by Hatch-Pallavicini (1965)

LATIN LOVER by Nannini-Paoluzzi

LATIN LOVER by Dalla

Sul Canal Grande resta una scia...
'Anima mia non mi lasciar'
Se mi vuoi bene pensami un poco,
scrivimi tanto, non mi scordar..."

gondola gondolì/ gondola gondolà.../ a wake ripples the Grand Canal.../ "My sweetheart, don't leave me"/ If you love me think of me a little,/ write to me a lot, don't forget me...)

Is it the moment of decline? Thus the figure of the Latin lover was found in the traditional repertoire of romantic songs, but was losing its distinguishing features. From the late Sixties onwards the presence of this character in Italian pop music became increasingly rare. The subsequent "sexual liberation" and feminism, which also influenced collective attitudes and behaviour, were to make the cliché outmoded. Instead we now witness sporadic examples of a critical approach to the subject.

◗ The recent song *Latin Lover* by Gianna Nannini, contains a collage of images, names, situations and citations which are part of the traditional repertoire; but they are combined in such a way as to produce an alienating and demystifying effect. "Marlon Brando questioni di tango/ mette in vendita/ il tuo sex appeal." "Sangue caldo profumo da sballo/ medaglione sotto la T shirt." "Jenny è fuori di testa stasera/ non capisce perché sei così/... mentre tu non hai voglia, non hai voglia/ più di questa canzone/ Latin lover... / stai con le tue foto, stai con i tuoi trucchi..."

(Marlon Brando questions of tango/ sells your sex appeal". "Hot blood heady perfume/ pendant under the T shirt". "Jenny's off her head this evening/ she can't understand why you're like this/... while you don't want, you don't want/ this song any more/ Latin lover.../ you stick with your photos, stick with your ploys...")

◗ The character seems to have that uneasy feeling of someone who has passed his prime and, lost in his souvenirs and memories, listless and passive, he withdraws from the female figure's demands. This decline seems to be confirmed in *Latin Lover* by Lucio Dalla: a character described as "coi capelli bianchi, le mani sui fianchi," increasingly disarmed and ready to discard his role. Here too we find the most traditional images of the genre: "il mare tra i taxi di Riccione e i motoscafi blu" (the sea with the Riccione taxis and blue motorboats) but they are used as a decadent backdrop: "il Latin lover con il suo cuore di cartone chissà cos'è stato in gioventù.../ solo un Latin lover e niente più" (the Latin lover with his cardboard heart who knows what he was in his youth.../ simply a Latin lover and nothing more). Does the Latin lover, as Gianna Nannini sings, "not want this song any more"? Or doesn't he even want to exist?

Renato Salvatori and Giorgia Moll in Mariti in città *(Husbands in the City), 1958 (Farabolafoto)*

Ugo Tognazzi, Venice, 1960 (Farabolafoto)

Renato Salvatori and Giorgia Moll in Mariti in città (Husbands in the City), 1958 (Farabolafoto)

A picture from Domenica d'estate *(Summer Sunday) (Archivio Brandini-Sanguinetti)*

LOVE AFFAIRS IN ROMAGNA

THE SOCIOLOGY OF BEACH BOYS

Giorgio Triani

The genre, with few exceptions, is picaresque. Or rather mock-heroic. Even when the stories of seduction are extraordinary and the protagonists legendary. From Don Juan to Casanova, from Rudolph Valentino to Rossano Brazzi right down to the Latin lover on the beach and the professional playboy there is a minimum common denominator, a trait that unites these very different figures of "lovers." This is the taste for excess and hyperbole which does not fear vainglory and which, in the field of literature, tends to make one think of *Gargantua* and *Pantagruel* rather than *Don Quixote*. Love binges that are quite incredible, also because the story escalates over time. A list of feats of passion in the style of a *miles gloriosus*, by narcissists oblivious to the etymological nobility of the term, to the original dignity and identity of the Latin lover.

Therefore let us begin with questions of etymology. Also because they permit model syntheses, immediate associations, as the first use of the word "playboy" by the playwright Ben Jonson in the seventeenth century indicates: "Pretty boy! Goes he to school?... He prates Latin, An it were a parriot, or a play-boy". The fact that at the time anyone who spoke Latin was either a priest or a play-boy, in other words a school-boy actor, allows one to grasp the close historical affinities (of genre) between the two words/figures (playboy and Latin lover); but also the evolution of this genre in our century, especially in art and the cinema, considering the close identification of the ultimate lover (from Rudolph Valentino to Rossano Brazzi) with the star system. Cinema loves, dream seducers (and seductions) which locate the world of the Latin lover and playboy in a dimension that is out of the ordinary, distanced from everyday life. A holiday of the mind (and of the body) in the sense of imaginary escapism, of immersion in the entertainment industry (by the way, a product of our century). From this emerges "the son of the sheik" as the prototype of a genre of great loved ones but especially great lovers. But also a holiday understood as a break from the usual occupations and affections, and especially as an escape to coastal resorts. This conjures up images of passionate, whirlwind affairs, of conquests that burn themselves out in a few days, or hours, of violent passion.

This association, which is a blend of fiction (the cinema) and escapism (the holiday), the set and the beach, emerged in the Twenties, when stars of showbusiness, art and fashion (who were

"unattainable," as well as champions of excesses not only in love) launched the fashion of meeting up in famous coastal resorts (where later — and this was not merely incidental — major film festivals were held from Venice to Cannes). And this also helps us to understand why the Côte D'Azur became the favourite haunt of playboys (in pursuit of film stars and third-rate actresses) in the Fifties and Sixties and more specifically how the beach (therefore nudity and a holiday atmosphere) produced the less élitist myth of the Latin lover as a *gallo italico* (Italian cockerel) and beach *cacciatore* (hunter), especially in Romagna. Later we shall consider in depth the emergence of this figure of the "seasonal" Latin lover — if I may be permitted to use this term — and the tourist myths that developed around him, in Rimini and particularly Riccione. But first we shall outline some other preliminary and introductory issues. First and foremost there are great and considerable differences between the Latin lover and the playboy, the former belonging to an élitist and literary context, and the latter to a popular and gossip magazine context. Refined, love craftsmanship on the one hand, industrial Don Juanism and a seduction assembly line on the other. The playboy in fact evokes modern times, the predominance of consumerism even in the field of sex and eroticism, to such an extent that he is confused with the gigolo and has a female counterpart: the playgirl. The Latin lover (always exclusively male) derives from the eighteenth- and nineteenth-century figures of artists and scholars who loved classical antiquity. Those on the Grand Tour, en route to the sun, who sought the monuments and vestiges of the past, but also the pleasures of the senses, physical delights. These were what Lawrence Sterne called "sentimental journeys," but also an escape from puritanical northern climes to more permissive and sinful lidos. And it is, in fact, in places that were later to become famous coastal resorts such as Venice Lido and Capri, that the chosen few found a warm sensual welcome. From Byron, great seducer of Italian women both of noble descent and peasant stock, to Fersen (to give an example of two extremes), the great homosexual aesthete who settled on Capri and took great pleasure in the local boys whom he forced to dress up as Ephebus and Narcissus. He was one of many English homosexual artists who, after Oscar Wilde's trial, left for this hospitable Italian island in order not to end up in Reading Jail.

In other words, the South as the latitude of pleasure and love affairs, was most in evidence along the coasts. It is here close to the sea, in fact, that "prey" and "predators" flocked in ever-increasing numbers as the fashion of holidays spread: "the sea, the beach and the rest... the rest is nearly always love," wrote the *Secolo XX* ironically in 1913. And the "rest" was well worth an illness: which may be sham of course. As the newspaper *Corriere della Sera* wrote in 1905: "It does not matter much if the waters are curative. They are a moral occasion: and there is no point in worrying about how much bromine and iron, soda and iodium they contain... The husbands do not even guess how much *petty morality* — as Nietzsche would say — a wife might absorb in fifteen swims, and how many bad resolutions may "pass" with a litre of healthy water..."
As early as the beginning of the century the press reported the feats of exceptional lovers, for example the legendary Cleanto Scarpa who broke in horses and women at Venice Lido. Even before the First World War the arrival of "foreign females" was announced in the newspapers and local rag sheets like an invitation to the hunting season. And at the Venice Lido in the Twenties the Chez-Vous nightclub often gave parties for the largest "colony of foreigners." But the "train bringing husbands" to join their wives who had been left alone during the week — though in the Thirties it was the subject of caustic allusions worthy of the novel by Achille Campanile *Agosto moglie mia non ti conosco* (Wife I Don't Know You in August), 1930 — still did not allow one to glimpse the ghosts that were to materialize from the Second World War onwards. The lifeguard — the typical figure of the erotic beach imagination — and the local lads, who as soon as summer came and with it foreign females broke off all their relationships with the local girls, marked the beginning of a phenomenon, whose development, in order to become significant from the point of view of social mores, necessitated mass tourism. The image of the Latin lover, the inimitable Casanova, the irresistible seducer, between the two world wars evoked cinematic horizons, literary myths and personalities who were absolutely exceptional. A territory in which Rudolph Valentino reigned supreme, but in which D'Annunzio and Mussolini may also be said to have played their part.
A lust for life, a need to make up for lost time and the hardships

suffered, combined with a bullet-proof optimism and a desire to re-establish normal life as soon as possible: it is in this climate that summer holidays, and especially the beaches, immediately became, as soon as the war was over, the symbol of a human condition desired, sought and loved above all others. Images of "obligatory" exorcisms: the first minute two-piece christened Bikini which, in 1946, a few days after nuclear experiments had been resumed in the Pacific atoll, was presented in a fashion show at the Molitor swimming pool in Paris. But also races (and chases) any old how (even in goods trains readapted for civilian service, because 90 percent of passenger carriages had been destroyed) to regain paradise lost. And the soundtrack of this migration was "scurdammece o' passato" (let's forget the past): a Neapolitan song that emerged from the rubble and was very popular during the reconstruction years. And, in fact, even if everything was not new, certainly the pre-war élitist rites and myths were swallowed up by the burgeoning industrial society. Though not yet a consumer society it was ready to copy the American way of life and leisure pursuits. Provincial Italy looked to the States. It was ready to go wild to the rhythm of the boogie-woogie in makeshift nightclubs and dance-halls. Americans in Rome and *vitelloni* (loafers) on the beach, who were poor but, if not good-looking, resourceful, especially where the sun and sea were a promise of sweet nights. Everywhere, Capri and Rimini, Viareggio and Venice Lido, Riccione and Santa Margherita, the beach liberation war denuded people who wanted to let their hair down and enjoy themselves to the full. But it was on the Romagna Riviera that this desire soon became a mass phenomenon and that the myth of the "handsome hunk," the beach version of the Latin lover, emerged in an original way that had no equal elsewhere. And this was due to several

Ugo Tognazzi in Venice, 1960 (Farabolafoto)

concomitant factors. First and foremost was the development of the hospitality industry at Rimini and Riccione, thanks to very enterprising local operators and the local community's prompt reconversion to (seasonal and family) tourism. This meant they were able to attract large numbers, the first of the mass holidaymakers who dreamt of the sea though they could not afford it. And these included many foreigners, especially Germans, who — not so much because they were in the habit of spending holidays by the sea, a custom that dated from the beginning of the century on the Riviera — came on a sort of pilgrimage to Romagna in the post-war years. They came back to see the places where the war had kept them on the Gothic Line, to remember fellow soldiers who had fallen. This was a commemorative tourism at the beginning, which also had its tragicomic side. For example, the German holidaymaker bumping into a local resident whose pig and chickens he had stolen, and who, in the meantime, had become a restaurant owner or lifeguard.

However, these bad feelings rapidly vanished when they came into contact with the hard and fast rule that "business is business," especially when pleasantly diluted by the bright carefree atmosphere of seaside entertainment. Sun and a suntan were the symbols of this new happy society that materialized in the summer and which fed on expectations and hopes which — as in the songs — married the sea and love. For the army of nordic beauties who invaded the Romagna beaches in ever-increasing numbers a love affair was not a mere whim, an extra, but was part of the "package." Guido Nozzoli from Rimini, the talented and famous special correspondent of the *Giorno*, says that the Nibelungs gave themselves with sunny, spontaneous rapture: they had no feelings of guilt or betrayal: sexual transgression was part of their holiday just like spaghetti, the sun, dancing and beach games. However, for the young and not-so-young local "handsome hunks" the summer and the arrival of the Vikings meant not only coming back to life after a long and boring winter in the provinces, but also a chance to discover that the world was a big place and to assert themselves.

It was *L'avventurosa estate dei birri* (The Adventurous Summer of the *birri*), from *bérr*, male turkey in Rimini dialect — according to Nozzoli in Fellini's book *La mia Rimini* (My Rimini), 1967, — who was the "resourceful, cocky, apparently cynical, rather exhibitionistic and aggressive youth, who pursues foreigners with the persistence of a collector and, in his spare time, between one love affair and the next, gets up to all sorts of exaggerated and irritating tricks." The *birro* might operate alone or in small groups and there was the "beach" and "dance" version. The beach *birro,* however, "must be tanned all over, even the soles of his feet, swim stylishly and dive in confidently, know how to play *alle assette*, do elegant exercises on the beach, row a boat out to sea without getting tired (especially on the way back)... and — last but not least — be liked by children, so they don't turn against him when he tries to make advances to their mother."

Of course you were not born a *birro* but became one. "To be ready for when the first foreign girls arrived the 'beach *birro'* — whether student, loafer or unemployed — takes advantage of every ray of spring sunshine, starts swimming when the water is still cold enough to give you a heart attack and, to repair the damage incurred from winter laziness and overeating, secretly does tiring exercises in his room in April and May and goes on painful diets." The *birro* was vain, but ready to face a challenge, whether he was a *superbirro,* a big shot, or a suburban *birro* who frequented "B circuit" dance halls, a woman was always seen as a conquest "to be judged by what she was worth and what she could give." And in fact there existed a precise classification of women in Romagnese slang. "Judging by age" — writes Nozzoli very amusingly — "and by appearance a woman could be: a *tubo* (ugly) or a *vallo* (ugly and deformed), a *ludero* (vulgar, ambiguous and not even attractive), an *osso* (thin), a *spippola* (small and lively), a *creatura* (very young), a *baldona* (shapely with sturdy legs), a *carampana* (an older woman getting on for fifty), an *orfanella* (modest, lost and ungainly), a *zingaraccia* (country or peasant woman), a *di prima* (beautiful), or a *patacca mondiale* (fake). All these *gnocche* (good-lookers) were then classified according to their personality: from the *gnorna* (complainer) to the *fanello* (crafty), from the *procaga* (sophisticated) to *una da battuta* (one who is willing without too many complications). Later you could decide if the Italian or *svizzera* (foreigner in general) was a *palmone*, in other words insensitive, a *tintinaga* or more commonly a *vigliacca* one who goes half way, a *sgolvonata,* thirsty for pleasure, capable of *ridurre sull'assa*, draining her partner." The *birri* much appreciated the *baldoni*, easy game, and feared the *freide* (wets) like the plague, those who had any illness from tonsilitis to *tincone.* "If you met a *birro* with a *freida* to warn him all you had to do was say, 'Catrani is looking for you.'" Catrani was the most famous doctor in Rimini for venereal and skin diseases. As an unrivalled protagonist of those years, Ivo Del Bianco, remembers — without regrets and vainglories to tell journalists in search of "local colour" — accidents on the job (more often connected with women from brothels rather than tourists) were normally treated by a nurse at the hospital. He was a specialist *sui generis* who, in the post-war years, going into the Bar Sport at Riccione (where the Green Bar now stands) carrying his penicillin (the new revolutionary antibiotic) shouted *Quel dà escol didre* (at the back was a makeshift surgery where patients were given injections).

But Ivo Del Bianco's account also shows the other side of Romagna *birrismo*, in other words, it was nearly always the foreigners who chose, though they pretended to let themselves be seduced. There was the fundamental difference between the *birri* who — and they were few — experienced the affair with a foreigner as a kind of apprenticeship, a way of broadening their horizons, improving the art of *savoir vivre,* and those who concentrated on the sexual act. As in the case — a caricature but true — of the lifeguard who, nudge-nudge wink-wink, invited the German girl to "*wollen sie spaziren*" (giving *spaziren* a much more down-to-earth meaning than "to walk"). The seasonal beach Latin lover was rarely great and often pathetic especially when — to go back to Nozzoli — "he had itchy fingers and absent-mindedly put a souvenir from his girlfriend's room into his pocket or laughingly asked for a loan at least to pay for a tonic."

We must, however, make another basic distinction — as regards mock-heroic philology — between the *birro* from Rimini and the *birro* from Riccione. The former had a greater historical background and a very prestigious tutelary deity, Paolo Mantegazza, the famous doctor, anthropologist, senator of the kingdom, successful popularizer, and, for a number of years after the Unity of Italy, director of the Rimini Bathing Establishment. A man of science and great epicurean, who, in recommending the sea — panacea of all ills and excellent tonic for sexual desire — invited

German tourists in Sorrento in the Fifties (Ullstein Bilderdienst)

bathers to visit the local sulphur factory, when the female workers were coming out, because contact with that substance, aroused them and made them ready for the act of love. But the Rimini tradition, celebrated in Fellini's *Vitelloni* and elevated to an art, was a very influential model. Especially for those from Riccione who, strong in the belief that the "Pearl of the Adriatic" was more exclusive and had a more fashionable clientele — especially in the early Fifties — tended to see themselves as a superior class of Latin lover. However, the memories of those in the front line at the time (found in the catalogue of the 1990 exhibition *Ricordando fascinosa Riccione* – Remembering Fascinating Riccione) do not support this claim. Or at least they lead one to think that in sunny Romagna from Cesenatico to Cattolica, there was only one type of *setacciatore* (sifter) in action. "At the beginning of the season, towards May, we went to the sea, normally in pairs and... began to 'sift' the beach, inch by inch, missing out some areas that were the hunting ground of certain lifeguards who snapped up all the foreigners. We looked for German and Swedish girls, preferably those who had just arrived, as we could tell from their pale skin... We avoided Italians, because of the danger of finding ourselves engaged... or in a serious relationship. Even though the Bolognese girls were very popular and the Ferrarese girls even more so. But we aimed particularly at the Swedish girls or the very rare Greeks and Spaniards. We had a points system that went from one to eight: the Greeks were worth eight points, the Swedish girls five, and Germans one because there were so many of them."

The elegant Corso Zanarini, for an aperitif and evening stroll, and particularly Dancing Savioli, the Saviolino, Villa Alta, the Paradiso, were the places where Riccione, unlike Rimini, could be seen as the Italian continuation of the Côte d'Azur. There was the constant parade of Ferraris, Maseratis and Lamborghinis in front of the Bar Canasta and the non-stop procession of film stars and celebrities from the entertainment world, and also authors and playwrights, who during the decade of the "economic boom," came to the "Perla Verde" to attend the Gran Premio Riccione — Theatre and Show Business Prize. This milieu of celebrities (which included Vittorio De Sica, Vittorio Gassman, Gina Lollobrigida, Totò, Silvana Mangano and Ugo Tognazzi) gave the tone to the Riccione nights and drew a large anonymous crowd eager to spy on them and try to copy them. Naturally there were rich prizes and favours for everyone, and every woman was admired by the good-looking local lads, the handsome natives who, having spent the day on the beaches making dates to go dancing at the Dancing Savioli, were all to be found round the bar in the same night spot. Beppe Savioli, the Riccione party king, gave them free drinks to boost his night-club. Apprentice Latin lovers, for the delight of French, Dutch and German girls, to whom the Savioli erected ephemeral monuments in the shape of a windmill or the Eiffel Tower, when parties were held in honour of foreign guests or for the election of a Miss Europe.

Singers with quiffs like Fred Buscaglione, whose famous song *Eri piccola, piccola così* was a hymn to beach machoism; or inimitable aristocrats like the ex-champion of swordmanship, Count Cornaggia Medici, who barricaded himself with his friends in the Paradiso demanding caviar and champagne and refusing entry to everyone, promising he would personally make up for any financial loss; and classy masters of cerimonies such as the above-mentioned Ivo Del Bianco (maître at the Savioli before becoming manager of the Paradiso and then going on to the "dolce vita" in Rome); not to mention famous scenes such as the one when Vittorio Gassman slapped Anna Maria Ferrero on the dance floor: these were some of the ingredients that made the food on the Riccione tables so tantalizing. It was a fashionable resort, which, to boost its reputation as number one in Italy, achieved renown by exalting the universal glory of that great Latin lover *par excellence*, Rossano Brazzi. It was 1957 and the actor received an award at the Savioli "for having publicized the image of the Latin lover throughout the world."

Evidently the attractions a coastal resort could boast and offer as regards *ars amatoria* were a tourist plus. This is seen in the conversation between Jean Sorel and Franco Maria Salerno in Dino Risi's film *L'ombrellone* (The Beach Umbrella), 1964: "In the high season I manage to have 70 or 80 women." "Listen, are they usually beautiful?" "Not all of them. Some are not so hot, but you can't be that choosy... We have to encourage tourism." "Do you prefer foreigners?" "Well, generally yes, especially Danes. For me Danish girls are the best. Germans are too sentimental. I don't go for Americans... oh, only if they're Jewish, otherwise they're not worth a light."

This conversation between the engineer on holiday with his wife and the local playboy shows how, in just a few years, the figure of the Latin lover (against a background of soft, sandy beaches, the Grand Hotel, and the discreet tinkling of champagne glasses) had been taken over by advancing Americanization and the new leisure culture, which Giorgio Bocca, in his book *La scoperta dell'Italia* (Discovering Italy) saw as "a synthesis of rich and poor, town and country, of polyglot studies, customs, swapped recipes, mixed marriages and twinnings." In other words a hybrid which was evident in all its vulgarity precisely where, by force of circumstances, it had to expose itself: on the beaches, on holiday. This can be seen from the emergence of an actual beach genre in the cinema (Italian style comedy) and music world. "Cinema in bikini" (as Giuseppe Ghigi described it in the book *Lido and Lidi*, 1989) whose soundtrack featured songs like *Sapore di sale* and *Rotonda sul mare, Love in Portofino* and *Pinne, fucili ed occhiali.* The forerunner of these films was *La spiaggia* (The Beach) by Lattuada and this was followed by *Le svedesi* (The Swedish Girls) by Gian Luigi Polidoro, *Leoni al sole* (Lions in the Sun) by Vittorio Caprioli, *Appuntamento in Riviera* (Appointment on the Riviera) by Mario Mattoli and *Il mare* (The Sea) by Giuseppe Patroni Griffi, to mention only a few. The movies were populated by playboys and wives on holiday, by "poor but good-looking" youths and industrialists who had made their money during the boom, by timorous foreigners and ageing Latin lovers, by porters and barmen, accomplices in the brief summer affairs. "The Capri/Positano/Ischia triangle" — writes Ghigi — "is teeming with drugstore cowboys from Naples, the Minùs, Cocòs and Sciusciùs who spend their brief, cynically carefree seasons with the Peppiniellos and Marisas. On the

Ostia/Fregene/Torvaianica coast we find the complete Trastevere bestiary... While on the Adriatic front you can find the whole range of the Michelin Guide to sex." And this brings us back to the coastal wrestling match — a real battle — which took place mainly in Romagna and was well summed-up in a comuniqué from a typical film by Risi, *L'ombrellone:* "Yesterday a hundred and fifty thousand Germans crossed the border. There were many accidents at the French frontier. Nothing new to the west. Riccione and Cattolica are completely overrun by English and Swedish girls. There were many accidents on the Autostrada del Sole. The death-toll on this first day was twenty." Needless to say it was this new mass phenomenon that shaped a new race of Latin lover. A type who, while his playboy side became accentuated, increasingly began to take on the aspect of the "hunted hunter."

Certainly Riccione in the Sixties could legitimately proclaim itself the "capital" or rather the "school" of the Italian playboy. Starting with Gigi Rizzi who did his apprenticeship there at that time before heading for Saint Tropez and became a gossip magazine celebrity because of his affair with Brigitte Bardot. But the light-hearted *de profundis* of the myth was pronounced by the Nordic Ursula, who, after seducing a Milanese lawyer and sending her fiancé back home, told the weekly magazine *Men*: "It's not true that Italians are *pappagalli* (literally "parrots," playboys), they are edible cockerels. You just have to know how to cook them." And with that the golden age of beach Latin lovers between 1947 and 1960 was relegated to history. What with revolutions in generations and customs, protests against the system and women's lib, sexual permissiveness became the norm. The *divertimentificio* (entertainment factory, a term coined by Camilla Cederna) still produced examples of extraordinary seduction. But there was a great gap between the gentlemanly Rossano Brazzi and the supermacho Zanza (provided a comparison is possible). It was like a great leap in the dark. Like going from Fellini's Rimini to Corbucci's *Rimini, Rimini*, 1986. On the tour operators' beach today the *vitelloni* have the face of Gigi and Andrea. They still laugh, but more loudly and neurotically. "This is because the future no longer has" — according to Ivo Del Bianco — "the flavour of promise and romantic adventure that it had for us in the Fifties. For us the foreign girl, the conquest, sex, meant living with the conviction that tomorrow would be even better. I think for example of all the many, too many remarks by psychologists and sociologists today and I ask myself: but do you think of the young people who have to go out with a condom in their pockets? It is the death of desire, of the pleasure of eating the forbidden apple." Yes; we look at the stereotyped icons of the latest Latin lovers (confined to the glossy world of male photomodels and fashion models) and only then, because it would not be possible otherwise, do we almost feel nostalgia for the heroic, unpolished Riminese *birri*. And also, in Guido Nozzoli's expert opinion, especially nostalgia for "the disappearance of the 'school ships,' the female soldiers of sex, generous valkyries who got all the boys within a radius of two kilometres to 'teach them to swim' or also trained up to six or seven pupils per season."

Two tourists in bikinis on the beach at Palermo, 1961 (Ullstein Bilderdienst)

Rome, 1960 (photo by Dino Jarach) ▶

Trevi Fountain, Rome, 1960 (photo by Dino Jarach)

Five English tourists in Sanremo, 1955 (Hulton Deutsch Collection)

Tourists in Florence, 1960 (photo by Dino Jarach)

Italians with tourists, 1963 (Ullstein Bilderdienst)

Initiatives such as the present, based on efficient, in-depth iconographic research, are praiseworthy. Keen researchers who tirelessly do the rounds of archives, photo libraries, newspaper offices and press agencies, permit Italian photography, characterized by a certain laziness, to momentarily shake off the apathy of decades, to confront itself with international photography and to embrace its own history, with a truly far-reaching determination.
Unfortunately, people like myself who frequent the Italian photographic world daily, and have done for years, are fully aware that an unrealistic image is presented today; an image that is biased, deceptive, and marred by too much expertise and painstaking research. Once again form has taken priority over content. There is nothing behind the formal brilliance that surrounds the visual representation of the famous Latin lover phenomenon. It must therefore be emphasized that the present symbolic show is merely descriptive and does not give an overall picture. However, it is the deceptiveness that fleetingly endows Italian photography with an alluring prestige, making the present project worthy of considerable attention. Paradoxical though it may seem, we should actually be grateful for the illusion displayed here, which will (would) enable a path to be traced and permit photography to be classified in Italy, as it has been in other countries.
Naturally, we cannot hope that Italian photography — a valuable, precise and searching testimony of the somewhat chaotic evolution of a society over the decades — will be celebrated with a programme of special events, like the ones organized in other countries, especially the United States and France. In fact, the favourable situation on the other side of the Atlantic, and the Alps, is quite unique.
The United States use the photographic image to document a history that is relatively recent — like the art of photography, in some respects. It is obvious, therefore, that the U.S. will adopt and express extremely high and absolute values that are, in fact, a celebration of America itself.
Similarly, the grandeur of the French can turn to generosity when they are allowed to believe that they own photography. The French

Previous page: Tourist Mercy Haystead in Positano, 1949 (Hulton Deutsch Collection) officially invented photography — although people in the profession know that what we understand as photography today (first and foremost, the possibility of making an infinite number of prints from an original negative) owes more to the invention of Englishman William Henry Fox Talbot than to the processes devised by Niépce and Daguerre — and made it available to the world, never letting anybody forget it. In strictly objective terms — if they can actually be applied — we have every right to complain about the way the United States and France, and also Germany and the U.K., celebrate their own photographers, whose talents Italians could certainly match if they were given the chance. Why doesn't this happen? Or rather, why does it happen so rarely? The present structure, created to visualize the Latin lover phenomenon, provides the answer: Italian photography has never been able to assimilate its History.

Trevi Fountain, Rome, 1960 (photo by Dino Jarach)

As long as photography is news, there are no problems. The narrative skill of so many national authors has always matched that of professionals the world over, and met the requirements of news magazines. When this infrastructural function is exhausted, Italian photography lacks the necessary ideas and formal concepts to develop its own specific structure. With one or two exceptions — that we will mention later — Italian photography does not find time for that moment of reflection that comes with putting things in order, with cataloguing. With regard to the observation made earlier, the present iconographic study has, above all, brought to light the following: mere existence counts for very little, unless accompanied by an awareness of possession. In other words, being is more important than just appearing.

To illustrate the evolution of the Latin lover ethos, the dust of years

In this page and in the two following: Gigi Rizzi doing a striptease at a party given by Maria Gabriella di Savoia and Marina Doria, 1976 (Publifoto)

was removed from many significant images which captured life magnificently, but had ceased to exist. Phenomenologies were classified with the painstaking care of the scholar who knows how to interpret and learn from past events. In a word, a card-index was compiled in which moments that can only be expressed in photography's vivid, visual language, were classified. There is an age-old lesson that Italy has never learned. Photography does not only exist by virtue of competent authors, but in relation to the entire apparatus responsible for managing and presenting the image. Nothing could be more simple, but it is still not clear to a class of professionals that has suffered, over the decades, from belonging to a country that has rarely had the courage to face reality. More particularly, years of futile debates on the presumed artistry of photography and distracting battles with the publishing world, have made us gradually lose sight of the one existing truth, that is, the important contribution made by people active in the sphere of management and presentation of visual communication.

It is certainly a known fact that behind the important phenomena that have gone down in History as major cultural events, there have always been personalities, as modest as they were talented, who remained in the background but, in fact, made a real difference. For example, Alexey Brodovitch, the mythical art director of *Harper's Bazaar* in the Thirties, was perceptive enough to engage, for the first time, photographers such as Richard Avedon (Dovima with the elephants, wearing a dress by Yves Saint-Laurent for Dior, in August 1955), Irving Penn, Lillian Bassman, Martin Munkacsi, Erwin Blumenfeld and Louise Dahl-Wolf. He was the first art director to realize how important the image was to a newspaper or a magazine. Brodovitch maintained that graphic design could express a way of thinking as eloquently as a text. He revolutionized *Harper's Bazaar* with bold, new layout concepts, seeking to combine photographs, texts and white space, in such a way as to give the page a more vivid, harmonious look, as well as overall aesthetic appeal. From 1934 to 1958 — twenty-four years in fact — Brodovitch's ideas dominated the look and image of the trendsetting American fashion magazine. He encouraged young photographers and saw the magazine as a launching pad for new concepts in fashion photography and graphic design. He knew how to successfully exploit the gifts of young artists (in the mid-Fifties he used Andy Warhol as an illustrator) and was extremely clever at directing great photographers, such as Henri Cartier-Bresson, Cecil Beaton, Bill Brandt, Man Ray and Lisette Model. The value of the photographic infrastructure, which in its turn is the infrastructure of different spheres of activity (fashion, publishing, advertising...) is a lasting one. Many internationally famous, award-winning photographs were originally selected from the wealth of material by photo editors with a keen eye. Being a baseball fan myself, the one that immediately springs to mind is the moving image of George Herman "Babe" Ruth's farewell to the public at the Yankee Stadium: holding his cap in his hands the hero, framed from behind, bowed to the roaring crowd, wearing that number 3 on his back which would never be assigned to another New York baseball player. Well, photographer Nat Fein was honest enough to say that he regretted not having been able to secure a better position among the thirty-four photojournalists sent to cover the event on that hot summer afternoon of 13 June 1948. While Arthur Glass, the sports editor of the *New York Herald Tribune*, immediately perceived the symbolic value of the unmistakeable figure silhouetted against the stands — and Nat Fein won the Pulitzer prize that year.

In Italy people still reminisce about the great days of news magazines, whose editorial offices were the training ground for generations of distinguished photoreporters — no names, please! The work of those same photographers, some of whom were intelligent and cultured, while others possessed great insight, or were just plain lucky,

vanished — sometimes without trace — when their days came to an end.

An important exhibition of Federico Patellani's work, which chooses to focus on the period of his career from 1939 to 1952 (even though Patellani continued to photograph until the day he died in February 1977) was held recently. His original photographs and important published features are accompanied by an excellent volume, with a richer and more detailed iconographical content, which for the first time presented the complete body of work of an author who was one of the founders of Italian photojournalism. This valuable photographic material has been preserved thanks to the efforts of Kitti Bolognese and Giovanni Calvenzi, who represent the exception referred to earlier. Believe it or not, many journalists and photographers were not familiar with Patellani's *oeuvre* before seeing this exhibition! It must be understood that he was more than a top professional, who deserves a position in the international hall of fame for his contribution to the development of photographic language and a place in Italian social history next to men of the calibre and substance of Buzzati, Pavese and Coppi. Despite the fact that the Patellani archive is well catalogued and preserved, he has gradually faded from the scene — which is evident from the amount of his work that has not even been listed, let alone catalogued.

Patellani is to Italian photography and social mores what Brassaï and Doisneau are to French society. What is the difference between the two worlds? Abysmal: France beats Italy hands down, seeing as our country often forgets it has so many top-notch photographers (Tino Petrelli, another ace, was only able to publish his monograph with the help of the Cassa di Risparmio bank), and even ceases to be aware that it has lived through as many periods of major importance: enough to mention the years of the Roman *dolce vita* (sweet life), that risks being cancelled forever by images that are difficult to locate. If this had happened in Paris or New York, you can imagine what a beating they would have given us with all their exhibitions, books, retrospectives, honours, and all the rest.

Thus the Latin lover, who achieved international recognition while living the many and varied exploits of the Italian lover, gives us a wonderful excuse to examine an Italian problem with a superior attitude, but a critical eye. The subject matter is epic indeed, and the research that has produced the present picture, was conducted accordingly. This scrupulous research has also brought surprising new facts to light. We hope that our modest but unwavering opinions on photography will not end here, but hit the mark and rouse our microcosm from the lethargy that has beset it for some time; a microcosm full of people with a will, but lacking common goals.

When I think back to the Fifties and Sixties, when the Latin lover was in his heyday, I also have another regret: that of not being able to listen to the story told by the real protagonist of that era. The twin lens Rolleiflex, which is presently enjoying a renaissance in the hands of fashion photographers. Reappearing trends in a creative language that is so magically bound to that fetish known as the camera. But that's another story.

Ostensibly, this essay is about the Latin lover; yet it is safe to say that the bulk of it will be about how the rest of the world perceives the Latin lover. After all, the Latin lover himself is entirely a function of the way the rest of the world perceives him.

As such, he is a consummate member of our late-twentieth-century, media-driven culture. Apparently unselfconscious, supremely unself-aware, entirely self-centered, and unabashedly self-promoting, the Latin lover was a media object and a media subject from his first appearance (he used cosmetics, pomades, and creams before it was even remotely hip). At the same time, the Latin lover has an unfeigned, timeless basic structure (he exhibits the self-propagating sexual behaviors that mitochondria cheer for; he is man as DNA designed him, the selfish gene writ large). But the Latin lover is, above all, a body of information, of linguistic organization. Let us first look at the words that surround and designate him.

"Every day, in every way, we are getting meta and meta," as the philosopher John Wisdom once said, in knowing parody of Emile Coué's self-suggestive mantra of self-improvement (pace HLG jr). Wisdom knew that little quirks of the language often reveal larger faultlines in the culture, and so he saw the word, and word-play, as holding germs of the larger ideas.

We can call it a food chain; we can call it the endless resemblance through orders of magnitude that underlies fractals; we can call it the incessant, parasitic construction of meaning by the chattering classes: but everything nowadays is built on something else.

Let us consider the various forms the Latin lover takes in the deafening international conversation that is our idea of culture. The Latin lover is not precisely the subject of the conversation; rather, he is an irritant, a grain of sand around which our cultural oyster secretes its lustrous nacre. So, to indulge a little more in the idea of the non-entity at the heart of the debate — the lover in the tennis sense of love: "zero, nought, nil, null" — the Latin lover is nothing without the effects he triggers.

Like a dangerous, ship-killing reef, the Latin lover would be meaningless in other surroundings, without the waters of the ocean and the ships that ply them. The Latin lover's existence is predicated on a testing of, and a concomitant indifference to, the results that he can trigger with virtually no effort. It is like that old routine from a musical revue, in which a woman, standing on the bridge of the Titanic with the captain, cries, "Oh captain, what would happen if that iceberg were to hit us?" He replies, "It would just go on as if nothing had happened, I expect."

The Latin lover, then, is a cultural construct, a meme; in particular, he is a product of cross-cultural confusion, of hybridization, of the conflict between national stereotypes and styles: relatively inert in his own little provincial backwater, but increasingly volatile in the conflicts of a growing, conflicting Europe. And the Latin lover is the response of the province to the growth of the cosmopolitan.

American girl in Florence, 1951

Vladimir Nabokov might have been thinking of the *gallo*, or strutting cock-o'-the-walk of Catania or Havana when he wrote, regarding Flaubert's *Madame Bovary*, "Her exotic dreams do not prevent her from being a small-town bourgeoise at heart, clinging to conventional ideas, or committing this or that conventional violation of the conventional, adultery being a most conventional way to rise above the conventional." Likewise, the Latin lover, for all his Captain-Blood fantasies (let us pay a passing homage to Rafael Sabatini as one of the great creators of the Latin lover image), is profoundly imbued with the ideology of middle-class comfort. As Aldous Huxley wrote, in *Antic Hay* (ch. 10): "There are few who would not rather be taken in adultery than in provincialism." Having placed the Latin lover in the solid comfort of the middle class (the oyster in which he is an irritant), and the irritating subaltern status of the late-nineteenth-century small town, let's look at the ways in which he is structured: first, through the words that describe him, and second through the tradition against which he conspires.

First the words.

The term "Latin lover," oddly enough, does not appear in most English dictionaries. Appropriately, where we do find the term is in the Garzanti English-Italian dictionary. The English "Latin lover" is identified in Italian by the term "Latin lover," with, as a gloss, the almost shame-faced "amante latino." In this way, the Latin lover

exists with greater solidity in the Italian language, than in English; one of those great untranslatables, like the Italian phrase "il Made in Italy," which in theory exists in English, though "Italian style" better translates the idea. "Latin lover" exists with two separate identities in Latin languages and cultures and Anglo-Saxon languages and cultures: it is a cross-cultural ricochet.

Three other synonyms are reasonably common: "Don Juan," "Lothario," and "Philander." Interestingly all come out of literature, and more specifically, out of theatre.

Don Juan is based on a pseudo-historical figure, a nobleman of Seville. He is of course the symbol of sexual profligacy, immortalized by Byron and Mozart. Please note that whatever importance Don Juan has as a cultural trope today comes, not from his clearly Latin real-life existence, but from the work of an Austrian composer and an English poet of Scottish descent.

Lothario comes from Nicholas Rowe's play, *The Fair Penitent* (1703), and is still the synonym for a fashionable rake. "A charming man who seduces and deceives women," is the dictionary definition of a Lothario. Lastly, Philander was, in the ancient Greek, a lover, and is now "one who carries on an affair with a woman one does not intend to marry, or carries on many affairs with frivolous intent." Interestingly, the term comes from "loving or fond of men" — this aspect of the Latin lover serves as a basso-continuo of suspicion throughout English treatment of the phenomenon. The more stolid Teutonic male inevitably questions the sexual orientation of his more colourful, flamboyant Mediterranean rival, as we shall see.

Casanova and Romeo are two other names — one of them from the theatre — that fit some part of the bill.

Whatever their origins — though the words are important signifiers determining the nature of this sprawling cross-cultural trope, or, to coin a term, metatrope — they all describe the same thing: someone who pursues women for the momentary conquest, not for the permanent bond; compare the old fashioned term "rake," from rakehell, akin to Old Icelandic, meaning "wandering, unsettled," or the French *roué*, related to the word for "wheel." And they virtually all come from literature: more specifically, from theatre.

Perhaps the first great figure famed as a lover was Mark Antony, as theatrical a warrior as ever lived. What made him a great lover, of course, was the woman he chose: the queen and vamp, Cleopatra. Yet, we would be wrong to think of Mark Antony in any way as a Latin lover — anyone who would divorce the sister of his boss (Octavia), fight and lose a major sea battle (Actium), and commit suicide, all on behalf of his beloved, hardly deserves the name.

Mark Antony was a great Romantic lover; Julius Caesar behaved far more like a Latin lover (being Latin in spades): when Cleopatra, at age 16, rolled herself in a rug and had herself unrolled at Caesar's feet, all indications are that he accepted the gift graciously — in terms that we moderns can certainly guess at. He then troubled himself no more over the girl, risking little for her in terms of military concerns or home life. In short, the perfect hypocrite and opportunist — the Latin lover.

Romantic lovers in later centuries are a dime a dozen, and that is largely because the dominant theme of our Judaeo-Christian civilization, which dates practically from Caesar, is the altruistic, committed, devoted lover: the thirteenth-century Palermo court of Frederick II, where the sonnet was invented; the Provencal troubadors; the Dolce Stil Novo poets of Bologna and Florence, a few decades later (Guido Cavalcanti, Dante Alighieri); the great love-poet Petrarch; and then Shakespeare, Goethe, and the weepy Romantics of the early nineteenth century: all worked together to create a collective narrative of heartbreak and devotion, not hard-boiled exploitation and adventure. And yet the forerunners of the Latin lover as literary construct can be found dotted throughout the same period: Cielo d'Alcamo, Marlowe's Faust, Byron himself, Foscolo, and so on, bringing us up to Rudolph Valentino and his cohorts. For every Julien Sorel and Fabrizio del Dongo, we find a hard-eyed descendant of Charles V, the first truly cosmopolitan emperor of all Europe, who reportedly said: "To God, I speak Spanish, to women Italian, to men French, and to my horse — German."

And part of it is surely the native culture of those places on the map that constitute Latinity: as Robert Burton, author of the *Anatomy of Melancholy*, so sobrely described one of those places: "Italy — A paradise for horses, a hell for women."

In a sense, part of the ethos of the Latin lover can be glimpsed by comparing the classic Latin lover with his opposite, the Anglo-Saxon composite Manly Man. Let's take John Wayne, and compare him with, say, Kevin Klein in *I Love You to Death* (in the priceless opening scene in a confessional, where he muddles his spread-sheet of sin while on his knees, speaking with his priest), or with the anonymous Roman Lothario of Daisy Miller, who squires Daisy to Rome's Colosseum at midnight, where she contracts a fatal case of malaria.

John Wayne: dangerous to men, safe for women.

Don Juan: dangerous to women, safe for men.

In a sense, the germ of much of the myth of the Latin lover can be found in Napoleon Bonaparte: an impetuous, self-absorbed, dashing genius with no scruples and no loyalties. His prowess on the battlefield was matched by his prowess as a lover, at least in the collective non-Latin view of him. Examine his formula for military success, and consider it in terms of seduction: "The whole art of war consists in a well-reasoned and extremely circumspect defensive, followed by rapid and audacious attack."

And it is more in that "well-reasoned... circumspect defensive" than in the "audacious attack" that we see the secret delicious thrill that the Latin lover stirs: his clear-eyed cynicism

Is it reasonable to think of Napoleon as a Latin lover figure in world literature? Clues abound to show us that, prior to Valentino, Napoleon was one of the members of the amatory Olympus of the mass subconscious.

Was Napoleon the Rudolph Valentino of his day? Consider a minor clue concealed in *The Age of Innocence*, where Ellen Olenska, the Polish countess with a past, can only be based upon Marie Walewska, Napoleon's devoted lover, a Polish countess, the mother of his bastard son, who in time became foreign minister of France. When Josephine wrote to suggest joining Napoleon in Warsaw, where he was engaged in an ardent dalliance with the lovely Polish countess, he fobbed off his wife with excuses: "Your grief affects me, but you must submit to events... The distance between Warsaw and Mainz is too great... I wish you would return to Paris, where your presence is necessary... I am more annoyed than you are. I should like to share the long nights of this season with you" (January 1807).

In the half century preceding Napoleon, two monumental figures — interwoven in the mass subconscious — had helped to nurture the myth of the Latin lover as genius, rapscallion, confidence man, and trickster. They are Giacomo Girolamo Casanova de Seingalt, and Count Alessandro di Cagliostro. Both were high-flying lovers and adventurers; though Cagliostro is less well-known than Casanova, he was perhaps a greater rogue and genius. Cagliostro's involvement in the Affair of the Diamond Necklace ruined the reputation of Marie-Antoinette and surely helped to precipitate the French Revolution. Cagliostro died in prison; Casanova, as a librarian in Bohemia, both in the late 1790s. Casanova merely had the foresight to write his memoirs; some of the episodes therein are clearly "borrowed" from the life of Cagliostro. When Goethe visited Palermo, the only landmark he wished to visit was the home of Cagliostro.

Now, having set the stage, as it were, for the evolutionary development of the Latin lover; that double-spiral of selfish genes that evolved in the primordial Campbell's broth of the twentieth century's entertainment-driven state of nature. If the myth of Romantic love is one fundamental underpinning to a grasp of the Latin lover meme, the pop nature of the twentieth century is another.

Fabio Lanzoni, 1992
(Grazia Neri)

This century was greenhouse to a subculture of image and icon; it was succubus to the dream factory — and that dream factory goes beyond just Hollywood, encompassing everything from ready-to-wear apparel to mass-produced wall paper and paper cups — wherein the slightest ghost of cross-cultural misunderstanding had consequences. Among the consequences of this new culture was a Tyranny of Convenience, a Freudian shorthand running through the new media; the Latin lover is a convenient character in the 24-hour movie theatre that passes for our mass subconscious.

In the endless film loop of twentieth-century culture, where plot-lines are twisted in double-helixes studded with three basic genetic building blocks — love, guns, and money — the Latin lover became something new.

He became film content. To give some idea of his new unrealness, consider that we can safely say that 007 — a later development — was a Latin lover with a steady job.

In the Twenties, the ur-Latin Screen Lover was certainly Rodolfo Alfonso Guglielmi di Valentina d'Antonguolla, or Rudolph Valentino. Valentino may have had competition from a few characters created by Rafael Sabatini (Captain Blood, Scaramouche, The Sea Hawk).

Since it was the actor, not the characters, who became immortal, let us look at the real life figure. Valentino was a remarkable figure in real life — remarkable for his unremarkableness. Before moving to the U.S. he was an overage student in an Italian agricultural college.

Consider the name, freely chosen and thus indicative: before Rudolph Valentino, there had been only one Valentino: Alessandro Borgia, who lived in sixteenth-century Italy.

Consider the figure that we have hypothesized of the Latin lover, ruthless, unsentimental, in prey to the DNA imperative, and yet self-absorbed, ingenuously vainglorious, and yearning for adventure; in reality, dangerous only to women. Consider the figure of Il Valentino, centrepiece of the lifework of Niccolò Machiavelli: Cesare Borgia, brother to Lucrezia Borgia, son of Rodrigo Borgia, Pope Alexander VI. Of the pope, the Florentine historian Guicciardini once said that Borgia's Rome had become a cesspool that would poison the world. Both Machiavelli and Guicciardini wrote in fairly lurid terms of the family: Lucrezia the poisoner and incestuous abusee; Rodrigo the corrupt pope; Valentino the pitiless, almost pathological Renaissance warrior.

Lucrezia we know; of Rodrigo, let us evoke him with two images: after a party he and other young clerics threw for the noblewomen and merchants' wives of Siena, a letter of the time supposed that many tonsured infants would be born in Siena in 9 months' time, and Guicciardini reported that the pope and his natural daughter were observed leaning over a Vatican balcony, cheerfully watching a stallion mounting a mare, making jokes and shouting encouragement. Valentino was less lewd than blood-thirsty; he was known for slaughtering his more trusting house-guests and his less popular lietenants.

Indeed, in a certain sense, three terrible events mark the career of Cesare Borgia, Il Valentino — a successful warrior who had created the foundation of a military papal state, under the protection of his father, the Pope, larger than anything else in Italy in the early 1500s. One was when he invited all his rivals to a banquet under truce, and had them slaughtered at table; the second was his use of a particularly harsh Spanish viceroy to subdue the populace of a town through reprisals; whereupon, he had the viceroy nailed to a board for his iniquities. Like something out of a Patricia Highsmith novel, this psychotic — who won Machiavelli's fervent admiration — then met with disaster when, at one meal, he and the Pope, his father, were both poisoned. When he most needed his father he least had his help, as Machiavelli notes; the dark romanticism of the disaster certainly appeals to a lover of Romantic brinksmanship like our Rudolph.

Rodolfo Guglielmi, then, took this name — Rudolph Valentino; when he was done with it, it would be used, variously, by the inventor of stiletto high-heels (Mario Valentino) and Nancy Reagan's couturier (a certain Valentino Garavani). Mutant memes.

How odd are the ways of film: our Valentino, the proto-Latin lover, was born in Castellaneta, Italy, studied agriculture, and emigrated to the United States at age 18, where he appeared as a dancer.

Six years after his American arrival, he made his film debut, but two years after that, in 1921, he created his classic role, as Julio, in *The Four Horsemen of the Apocalypse*. He — or rather, the Latin Screen Lover — had the good fortune to die of peritonitis at the height of his career. He was buried in state.

The good fortune, did we say? Well, Valentino avoided becoming a scaly old man, as did, say, his contemporary, the dashing yet horrible Gabriele D'Annunzio; in time, too, his fey, Oscar Wilde-ish side might have come to the fore. After all, the dancer and author of slim books of poetry, one of them entitled *Daydreams*, never really had a clear sexual persona, anyway. Under the pressure of entertainment-driven culture, the pumped-up, frenzied Latin lover began to acquire an hysterical edge, and a sexual ambiguity that could only be tempered by the subtlest of irony. Thus, as the century progressed, we see the image begin to decay.

Let us see how that happened, through some of the outstanding works of the Latin lover's hagiography of the period.

Some of it was openly disputatious. Let's look at Helen Lawrenson's *Latins Make Lousy Lovers* (*Esquire*, 1936).

Although occasionally sneering in tone, the article is startling for its cool evaluation of sexual politics. Lawrenson opens with a caveat: "This is not the wail of a downhearted frail who was scorned and is therefore taking a cad's revenge." She points out that the article is based on her personal experience, as well as the testimony of other "disillusioned damsels ... those unwept, unhonoured and unsung American women who have trusted and Given All in Cuba and Mexico, Central and South America, Spain and Puerto Rico — not to mention various encounters with visiting Latins on their own hearthstones in Ohio, Maine, Mississippi, and both Dakotas." Saying that it is "high time someone exploded the mythical superiority of Latins as lovers," she declares, adding that "with an American flag of washable bunting draped prominently — but with careless grace — around my chest, and balancing an American eagle on my head, I hereby rise to state that the ... belief ... that Latin men are the best lovers and Americans the worst ... is a hoax." Lawrenson then goes on to dissect her subject, in three chapters, under the headings: The Latin at Large, The Latin at Home, and The Latin in Bed. Dissect is the term to use, though "flay" might do nicely.

The Latin at Large: "They are generally short... they are thin, too, with narrow shoulders and wide hips... their teeth, if any, are either frayed stumps or dazzling with gold... badly fitting suits, and shoes that pinch their feet — and they have little feet. ... Their hair is oily and usually needs cutting. They spit a great deal. They are always scratching themselves. ... It makes my heart bleed to think of the boatloads of hopeful females who go down there every year on cruises, trusting to find a nation of Cesar Romeros. ... They pay you fantastic compliments that no half-wit would believe, but they never send you flowers or give you presents."

The Latin at Home: "In his own home, [he] is absolute king, lord and master. ... He goes out night after night, to political meetings, the club, poker games, jai-alai games, cock fights, cabarets, dances, parties, dinners, sidewalk cafes — or to visit his mistress — and his wife stays home. ... One man I know married his wife when she was sixteen and has never let her out at night since. She is now thirty-two. ... Night after night, she used to sit at an upstairs window alone and watch him sitting in a gay party at the sidewalk café across the street."

The Latin in Bed: "And now we come to the point of the piece. ... He devotes his life to it. He talks it, dreams it, reads it, sings it, dances it, eats it, sleeps it — does everything but do it. ... They boast of their prowess, their anatomical proportions, and their methods. ... But if you believe the testimony of their women-folk, when it actually comes to the test, they apparently suffer from tropical amnesia. In other words, they're talkers, not doers. ... In short, as the result of an extensive female survey, my conclusions are that offhand I would swap you five Cubans, three South Americans, and two slightly used Spaniards for one good Irish-American any night of the week."

Lawrenson's diatribe — and it was not quite as mean-spirited as this distilled version might suggest — was strong stuff; the rise of Mussolini did relatively little to shore up the idea of Latin lover as friend of women and democracy. Even in Italy, a writer like Vitaliano Brancati begins to attack the myth of the Latin lover. *Don Giovanni in Sicilia*, written in 1940.

It was the story of Giovanni Percolla, a young man from Catania; in some sense, it was a psychological study of the real human being behind the puppet-like caricature portrayed in the essay by Lawrenson. Percolla, a taciturn, handsome, exceedingly self-regarding, and indolent young man, lives in Catania.

It traces Percolla's career. This means tracing Percolla's perfervid and largely frustrated career of Latin lover, rather than his dead-end, no-show employment in a store owned by cousins.

The career begins amidst the same group of four friends who progress from squatting in dark alleys and peering through windows — "scuttling like cockroaches," as Brancati puts it — to brothels, to long days of chasing after every lovely woman sighted in Rome, a city that was a cornucopia of beautiful women, after Catania. Brancati knows his high farce; in one lovely scene the group of four at midnight, stumbling from exhaustion, have reached the hotel and have the key in the front door lock when ANOTHER Roman beauty strolls past swinging a purse; the tired chase was on again, with cries of "uhuuu!"

"For that matter, every time a lovely woman walked out of their view, they felt as if they had been betrayed and abandoned. There was something widowish that haunted their hearts during their entire stay in Rome."

Brancati paints a pitiless portrait of the provincial Latin lover — the same one painted so coolly by Fellini a decade later, in *I Vitelloni*. It is the Latin lover portrayed by Alberto Sordi in his finest roles.

Brancati portrays the authentic falseness of the character, as it were, in a scene of idle Latin-lover café chatter.

"Giovanni was becoming ever more enthusiastic in his appreciation of the pleasure women offered, and correspondingly generous in the lengths to which he offered to go in order to win that pleasure (I would give ten years of my life! ... I would let them beat me like a rug... I would lick the soles of the shoes of her father, the man who put her on this earth! ... I would drink this, I would drink that! ...), but at the same time, he was beginning to have a low opinion of women in general." Concluding that "God's given a bunch of cretins total control over the finest thing on earth," Giovanni Percolla sets off on a remarkable marriage that is destroyed by his own jealousy and immaturity, whereupon he renews his poor opinion of women, ending the book.

In 1949, Brancati's next novel — *Il Bell'Antonio* — won the Bagutta prize, Italy's most prestigious, beating out the great and tragic author Cesare Pavese, who killed himself in 1950.

The book is a delightful satire of the Latin lover of a small town in Sicily: to explain succinctly, in the film version, the two leads were Marcello Mastroianni and Claudia Cardinale. The wonderful twist given, however, is that the Bell'Antonio, who has haunted the dreams of every girl in town, and boasted with the best of them, is entirely and absolutely impotent (with Claudia Cardinale!).

This is the newest twist on the Latin lover: a figure, or *maschera*, from the Commedia dell'Arte, along with Pulcinella and Harlequin.

In part it was certainly a reaction to the "maschio italiano" image of Benito Mussolini, one of the most unemulated males in Italy in 1949: he had crowed that he was cock o' the walk for 20 years, and no one wanted to hear it any longer.

With that came a new Latin lover, and Marcello Mastroianni was it. He was a bit mild-mannered for a Latin lover, perhaps, but Mastroianni knew well of Giovanni Percolla, and loved his character of ineffectual dreamer.

There were other Latin lover figures at the time, finest among them Vittorio Gassman, but Mastroianni rules them all.

His trademark moment was his jittery goggle-eyed panic in moments of close encounter or emotional stress.

And one of Mastroianni's most notable moments as a Latin lover comes in Fellini's *Otto e mezzo*. It may be loading too much meaning into a fairly ambiguous scene, but that's what pop criticism is all about: the scene is one of Guido's dream sequences. A child is chanting Asa-Nisi-Masa over and over again. Asa-Nisi-Masa is Italian child's Pig Latin for A-ni-ma, or soul. Guido, the Latin lover, was completely mystified by anything spiritual, understanding only the corporeal. And this is the same slowly unravelling Latin lover who in the fullness of time would give us Ettore Scola's *A Special Day*.

Which sets us up for the last two figures in this Latin-lover pop revue: Tennessee Williams and Pier Paolo Pasolini.

About Tennessee Williams, suffice it to offer two or three passages from *The Roman Spring of Mrs Stone*. The character, Paolo, was played in the film version by Warren Beatty in one of his first big-screen roles. But the film version was not as explicit about Paolo's predilections as Williams' book was. It becomes clear why Paolo is unable, shall we say, to commit.

It is done with subtlety. Early on, Paolo is described by an ageing doyenne as a "marchetta," a cheap trick off the sidewalks of Rome. As the wealthy American widow becomes involved with the young Roman Latin lover, "Mrs Stone found herself thinking that surely such beauty was a world of its own whose anarchy had a sort of godly licence. She knew that she, too, had once had beauty like that and had enjoyed the anarchistic privileges of such beauty, but that her licence to enjoy them had been revoked by the passage of time. She lived, now, in a world that was subject to worldly laws." That perfectly summarizes the idea of the Latin lover; but the Latin lover need not even be beautiful (in his fervid imagination, at least). But he is best skewered in this scene at a haberdashers, where Mrs Stone is treating him to any suit he desires: "Paolo ordered not only a suit of dove-grey flannel, but two others, a midnight blue tuxedo and a suit of shantung silk the colour of a yellow pearl.

"Mrs Stone had never seen, even in a child, such a degree of excitement as he exhibited at the tailors."

And Williams is perhaps best in his depiction of those who prey on these sidewalk Latin lovers: the "collection of 'stately witches and epicene dandies'" that moved in a "great empty circle."

Moving us then to the final, furious extreme of Pasolini, with his *Ragazzi di vita* (1955; among other works). In Italian literature, such raw depiction of harsh, sexual predation and pointless lives had never been heard before. And this was the Latin lover described by an openly gay Italian communist; this time, the Latin lover was a penniless loser from bombed-out postwar Rome.

There is one scene in which the usual group of five young men have found a cruising gay, to whom they will pimp themselves for a buck. "He stopped for a moment by the opening in a public urinal, and looked around. Begalone and Alduccio examined him thoroughly. He was pretty well dressed, wearing a fine shirt and handsome sandals. Undecided, the queer went on toward the Piazza Farnese and then up again to the Campo dei Fiori by a dark little street — and so on, two or three times running. He went around and around through those streets like a mouse drowning in a bucket." (translation by E. Capouya)

It is Don Giovanni meets Mean Streets meets My Own Private Idaho. Grim, chilling stuff. Which brings us, really, to the present. The Latin lover has become credible again in the media, but in the person of Antonio Banderas. And Antonio Banderas, say what you will, is not entirely a Latin lover. He is Latin, and he plays a lover most of the time. All true. But in the clinch, when the flames are searing and the kisses are steaming, Banderas has that unmistakable slight goggling of the eyes, the fish-out-of-water stare, that nervous twitch that he has stylized — the Marcello Mastroianni "I-can't-believe-this-is-happening-to-me" look.

No, the Latin lover is through. Washed up, history, out of business. You still have your Fabio, but he is a caricature of himself (see the "I-can't-believe-it's-not-Butter" ad).

The only credible Latin lover left to the American pop imagination — until Martin Scorsese films the life of Porfirio Rubirosa, anyway — is in exceedingly fine fettle: Linda Fiorentino.

Linda Fiorentino in *The Last Seduction*, to be specific. She is the only one around who can do the Latin discard, the Latin swoop, the Latin you-are-under-my-power routine. She has turned it around, finally melding Theda Bara's "Demon Lover" meme with the "Heartless Adonis" meme that we have been examining in this essay.

Well, it's just nice to know somebody smart got the franchise.

TELEDISILLUSIONMENT
SLEEPING (MALE) BEAUTY ON ITALIAN TV

Norma Rangeri

Fiorello, star of Italian television (Grazia Neri)

Give up hope all you dear female viewers who need to be cuddled and seduced. In the year of the phallus triumphantly exhibited on the pages of all the glossy magazines, the small screen has decided to let you go without. Exactly. While the male organ seems to be experiencing its magic moment and the champions of machoism (from Tyson to Tomba) are displaying their fighting strength or their mystical eroticism (Sting), while the paparazzi's flashes are immortalizing VIPs' phalluses (Casini nude), in the virtual world of TV the male is a rare species and the small screen leaves women at the mercy of teddy bears who leave a lot to be desired as far as sex appeal is concerned. Let us admit it, TV does not stimulate female fantasies. Quite the opposite; it leaves them completely unsatisfied. Instead of Alberto Lupo's warm voice and virile gaze (in those legendary Sixties one lived in a period of post-radio and sublimated sex), today we have to be satisfied with Ridge Forrester's square jaw and his rapid consumption of sex in scenes with his numerous stepmothers, wives and girlfriends. Agreed Ridge is not Kevin, but he does what he can in his little, gilded, obsessive world, and it is especially thanks to him and his women that *Beautiful* is the only soap to have survived (the audience ratings of all the others are plummeting, a telltale sign of the viewers' unsatisfied dreams). Women have developed, women are demanding, women want satisfaction. Yes, everyone has realized this except our beloved misogynous TV. And this is a real injustice, because the female public are the solid foundations of the audience. Italian housewives who made the fortune of soaps and anchorpersons such as Patrizia Rossetti, Baudo and Magalli, are definitely the majority of small screen viewers. The reason for this neglect of female desire is simple. We only have to ask who the programme planner eggheads are. The answer is men. Or rather males. Real bosses of remote control (we don't actually think that it's the demand that creates the supply of programmes, do we?), getting on in years (to mention just two names, Michele Guardì and Pippo Baudo), champions of family TV and the basest emotions, at best, examples of national voyeurism (to mention just one of many, Gianni Boncompagni) at worst. So the old male chauvinist culture that produces game and variety shows revolving round showgirls like Valeria Marini, Alba Parietti, Lorella Cuccarini, Laura Freddi, Wendy, Ambra and all the rest, still persists. However you see it, whether you are one of those people who think we live in a phallo-critical or phallocratic society the result is the same. It may well be true that men are going through an introspective phase (strengthening the ego, cutting the superego down to size, and listening to the id), but the conclusion as regards television remains the same: on the one hand provocative showgirls with legs up to their navel and buttocks exposed, on the other, unvirile, virtually sexless presenters. Frizzi, Castagna, Bonolis and before them Columbro and Predolin are at most reproductions of the homely *vitellone* (loafer), lions in carpet slippers, pale copies of the Latin lover that was. And where there's no substance, superficiality and deception reign. Even a programme like *Beato tra le donne* (Blessed among Women) — last summer's big hit with an audience of 8–10 million — which on paper was to have reversed the traditional roles by putting pectoral muscles and biceps on show for the enjoyment of the opposite sex, in actual fact turned out to be the same old thing. The boys competing for the title were simply part of the show's trappings, they didn't play the lead. It was yet again played by an excited female audience (crowded into the Bandiera Gialla at Rimini) in search of the lost male. We saw girls with their skin gleaming with oil and perspiration, hungry for sexy males, jigging up and down, dancing, and showing all they've got. In the end it was they who held the show together, they were once again the favourite object of the voyeur in front of the screen. Nothing in common with the new heroes of the "no-generation," with Ethan Hawke (hero of "Captain my captain" in *Dead Poets' Society,* now hailed as the future Robert De Niro), an angelic version of Kurt Cobain and Vasco Rossi, a specimen purged of the excesses of drugs and reckless living. The small screen which reduces everything to the same level, at most proposes trashy models, (long hair and pumped up muscles), exposed on the edge of the pool or on the catwalks of the spa at Castrocaro, under the eye of the camera which, alas, can't reveal what isn't there. Only once has TV managed to spawn a specimen of a vigorous male with the characteristics both of the "Latin" and of the "lover": Fiorello. With his hairy appendage (varying in size), his floppy Armani clothes, his girlfriends chosen from the most voluptuous showgirls, he discarded the model of a TV white-collar worker to become the idol and model of real white-collar workers. Fiorello's mask worked until television wore out his powerful batteries charged by years of hard work as a holiday camp host. What made him a hit on screen was his image of a provincial boy, bursting with energy, not very bright academically, but full of generous enthusiasm. A typical case of emancipation, a poor, good-looking boy, a Maurizio Arena or Renato Salvatori of the Eighties. A few seasons spent in the cathodic washing machine then inexorably wore him out and faded him, to the point when he became a ghost of his former self (only good for flops and television commercials). Yes, tele-

vision commercials! Can you think of anything less erotic? How can you get turned on by Bonolis busying himself with parmesan, Castagna buried under a pile of pots, and Frizzi trapped by biscuits? The television machine doesn't make any exceptions and, like a washing machine, washes and wrings out its rags pitilessly. This is why champions of emotional bleaching, of the sentimental desert, Frizzi, Bonolis, Castagna & Co with their depressed bank-

Italian TV programme Beato fra le donne *(Blessed among Women), summer 1995 (Grazia Neri)* teller blue and anthracite double-breasted suits, are the closest thing to battery chickens: dressed or nude, it makes little difference. Jean Baudrillard has described something similar in referring to the communication society: "We are in the stage subsequent to alienation. As long as there is alienation" — wrote the semeiologist in 1985 — "there is a show, action and a stage. Obscenity begins precisely where there is no more show or stage. Obscenity begins precisely when everything becomes visible, immediate and transparent, when everything is exposed to the cold, harsh light of information and communication." Paolo Bonolis is "obscene," with his little Pinocchio face pumping adrenalin, capable only of directing, like an old *maîtresse*, the traffic of disco girls and boys, faithful to the script larded with lines from the Bagaglino satirical cabaret company. Put your hand up if you've managed to perceive a glimmer of his soul, if you've managed to capture a real-life feeling born outside the boob tube. Fabrizio Frizzi is "obscene," when, the eternal joker, he bombards viewers with his constant empty laughter, revealing a mindlessness since birth. In conclusion, the television presenter only presents the emptiness accumulated in years of virtual life, which have removed every humanoid trace without replacing it with a cyborg. Who is Bonolis? A bit of Milly Carlucci (the glib talker), a bit of Gianfranco Funari (the Roman accent and heavy-handed nudge-nudge, wink-wink), a bit of Castagna (wide-open blue eyes and the latest Berlusconi showgirl in tow). In other words, the thirty-year-old electronic man has no powers of seduction. He's like a Russian doll, once you've seen one you've seen them all. All is revealed, like in a blue movie which leaves no room for imagination. It is not by chance that the erotic charge (?) of the small screen's golden boys depends entirely on their respective consorts, lovers, fiancées, lovely figures all from the same mould, but not yet completely sterilized. Rita dalla Chiesa (Frizzi's fiancée), Laura Freddi (Bonolis' fiancée) and Francesca Rettondini (Castagna's fiancée) wear out their lingerie in the gossip press in an attempt to create an unlikely aura of "tombeur de femmes" around their males. The only one who has tried to explicitly play the role of the last seducer is Berlusconi's moustachioed, Alberto Castagna. But his fortunes, if you look closely, do not rest on an allusion (so exaggerated it becomes a caricature, and in the end comic) to hidden virility. The success of programmes such as *Stranamore* (Strangelove) does not lie in the greased hair, vacant blue eyes, chunky bracelet and jacket with vents. No. Castagna is the mirror that reflects, exploits and recycles the emarginalized tribe of young people covered in gel, those in jackets with enormous padded shoulders who, as sociologist Carlo Donolo writes, "grew up in the swamp of the Eighties, who are devotees of consumerism and discos, whose visibility is measured in decibels, and who are not to be confused with the vast majority of disorientated and disillusioned youth who prefer invisibility and silence." Therefore Castagna has become the idol and model of emotions experienced according to TV soaps, the "people show." The one where (as happened in a peepshow like *Complotto di famiglia*, Family Plot) a hidden camera films husbands and wives instigating their partner to be unfaithful. However, if these are the trump cards that draw the audience, if despite everything, these are the objects of desire preferred by female viewers, there's a reason for this. In spite of the rivers of ink used to describe the new media and imagine the future of "homo ciberneticus," television is not a game for children, but the strongest, most reliable, irreplaceable staff of the female or male pensioner, seeing that it's the sixty-year-olds that top the audience ratings with five hours a day viewing time (data Mediapolis, Milan). Besides what is the average age of the small-screen gurus? Bongiorno, Vianello and Corrado have past the seventy mark and could open the Villa Arzilla (home for retired actors) club. So the grannies' dreamboats remain the young boys of 1938: Baudo and Costanzo, Lubrano and Funari. The harlequin-like imagination of an artist like Arcimboldo would paint the typical television personality with Bongiorno hair (bluish blond), a broad Baudo forehead, two little Costanzo eyes and a large Funari mouth. What can you do?

LATIN LOVER 2000
THE DISCO LATIN LOVER

Laura Piccinini

Latin lover 1995 going on 2000, the remix. Just like the title of an Italian dance music compilation, on cassette and Cd. Or else a trial label for a hypothetical discotheque renaissance of the favourite stereotype of carefree women on holiday far away (in time). Perhaps among the lads who will be in their Twenties next millennium: lethargic and studied... Who should have drawn upon that Mediterranean appeal to try and make politically incorrect approaches. Where are we — perhaps at the better-than-Ibiza resort of Riccione, acclaimed in recent summer reports by our correspondents on the Adriatic front?
"Latin lover? No way! You're joking. What the...? Naah!"
Summer/Winter 1995–96.
When pressed, likely candidates for the "Italian champions of the conquest" answer, giggle and talk about past glories. Luca, 23, is a Dj in Modena: "I think that the younger generation has other models, they're not into going out on the pull. Other values, different interests, thanks to TV and how the mass media have changed the way people think..." Simone does the public relations for several discos from Milano Marittima southwards. He wastes no time in admitting "nowadays it's them, the women, who make the first move. But when I and my mates went on holiday abroad, to Portugal... the girls seemed almost afraid that we'd go up to them, they called us pigs and then left. But as soon as they saw a tanned guy with dark hair and an intense gaze... they did a triple take. It's not that the Italian type doesn't appeal anymore. It's that so many things have happened to put a brake on certain things. Aids, the fear of sexual violence..." His view is confirmed by the most seasoned planners — too old to be part of the target age group — of Rimini and Riccione night-life (and similar fun places). And, figures in hand, with light-hearted neo-yuppie brio they point the finger directly at the events and phenomena that have determined the change, the end of an era. Each of them answers without hesitation from the standard issue mobile phone: "Picking up foreign women is a sport of times gone by. It's over. Yes, you still find the handsome Italian lad, the most self-confident one in the group, and sometimes he might have a go at scoring with the foreign woman of the moment, but practically every time the thing goes no further than a superficial chat-up, it's just a matter of keeping up appearances, an act for the benefit of the group that does not have to be taken to its conclusion. Nowadays there's more desire to measure success

in other ways, in terms of money, which always comes before the number of conquests. That's no longer enough on its own. Or else it's just the desire for a one-night stand, a night without too many strings attached, so off to the rave or the after-hours, where you dance until you drop, by which time you couldn't do it anyway, you have got no desire to take any kind of sexual initiative... you swallow the little pill and nothing else matters. At least, that's the way it's been the last few years." They all agree on one thing: you just don't see that many unaccompanied foreign women on holiday anymore. "It's because of the algae," says Macho, Pr man for the Ekos and Pascià discos at Riccione. "When the algae arrived here in the Adriatic that was the end of foreign tourism, since 1987 the German and American women have vanished... and then there have been all those terrorist articles in magazines such as *Newsweek* or the German magazine *Stern*." Right. Without the foreign women, what's the point of having a European Cup of Love, a Conquest Championship?" So: a vacuum. Or just a little affair here and there, faded fragments of legendary Italian holidays. Only this last summer have things begun to pick up a little. The figures show there has been a 20 percent increase in foreign tourists. The mid-summer newspapers this year were full of magniloquent parallels between Riccione and Ibiza, London and Los Angeles (this last comparison probably because of the nights of rioting along Viale Ceccarini). A whole set of circumstances have paved the way for the suspicion that the worm is turning. An example? Well, what about the Pet Shop Boys from England — an extreme glossy pop group, of a markedly intellectual (and often clairvoyant) stamp — who have relaunched their anthem for the "paninaro" generation of ten years ago, a little more cyber this time round: the paninaro '95 remix. Then there's the boom of wearing Gucci, after the big family crime stories which for the way they were carried out came as almost the apogee and catharsis of the decadent phase, followed by a return to the good old ostentation of fashion which in the Eighties was ruled by the "Italian J.R. [Armani]," when the "Japanese asked the visiting Italian president Pertini about those moccasins with the double 'G' — an item beloved of the classy Sixties lover — which Reagan also loved" (that's what it said in newspapers of the time). An Eighties thing, you think? Back then: it was the mid-Eighties, the tradition and legend of Latin charm had suffered some but not too much — depending mainly on the loca-

Andy Garcia (Grazia Neri)

Diego Abatantuono (Farabolafoto)

Scene from the film Truth or Dare in Bed with Madonna *(Grazia Neri)*

Julio Iglesias (Grazia Neri)

Antonio Banderas and Selma Hayek in Desperado, 1995 (Farabolafoto)

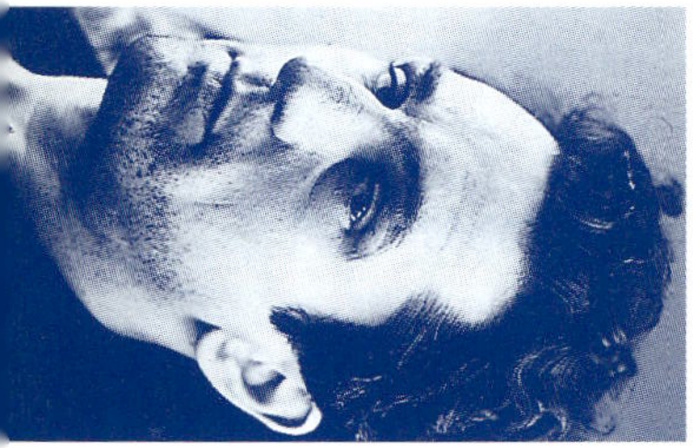

Robert De Niro

John Travolta and Karen L. Gorney in Saturday Night Fever, *1977 (Grazia Neri)*

Johnny Depp in Don Juan de Marco, *1995 (Grazia Neri)*

Marco Leonardi in Like Water for Chocolate, *1992 (Farabolafoto)* tion and social context — as a result of the inroads made by feminism. Perhaps what saved the retro(grade) appearance of any continuity was the extenuating circumstance of the post-modern salvage of the skill. Enrico, a twenty-six-year-old student who has done Pr for a number of clubs, recalls his sixteenth birthday at the Savioli disco, when the "championships of the conquest of foreign women, just like 'real' championships with rules and records, were still going strong..." A "typical" phenomenon incorporated into the all-inclusive export of the "made in Italy" myth of Italian style: before the Armani label came Pininfarina cars ("Italians have always preferred cars to trains" was an advertising slogan that was to continue to circulate in *Esquire* and magazines of the kind) and black, naturally wavy hair. The singer known as Madonna, before becoming a star and jettisoning her surname (Ciccone) which gave away family origins in Abruzzo, sang "Italians do it better," went jogging and did concerts with that same slogan written on her T-shirt (the most popular of the moment, especially among American women, who were often to be seen wearing it as they arrived at Italian airports). Of Madonna's lovers the place of honour went to a certain Santaniello, most definitely not the only Italian to be snapped at the side of this determined blonde. And when she went to see her relations in the land of her forebears... Italian pride, souvenir-format as a guarantee of quality, reached its zenith. In the meantime a new type of youth — a rather anomalous thing for the country, less rebellious and estranged from the sub-cultural trends of aggregation — caught the attention of the trendy "Brit" magazines (*The Face* and *I-D*).

But was this new Latin lover the "paninaro" revisited? The typical young man of the over-sweetened (many of the trendiest clubs and discos of the time were called "dolce vita") life of the Eighties? He seemed more interested in his original Timberlands than in getting his leg over. The "Rimini" version, according to the "lookologist" Mr D'Agostino in *L'Espresso*, 1985, was a "middle-class consumer."

But "in competition with the 'paninaro', the most refined type of Latin lover," continues Enrico, "there were also the so-called 'maragli' or 'maranza,' long hair greased with third-rate gel, faded jeans jackets and fake cowboy boots. And in the end they were the ones who did best with the foreign girls, the guys who looked most like hicks." The division here is very similar to the one noted by one of the characters in Arbasino's *Fratelli d'Italia*, a brilliant literary survey of the vices and virtues of the generation that came twenty years earlier: "Enough, we've had enough of the same old story, of the beautiful foreigner... young or old it doesn't make any difference... But she comes to Venice or Rome with some ideas in her head and a flutter in her heart: wide-eyed and swinging her handbag as the pigeons take off. There between Bernini and Borromini she finds that Latin-Mediterranean charm in one of its two invariable varieties: the dark curly proletarian or the elegant man, greying at the temples... Is there no possible alternative between spring lamb and silver fox?" That was then.

Now, after the Sixties and Eighties: Algae and Aids. As if the algae were nothing less than an epiphanic materialization of the terror spread by the disease. In the collage of national idiom, dialect and language (of the foreigner) — the pidgin of the Mediterranean pick-up — any attempt to translate "safe sex" sounds truly odd. Then came the thoughtful Nineties: think more and keep a greater distance from self-introspection, plunge into the void like Alice in wonderland, or else take a running bungee jump. Check out the videos: Jovanotti sings a rap serenade swinging from scaffolding, and the faux-romantic girl (new-style Alice, if not Alicia Silverstone in the Aerosmith video) throws herself off a bridge only to get away from the guy who's chasing madly after her. And what of riott grrrls? Nothing like the Ambra we have here in Italy, we're talking Washington DC, not the Adriatic Riviera. Yes, but at least Jovanotti was in the Pilastro district of Bologna, which is not so far from Rimini, and in the end videos are broadcast everywhere. Exactly.

"As long as Zavoli was still filming teenagers, a janitor from Bari could get on a train every day and arrive in the evening and decide which one of the 117 discos to go to for the rest of the night, then take the train and be back in time for work": so it went in the newspaper *La Repubblica* during the first summer of the Nineties. After this apparently peaceful beginning things were to become ever more complicated, in proportion to the number of "X"s obsessively exploited ad editorial nauseum for the purpose of labelling the new unassailable generation. The unknown factor is no longer simply just the future, rather it's the choice — currently being made — of self. A matter of identity, of sexual identity. What sex are Nineties teenagers? Him and her are ever more confused: androgyny and bisexuality wink down from giant Calvin Klein advertising posters, from fashion spreads on the new "weird" exemplars, or the "girlie

Joaquin Cortés (photo by Nacho Pinedo)

boys" that appeal so much to the girls, and also to the boys. Lost, fragile and covered in glitter... likely lads have taken up the positions abandoned by the "men in crisis." "Zanza," a veteran Latin lover, looks on and sighs. Ten years ago, true blue conservative male that he is, he was up in arms at the suggestion of launching Riccione as a gay destination. This sex bomber, the last in a long line of Adriatic lifeguards, expressed his anger as a spokesman for the genuine Latin lover in an interview for the daily *La Repubblica*: "'Latin lover' is the only label the world knows from this part of Italy, Romagna." At the time he said... "making love to the women tourists is a job, it's a sport, a heavy flirt that doesn't go the whole way, doesn't count, and you don't get any points for going with local girls."

In the meantime the gays — Latin ones too — have used the macho myth to camouflage themselves, in the process turning it into a larger-than-life stage costume: sleek, oiled muscles and designer singlet, an interpretation of an article of clothing that used to be concealed, or at best worn by builders blasted by the sun or muscle-men under the neon lights of the gym. Then came Armani, and then came Dolce & Gabbana, & the new interpretation of the Mediterranean male: on the clean singlet is the message "Italian lover/24 hour service/pasta & wine included" (bread, love and not too many dreams, if you remember what Moschino managed to do with his mish-mash of stereotypes for export) worn by a Latin-American model, the 18-year-old Cuban Hansel. And on the chest, there had to be the cross, to exaggerate the little red good-luck charm, and then to mix things up further, the "peace symbol," mid-way between icon and inspiration. Ready-to-wear collections designed for international catwalks come to the rescue of the image of the "real Italian" (forget about Toto Cutugno singing in the Italian song contest). To be worn for a season or even less, and then to be taken up two or three seasons down the line, interpreted by yet another designer.

Antonio Banderas in Desperado, *1994 (Grazia Neri)*

As ever, it's more than just a simple matter of "image." So, back to the prowl, lads? Latin loverism burst into a million pieces and then disappeared — although it took a detour through the wardrobe — because it was pigeonholed as belonging to standard heterosexuality, and then it fragmented to pass among the genders (understood as the, sexual classification to which each of us chooses to belong). Is the ultimate conclusion that the "Latin" legacy has been

taken over by the "transvestite," the figure so beloved of fin de siècle theorists? "I'd see him in size nine, very high Vivienne Westwood shoes," says the young writer Isabella Santacroce, then adding a pin-stripe Jean Paul Gaultier suit (skirt or trousers), a see-through body, with "extreme attention to dressing and looking after his appearance," adds Vania Arcangeli, who has worked in casting for many Italian directors. She/he strolls along Viale Ceccarini, prefers the Mediterranean overgrown-boy type and is crazy for Antonio Banderas, it is to him that he dedicates the tormenting *J'adore* sung by Boy George. Latin Trans Appeal. New-style Latin loverism is free and politically correct; (the flip side of drag cockiness is the melancholic gaze of Fabrizio Bentivoglio, cast in the video for the Lucio Dalla song *Latin Lover*, from the soundtrack to Giacomo Campiotti's film *Come due coccodrilli* (Like Two Crocodiles), adds Arcangeli, who worked on it.

And beyond... What fashion in the Eighties did was create space for the existential and nihilistic transvestism of Nineties rockstars, one day grunge, the next bedizened like profane drag queens, all diluted in the most sexually ambiguous pop of the male dolls (though some of the people concerned have had enough of playing a toy) of Take That (and also the aptly named "Menswear"). Lovable little boys like little girls, they come complete with a set of interchangeable little clothes. Plastic surgery now seems to be about as big a deal as a session at the beauticians. Take a performer/artiste like the Frenchwoman Orlan, who has put herself through endless plastic body surgery to make her look like Jane Fonda or Botticelli's Venus. She might one day wake up and decide she wants to look like a Latin lover, and with enough grafts and transplants she'll succeed. More and more men are turning to plastic surgery, for silicon chest implants or to improve their sexual attributes. A Latin male model: a total of fourteen operations so far... "Given the sexual identity crisis of the white Western male," writes Helena Velena, a theorist of alternative sexuality, in *Dal cybersex al transgender* (From Cybersex to Transgender), the anthem of "transgendering" is "free choice of being a masculine male or feminine female. And that means any possible gradation, variation or transformational flux in between these two vague parameters." She keeps focusing back on the infinite mutant possibilities offered by cybersex. How will what is left of the Latin lover survive in an on-line incarnation? The flavour of the year, analyzed to death, and in the end a compulsory stage of any discussion of the history of approaches to loving that is right up to date. Thanks to the many possibilities of plastic surgery, and perhaps the even greater potential of genetics, it is easy to pass to the virtual opposing party; this would appear to be the finishing line for this millennium. In the on-line world role exchange is so very easy it may be obligatory. If, at this point, you are thinking that the Latin lover is completely lost, there is a simple question that begs asking. What is the first thing that an Italian student thinks of doing when he gets his Internet connection? Might it not be chatting up a foreign girl? "I spent last night with a girl from Oklahoma!" says the high-school kid to his classmates the day after, eyes bleary from hours of monitor glare. Right. Latin charm strikes back! Who says? All it would take is an e-mail address such as "rudolph latin lloveyou.com..." or else, when she asks you to pixellate your photo and e-mail it so she can see it on her screen, you could pick a photo of Ramon Novarro or Antonio Banderas. Before she has a chance to check you out in the flesh she has to physically fly the ocean. Latin loverism on the information highway: enough to horrify our Zanza. But think again. It's perfect: if the lover is compatible with your PC (personal computer), everything's PC (politically correct). There is still hope for less cyber-savvy new Zanzas. At least, as long as he buys you an ice cream from the little bar next to the sunny beach. And as long as advertisers in the infinite wait for the future bring back traditional bodies and patterns of behaviour: the Latin lover lives on, less virtual then ever. If anything, tongue in cheek. The result? Remember the advertisement for a certain Maxibon? Italian boy spots foreign girl and homes in for an Anglo-Romagnese chat-up line that would make his illustrious ancestors blanch. It all rhymes, naturally: "You are... bell', com'un tocc'de stracciatell..." Zanza would probably approve...

And if advertising is not enough, there are other creatures/personalities, cloned from TV talk-shows, such as Walter Nudo — the world's most handsome man — 50 percent Latin charm, and cascades of black curls: one word in Italian, half a word in American, and a smothered cough... listening to him he seems to be the ideal heir to Alberto Sordi in *Un americano a Roma* (An American in Rome), or to any of the exponents of the old-style Latin-style romantic pick-up. And what about the Italian TV star Fiorello? According to Gianluca he is the one who is the "new Latin, the heir to the Cecchetto style of the Eighties, he always wears Walker boots, old

Levis and he works out in the gym: you see some like that around. Especially on the nights dedicated to 'the hunt.'" Here too — as for Arbasino and Eighties commentators — there is a counter-balance in a more elegant and fashion-conscious flavour: "Streetstyle, rollerblades, surf glasses..." Just like in the last Pet Shop Boys video: cyber-scratch, muscles glistening like the silver foil around chocolates, post-irony, spectacular auto-eroticism and gay flirtation. In the boys of today there is always that "measured being in love with themselves," comments Gianluca, which makes the complete conquest of the other almost irrelevant... If it doesn't happen, it's no big deal... Zanza sighs, though there is some consolation for him in this year's crop of end-of-summer articles: the Venetian with a motorboat who swept Julia (*Pretty Woman*) Roberts off her feet during her stay at the Venice Film Festival; Naomi (*Black Venus*) Campbell who confides to a friend that she has found an Italian lover. Her next-day denials count for little, for a moment the tradition was back with a vengeance, without any strange mutations... After all, thousands are in love with the VJ Hugo — a blend of Latin charm and Spanish-lilting English, or in love with anybody who presents a video of the Italian Raf, pronounced with an English-style "R," not the Italian rolled version. All you have to do is avoid getting in too deep. In her "stories of young people at Riccione" Santacroce assures us that we can be sure of one thing: "a molto cosmopolitan dinner in a disco in the hills... a molto red-neck, Zanza style, and a Swedish girl per second, as long as she's breathing he'll have a go... the Dutch guy he's sharing the flat with, along with his Chihuahua, has disappeared with the twin German girls, the semi-nude blondes who have fled from Munich to have an exciting holiday in the arms of hairy, passionate Latins," and then flashbacks to a past inhabited by "a certain Massimo Ciavarro in a molto photo-romance style, mon cher, goes ape-shit for foreign tits and then ends up marrying a totally tradizionale girl-next-door type." Ambiguous and hyper-consumer Italian twenty-somethings of the Nineties reduce the Latin lover to a kitsch plasticine icon, somewhere between the style of a scandal rag and a "we wanted to be Kerouac or Arbasino, Alex from *A Clockwork Orange* and a local version of Bret Easton Ellis." The Latin lover has gone cyber; the Latin lover has gone camp. Zanza looks on, sees, and plunges his hands into his greased-back hair.

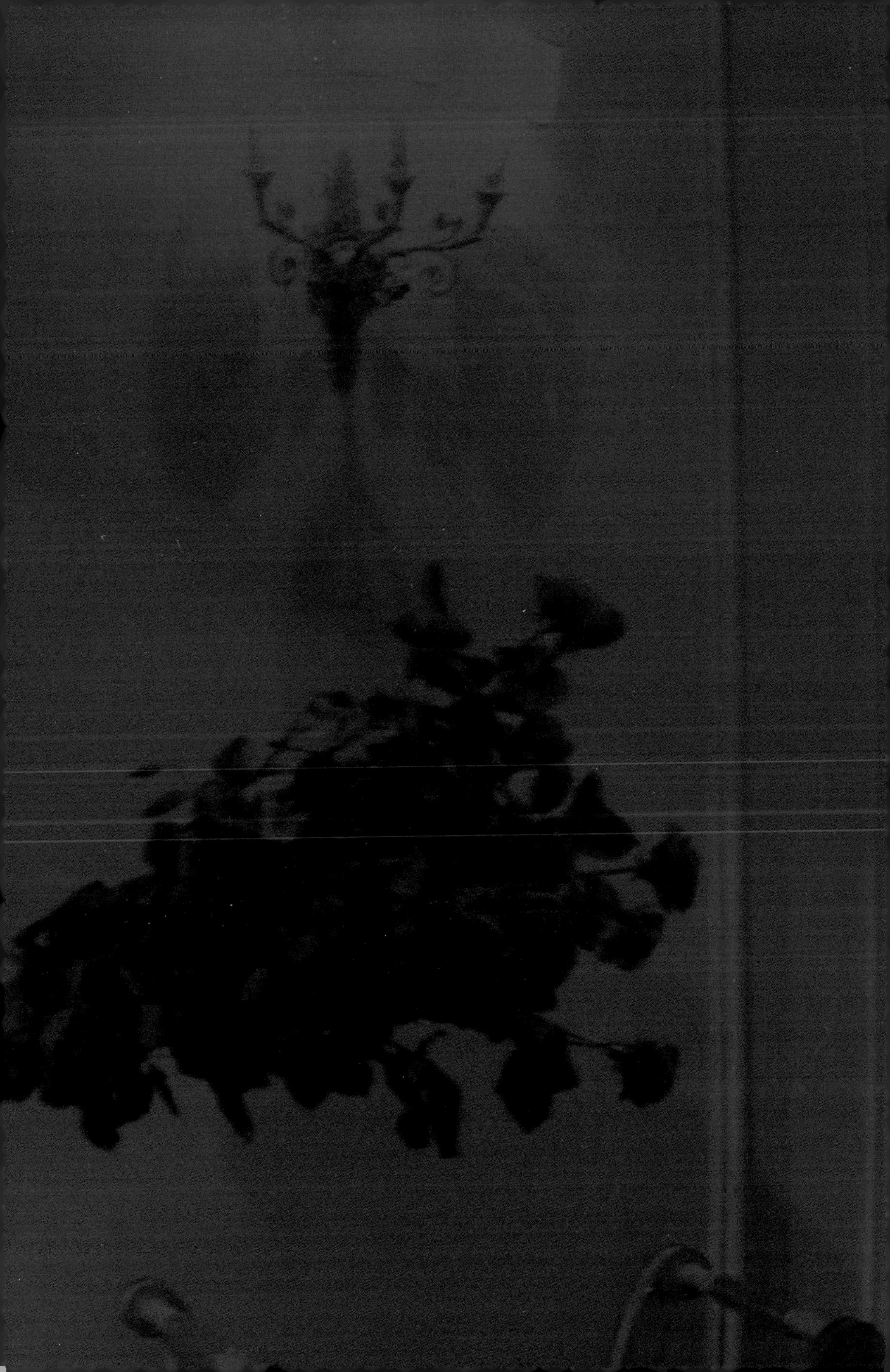

Giannino Malossi

Specializes in interdisciplinary activities in overlapping areas of fashion, mass media and culture. Editor of *Apparel Arts, la moda è la notizia* (1989), *This was Tomorrow, pop da stile a revival* (1990), *La Sala Bianca, nascita della moda italiana* (1992), *La regola estrosa, cent'anni di eleganza maschile italiana* (1993).

Italo Lupi

Architect and graphic designer. For six years he was Art Director of *Domus* and IBM's in-house magazine, and is now Art Director and Chief Editor of *Abitare*. He was also in charge of IBM's image and of the Triennale di Milano.

Luigi Settembrini

Managing Director of the Biennale di Firenze, he is held to be one of the foremost Italian experts in the field of communication and the image. In recent years he has been instrumental in relaunching the Pitti Immagine clothing textile fairs. Author of *Vestiti usciamo* (1986) and *A New York non si muore di vecchiaia* (1992), he has written various essays on social mores and fashion.

Carlo Romano

Researcher of marginal trends in modern culture, he also writes for the literary section of *Il Giornale*.

Franco La Cecla

Professor of Cultural Anthropology at the University of Venice, he has published *Perdersi* (1992), *Mente Locale* (1992), *La Pornoecologia, Media e natura* (1993), *Dormire, un'antropologia del sonno* (1993) and *Bambini per strada* (1995).

Previous pages: Don Jaime de Mora y Aragon, 1961 (Publifoto)

Loredana Leconte

A journalist who writes for various film magazines, including *Panoramiche, Film, Cinema Zero*, as well as newspapers such as *La Gazzetta del Mezzogiorno, Il Piccolo*, and *Il Manifesto*.

Alberto Panaro
Author of the novel *Corpo Celeste* (1994), essayist and translator who made the first translation of the fantastic work of French libertine Savinien Cyrano de Bergerac.

Lorenzo Pellizzari
Film critic, essayist, and historian. Contributor to *Cinema nuovo* and editor of *Cinema e Cinema*. Books include *Cineromanzo* (1978) and *Il romanzo di Alida Valli* (1995, co-written with Claudio M. Valentinetti).

Giuliano Accordi
Teacher, writer, and author of the novel *Zero a zero* (1995), he specializes in contemporary literature.

Giorgio Triani
A sociologist and journalist, he writes for the cultural sections of *L'Unità*, *Corriere della Sera* and *Italia Oggi*. Triani is the author of *Pelle di luna, pelle di sole: nascita e storia della civiltà balneare 1750–1946* (1988), *Lido e Lidi* (1989) and *Bar Sport Italia* (1994).

Maurizio Rebuzzini
Photographer, journalist and editor of *Fotographia magazine*.

Antony Shugaar
Freelance journalist and translator, he studies the relationship between Italian and American Pop culture.

Norma Rangeri
Journalist and TV critic of *Il Manifesto*.

Laura Piccinini
Journalist who writes on fashion and youth culture for *Il Manifesto* and its weekly magazine *Extra*, and other newspapers.

55 Gute-Laune-Spiele für Plapper- und Plauderstunden

BILDNACHWEIS

Freepik.de
S. 5/8/9/19/29 rawpixel.com
S. 58/59: irikul
S. 58: saravami
S. 18/19: pikisuperstar
S. 80: Sketchepedia

GettyImages.de
S. 5: KatBuslaeva
S. 30: dvoriankin

Fotolia.de
S. 30/31/74/75: Tapilipa

Umschlag:
GettyImages.de/exxorian, MicrovOne, Ozpk
Freepik.de/brgfx

IMPRESSUM

ISBN: 978-3-96046-074-9

55 Gute-Laune-Spiele Band 4

Klett Kita GmbH
Rotebühlstr. 77
70178 Stuttgart
Internet: www.klett-kita.de

Geschäftsführung Silke Wiest, Malte Kullak-Ublick
Redaktion Myriam Bork
Redaktionelle Mitarbeit Nicole Woratz
Autoren Britta Bartoldus, Marion Bischoff, Heike König, Ute Langhammer, Margot Lindner, Leah Schäfer, Karin Schäufler, Tina Scherer
Gestaltung und Satz DOPPELPUNKT, Stuttgart
Druck Paper & Tinta, Nadma

Kontakt
Telefon: 07 11 / 66 72 58 00
Telefax: 07 11 / 66 72 58 22
kundenservice@klett-kita.de

Gedruckt auf chlorfrei gebleichtem Papier.

Für jedes Material wurden Rechte nachgefragt. Sollten dennoch an einzelnen Materialien weitere Rechte bestehen, bitten wir um Benachrichtigung.

Bibliografische Information der Deutschen Nationalbibliothek. Die Deutsche Nationalbibliothek verzeichnet diese Publikation in der Deutschen Nationalbibliografie. Detaillierte bibliografische Daten sind im Internet über http://dnb.d-nb.de abrufbar.

Inhalt

55 Gute-Laune-Spiele

Seite

KAPITEL 3: GESCHICHTEN ZUM ERZÄHLEN UND MITMACHEN .. 43

KAPITEL 4: REIME & RÄTSEL 69

Liebe Leserinnen und Leser,

im Spielhäuschen sitzen Vincent und Linn und flüstern aufgeregt miteinander. Was die beiden wohl aushecken? Rafael sitzt gedankenverloren in der Leseecke und betrachtet ein Buch über Dinos. Was wäre, wenn es die heute noch geben würde? Carlotta singt ein Lied in einer selbsterfundenen Sprache und Amir und Lilja sind sich gerade nicht ganz über die Regeln des Spiels einig, das sie miteinander spielen. Allen Kindern in dieser Situation ist eines gemeinsam: Sie trainieren ihre Sprache – und merken das gar nicht!

Unsere Sprache ist der Schlüssel zur Welt. Sie lässt uns an einer Gemeinschaft teilhaben und gibt unseren Gedanken, Wünschen und Gefühlen eine Gestalt. Wir interagieren miteinander, verstehen uns, lernen die Umwelt ein bisschen besser kennen. Und manchmal erschaffen wir sogar ganz neue Welten.

Kinder denken oft noch laut und lassen uns an ihren Vorstellungen teilhaben. Dabei sprudelt das eine Kind vor lauter Wörter über, ein anderes ist vielleicht zurückhaltender. Die Freude am Sprechen kann man aber ganz spielerisch bei allen Kindern wecken. Denn Sprache im Alltag zu fördern heißt nicht, Grammatikregeln zu pauken, sondern Geschichten zu erzählen, Wörter zu erfinden, die Zunge witzig zu verrenken, zu lachen, zu singen und rumzuquasseln.

Dieses Buch will Ihnen dabei eine Hilfe sein: Mit neuen Fingerspielen, Liedern, Fortsetzungsgeschichten, Reimen, Rätseln, Klatschspielen und vielen Ideen mehr sind Sie bestens für den Alltag gerüstet.

Ich wünsche Ihnen und Ihren Kindern viele schöne Plapper- und Plauderstunden!

Herzlichst, Ihre

Myriam Bork

Redaktion *55 Gute-Laune-Spiele*

Kapitel 1

Fingerspiele & Mitmachgedichte

Fünf kleine Räupchen

Fingerspiel

Alter: ab 3 Jahren
Dauer: 5 Minuten

Fünf Räupchen kriechen über ein Blatt,
rülpsen ganz leise, sind richtig satt.
Mit den Fingern über den Oberschenkel kriechen.

Sie kringeln sich ein und schlafen ein Stündchen,
die Räupchen, sie schnarchen durch ihre Mündchen.
Finger in der Faust verstecken und dazu Schnarchgeräusche machen.

Da wacht das erste Räupchen auf,
das zweite folgt ganz bald darauf.
Den Daumen, dann den Zeigefinger aus der Faust ziehen und damit wackeln.

Ein drittes Räupchen kommt dazu,
das vierte erwacht aus seiner Ruh.
Mittelfinger und Ringfinger hervorziehen und damit wackeln.

Das fünfte wacht jetzt auf und singt:
„Schaut nur, ich bin ein Schmetterling!“
Den kleinen Finger zum Schluss herausziehen und beide Hände aneinanderlegen; wie ein Schmetterling flattern.

Idee: Tina Scherer

Oh Schreck, das Küken ist weg!

Fingerspiel

Alter: ab 3 Jahren
Dauer: 5 Minuten

Schwebt herab ein Blatt vom Baum,
bedeckt das Ei, man sieht es kaum.

Eine Hand liegt als Faust auf dem Tisch oder dem Oberschenkel, die andere Hand kommt als Blatt angeschwebt und legt sich leicht darüber.

Im Ei, da reckt sich's, eins, zwei, drei,
ein Küken schlüpft jetzt aus dem Ei.

Mit der Faust wackeln, dann ein Küken darstellen, indem der Zeigefinger als Schnabel gekrümmt aus der Faust gestreckt wird.

Die Kükenmama guckt sich um,
guckt um das Blatt vom Baum herum.

Die andere Hand als Kükenmama auf Zeige- und Mittelfinger laufen lassen.

„Da ist mein Küken, ach, wie schön,
ich hab es nur nicht gleich geseh'n!"

Die beiden Hände gehen aufeinander zu und berühren sich; laut „Juhu!" rufen.

Idee: Tina Scherer

Dibbedibbedib, bist du schon fit?

Mitmachgedicht zum Reimen

Alter: ab 4 Jahren

Dauer: 10 Minuten

Dibbedibbedib – bist du schon fit?
Ganz egal – mach einfach ______(mit).

Mit der Hand einladend zu sich herwinken.

Dibbedibbedib – das ist kein Topf.
Jetzt bewegen wir den ______(Kopf).

Den Kopf vorsichtig mehrmals nach links und rechts bewegen.

Dibbedibbedib – schau, was ich kann.
Jetzt sind schon die Schultern ______(dran).

Die Schultern hochheben und fallen lassen. Danach zuerst einzeln nach vorne wund hinten kreisen lassen. Anschließend beide Schultern zusammen kreisen.

Dibbedibbedib – da hilft kein Rütteln.
Wir wollen nun die Arme ______(schütteln).

Die Arme schütteln.

Dibbedibbedib – kannst du das auch?
Dann schüttle jetzt mal deinen ______(Bauch).

Mit dem Bauch wackeln.

Dibbedibbedib – bist du denn froh?
Dann wackle jetzt mit deinem ______(Po).
Mit dem Popo wackeln.

Dibbedibbedib – willst du verreisen?
Oder mit dem Becken ______(kreisen)?
Die Hände in die Hüften stemmen und mit dem Becken kreisen.

Dibbedibbedib – schon ganz alleine,
schüttle ich jetzt meine ______(Beine).
Zuerst das linke Bein ausschütteln, danach das rechte.

Dibbedibbedib – und ganz zum Schluss,
kreisen wir noch mit dem ______(Fuß).
Zuerst den linken Fuß kreisen lassen, danach den rechten.

Dibbedibbedib – o weh, o weh,
vergessen haben wir den ______(Zeh).
Mit den Zehen wackeln. Zuerst am einen, dann am anderen Fuß.

Dibbedibbedib – jetzt sind wir fit.
Mach beim nächsten Mal doch wieder ______(mit).
Den Daumen hochhalten.

UND SO GEHT'S:
Sprechen Sie den ersten Reim. Die Kinder versuchen, das Reimwort zu erraten und rufen es Ihnen laut zu. Wiederholen Sie den ganzen Reim gemeinsam. Führen Sie anschließend die dazugehörigen Bewegungen aus.

Idee: Leah Schäfer

Huhn und Osterhase

Fingerspiel

Alter: ab 3 Jahren
Dauer: 10 Minuten

Grüß dich, ich bin der Osterhase.

Mit einer Hand eine Faust machen und Zeige- und Mittelfinger aufstellen.

Gack, gack, ich bin ein Huhn.

An der anderen Hand mit Daumen und Zeigefinger den Schnabel formen; die anderen drei Finger stehen als Kamm.

Schenkst du mir heute deine Eier?

Osterhasenhand bleibt, mit der anderen ein Ei formen.

Warum soll ich das tun?

Hühnerhand bleibt, mit der anderen am Kopf kratzen.

Zu Ostern will ich Eier malen.

Osterhasenhand bleibt, die andere schwingt, als würde sie malen.

Und meine sollen's sein.

Hühnerhand bleibt und nickt zustimmend.

Ich freu mich, das ist fein.

Hühnerhand bleibt, Osterhasenhand bleibt – schauen sich an.

Ich danke dir, mein liebes Huhn.

Die Hände ineinander falten, wie bei einem Handschlag.

Nun muss ich los, hab' viel zu tun.

Die Osterhasenhand hoppelt weg, die andere winkt nach.

Idee: Marion Bischoff

Der Krabbelknecht

Tisch-Fingerspiel

Alter: ab 3 Jahren
Dauer: 5 Minuten
Material: Laub

Der Krabbelknecht, der Krabbelknecht,
das ist ein dürrer Weberknecht.

Auf einem Tisch Laubblätter verteilen, mit der Hand über den Tisch krabbeln.

Er krabbelt über Laub und Blätter,
bei Sonne und bei Regenwetter.

Mit der Krabbelhand über die Blätter krabbeln.

Doch kommt ein Vogel mit Appetit,
bekommt der Weberknecht das mit.

Mit der anderen Hand über dem Tisch einen Vogel darstellen.

Schwupps, ist er im Laub versteckt!
Und der Vogel? Der fliegt weg.

Die Weberknechthand unter dem Laub verstecken, mit der anderen Hand „wegfliegen".

Idee: Tina Scherer

Eine Reise in den Dschungel

Mitmachgedicht

Alter: ab 4 Jahren
Dauer: 15 Minuten
Ort: Bewegungsraum

Heute wird es wunderschön,
wir werden viele Tiere sehn.
Daumen nach oben. Die Hand an die Stirn über die Augen legen und sich umsehen.

Denn, hört gut zu und seid ganz leise,
wir gehen heut auf Dschungelreise.
Den Zeigefinger vor den Mund halten.

Wir steigen in das Flugzeug ein
und werden bald im Dschungel sein.
Wie ein Flugzeug durch den Raum fliegen.

Als wir am Ziel sind angekommen,
haben wir ein Rauschen dann vernommen.
Die Hand hinter ein Ohr legen.

Wir laufen los, doch dann ist Schluss,
wir stehen vor 'nem großen Fluss.
Mit beiden Händen Schlangenlinien vor dem Körper machen und so den Fluss imitieren.

Und was schwimmt denn da in ihm?
Ach, das ist ja ein Delfin.
Schwimmbewegungen machen.

Wir gehen weiter durch den Wald,
das nächste Tier sehn wir schon bald.
Durch den Raum gehen.

Ein Affe, der ist ganz schön satt,
schläft unter 'nem Bananenblatt.
Auf dem Boden zusammenrollen und schlafen.

Da kitzelt ihn ein Sonnenstrahl.
Er niest und dann auch gleich noch mal.
Zweimal niesen.

Er schwingt sich schnell von Ast zu Ast,
immer so wie's ihm grad passt.
Mit Lianen durch das Zimmer schwingen.

Es dauert überhaupt nicht lange,
da kriecht aus dem Gebüsch 'ne Schlange.
Auf den Boden legen und wie eine Schlange kriechen.

Sie sieht uns, kriegt 'nen Riesenschreck,
mit einem Satz ist sie schon weg.
Schnell in eine Ecke kriechen.

Ich bin müde und muss schlafen gehen.
Doch wo kann ich schlafen? Das muss ich noch sehn.
Gähnen.

Ich mach's wie das Faultier und schlafe am Baum.
Bestimmt hab ich kopfüber den schönsten Traum.
Auf den Rücken legen, die Arme und Beine um einen imaginären Ast schlingen und schlafen.

Idee: Leah Schäfer

Fips, der Floh

Fingerspiel

Alter: ab 3 Jahren

Dauer: 10 Minuten

Das ist Fips, der kleine Floh,
der ist gerade gar nicht froh.
Er hat Hunger – und zwar sehr,
es muss jetzt was zu essen her.

Den rechten Zeigefinger in die Luft halten und bewegen. Mit der linken Hand den Bauch reiben.

Da vorne stehn zwei graue Katzen,
man hört den Fips vor Freude schmatzen.
Er sucht sich eine davon aus,
nimmt dann Anlauf und springt drauf.

Die linke Hand vor den Körper halten, dabei die vier Finger auf den Daumen pressen. Der Zeigefinger der rechten Hand springt auf den Handrücken der linken Hand.

Fips, der gräbt sich ganz schön schnell
in das strubbelige Fell.
Doch die Katze schüttelt sich,
sie will den Flohbesucher nicht.

Mit dem rechten Zeigefinger über den Handrücken der linken Hand fahren. Die linke Hand schütteln.

Fips, der kommt in hohem Bogen
ganz schnell durch die Luft geflogen.
Und er landet auf dem Bauch,
mittendrin in einem Strauch.

Den rechten Zeigefinger in einem großen Bogen von der linken Hand nehmen und mit dem Fingernagel nach unten vor den Körper halten.

So, denkt Fips, jetzt hab ich's satt,
ich fresse lieber hier ein Blatt.
Er kaut und schluckt und ist ganz froh,
die Blätter schmecken unsrem Floh.

Mit dem Daumen und dem Zeigefinger der linken Hand einen Kreis bilden. Den rechten Zeigefinger in die Öffnung halten und bewegen. Bei der letzten Zeile den rechten Zeigefinger auf- und abhüpfen lassen.

Leah Schäfer

Das schönste Blümchen

Fingerspiel

Alter: ab 3 Jahren
Dauer: 10 Minuten

Fünf Blümchen dort am Wegrand stehn.
Sie blühen wirklich wunderschön.
Die Finger der linken Hand spreizen.

Das erste sagt: „Ich bin so toll!
Mein Blütenkleid so rot und voll.“
Den Daumen nach oben strecken und hin- und herbewegen.

Das zweite meint: „Du bist zwar schön,
doch ich bin hübscher anzusehn.“
Den Zeigefinger nach oben strecken und hin- und herbewegen.

Das dritte sagt: „Seid doch mal schlau,
ich bin schöner – ganz in blau!“
Den Mittelfinger nach oben strecken und hin- und herbewegen.

Das vierte ruft: „Das ist nicht nett,
ich bin die Schönste – in violett.“
Den Ringfinger nach oben strecken und hin- und herbewegen.

Das fünfte sagt: „Das ist nicht wahr,
denn ich bin schließlich auch noch da!“
Den kleinen Finger nach oben strecken und hin- und herbewegen.

Da kommt ein Kind und denkt bei sich:
„Welche Blume pflücke ich?
Der Zeigefinger der rechten Hand bewegt sich langsam auf die linke Hand zu und berührt kurz einen Finger nach dem anderen.

Jede sieht so prächtig aus,
ich nehm sie alle in einen Strauß.“
Die rechte Hand umfasst die Finger der linken Hand.

Da freuen sich die Blümchen sehr,
zusammen leuchten sie noch mehr.
Die linke Hand hin- und herdrehen und die Finger dabei zappeln lassen.

Leah Schäfer

Eine Weltreise

Mitmachgedicht

Alter: ab 4 Jahren
Dauer: 20 Minuten
Ort: Bewegungsraum

Psst, ihr Kinder! Seid mal leise,
kommt ihr mit auf eine Reise?
Wir fahren einmal um die Welt.
Ich bin sicher, dass es euch gefällt.
Den Finger auf die Lippen legen und psst! machen.

Zuerst geht's nach Amerika.
Mit dem Flugzeug sind wir ganz schnell da.
Flügel spreizen, Propeller an,
durch die Lüfte sausen – seht wie ich das kann.
Wie ein Flugzeug durch den Raum fliegen.

Gut gelandet, ach wie schön,
jetzt können wir mal wandern gehn.
Im Grand Canyon ist es heiß,
ich wandre lieber mit 'nem Eis.
Durch den Raum wandern, dabei ein Eis schlecken.

Amerika ist wunderschön,
doch jetzt wolln wir Koalas sehn.
Mit dem Schiffchen übers Meer geschwommen,
sind wir in Australien angekommen.
Mit Schwimmbewegungen durch den Raum laufen.

Ich denk' so bei mir: Ei der Daus!
Da vorne steht der Vogel Strauß.
Und das ist wirklich allerhand,
sein Kopf der steckt im warmen Sand.
Die Arme zu Flügeln an die Seite nehmen und
den Kopf nach unten strecken.

Wir gehn weiter, haben keine Ruh,
da sehen wir ein Känguru.
Sein Beutel wippt beim Hüpfen sehr,
wir hüpfen einfach hinterher.

Wie ein Känguru durch den Raum hüpfen.

Ach, das ist ein schönes Spiel
und Afrika ist unser nächstes Ziel.
Mit dem Fernglas in der Hand,
gehn wir auf Safari durchs ganze Land.

Die Hände wie ein Fernglas vor die Augen halten und durch den Raum gehen.

Die Sonne scheint, es ist sehr heiß,
auf meiner Stirn, da steht der Schweiß.
Ein Elefant bemerkt's, hat einen Plan,
spritzt mich mit kühlem Wasser an.

Mit der Hand den Schweiß von der Stirn wischen.

Jetzt wollen wir nach Asien reisen,
und hier ganz viel Reis verspeisen.
Auch vieles andre noch probieren,
auf der Chinesischen Mauer balancieren.

Balancierend durch den Raum laufen. Dabei die Arme für das Gleichgewicht ausbreiten.

Ach Kinder, wie die Zeit vergeht,
es ist ja nun schon ganz schön spät.
Schnell aufs Fahrrad, jetzt geht's heim,
unsre Familien freun sich – das ist fein.

Die Arme wie ein Rad kreisen lassen und so durch den Raum laufen.

Leah Schäfer

Erntedank bei den Mäusen

Fingerspiel

Alter: ab 3 Jahren
Dauer: 10 Minuten

Das ist Papa Maus,
der geht täglich aus dem Haus.
Daumen nach oben strecken.

Das ist Mama Maus,
die geht täglich aus dem Haus.
Zeigefinger nach oben strecken.

Das ist Bruder Maus,
der geht täglich aus dem Haus.
Mittelfinger nach oben strecken.

Das ist Oma Maus,
die geht täglich aus dem Haus.
Ringfinger nach oben strecken.

Sie schleppen Körner in den Bau.
Die Hand zu einer Faust ballen, als würde man etwas tragen.

Das Mäusebaby, superschlau,
Kleinen Finger in die Luft strecken.

futtert viele Körner auf
Daumen und Zeigefinger der zweiten Hand schnell aufeinandertippeln.

und reibt sich dann den vollen Bauch.
Zurücklehnen und mit der Hand über den eigenen Bauch reiben.

Idee: Marion Bischoff

Eichhörnchen Finn

Tisch-Fingerspiel

Alter: ab 3 Jahren
Dauer: 5 Minuten
Material: Laub

Wo ist denn bloß mein Essen hin?
Das fragt sich heut der kleine Finn.
Mit der Hand in den Blättern wühlen.

Vielleicht auf diesem hohen Baum?
Ganz schön weit, er schafft es kaum.
Mit der Hand am Arm des Kindes hinaufwandern bis zur Schulter.

Zwischen Ästen und Zweigen sucht er schnell,
kratzt sich dann an seinem Fell.
In den Haaren wühlen und das Kind etwas kitzeln.

Hüpft den Baum herab, padauf.
Stolpert, landet auf dem Bauch.
Hand herabfallen lassen.

Idee: Tina Scherer

Fünf Schneeflocken

Fingerspiel

Alter: ab 3 Jahren
Dauer: 5 Minuten

Fünf Schneeflocken fallen auf die Erde nieder.
Fünf Finger wackeln von oben nach unten.

Das erste Schneeflöckchen macht sich den Spaß
und setzt sich mitten auf deine Nas.
Den Daumen zur Nase führen und diese berühren.

Das zweite Schneeflöckchen setzt sich aufs Ohr
und kommt sich dort ganz lustig vor.
Den Zeigefinger zum Ohr führen und dieses berühren.

Das dritte Schneeflöckchen klettert hoch hinauf
und setzt sich auf dein Köpfchen drauf.
Den Mittelfinger auf den Kopf legen.

Das vierte Schneeflöckchen setzt sich auf die Wange
und bleibt dort kurz, aber nicht lange.
Den Ringfinger auf die Wange legen.

Das fünfte Schneeflöckchen setzt sich auf deinen Mund
und glaubt, der Schnee, der sei gesund!
Den kleinen Finger auf die Lippen legen.

Idee: überliefert

Der Nikolaus im kleinen Haus

Mitmachgedicht

Alter: ab 3 Jahren
Dauer: 10 Minuten

Aus einem klitzekleinen Haus,
da schaut der Nikolaus heraus.

Die Hände über dem Kopf spitz zusammenführen und so ein Hausdach andeuten.

Er trägt 'ne Brille, klein und rund,
ein langer Bart verdeckt den Mund.

Mit den Daumen und Zeigefingern eine Brille formen und vor die Augen halten. Danach mit den Händen einen großen Bart vor dem Mund andeuten.

Er zieht nun seine Stiefel an,
damit er losmarschieren kann.

Pantomimisch die Stiefel anziehen und mit den Füßen auf der Stelle gehen.

Auf dem Rücken liegt ein Sack,
den trägt er heute huckepack.

Pantomimisch den Sack über die Schultern werfen.

Er holt ganz leis vor jedem Haus
ein Päckchen aus dem Sack heraus.

Mit den Händen kleine Kisten zeichnen.

Der Sack ist leer, wie ist das schön,
nun kann er schnell nach Hause geh'n.

Mit den Füßen auf der Stelle gehen.

Der Nikolaus ruht sich nun aus
und kommt erst morgen wieder raus.

Zusammengelegte Hände an eine Wange halten, dabei den Kopf neigen, um das Schlafen anzudeuten.

Idee: Britta Bartoldus

Der Rabe Hugo

Mitmachgedicht zum Aufwärmen

Alter: ab 3 Jahren

Dauer: 5 Minuten

Rabe Hugo friert so sehr,
der Winter fällt ihm heute schwer.

Das Frieren und Bibbern nachstellen: zittern, die Arme reiben.

Er schüttelt seinen Flügel aus,
schüttelt Kälte und Regen heraus.

Einen Arm ausschütteln.

Der andere Flügel kommt dann dran,
das fühlt sich doch schon besser an.

Den anderen Arm ausschütteln.

Der Rabe schüttelt schnell ein Bein,
er möchte warm im Winter sein.

Ein Bein ausschütteln.

Das andere Bein kommt auch noch dran,
das fühlt sich wirklich besser an.

Das andere Bein ausschütteln.

Er reckt den Kopf, krächzt Guten Morgen,
vorbei sind seine Kältesorgen.

Laut „Guten Morgen!" rufen und krächzen wie ein Rabe.

Idee: Tina Scherer

Kapitel 2

Lieder, Klanggeschichten & Klatschspiele

Tausendfuß, der Tausendfüßer

Klanggeschichte

Alter: ab 3 Jahren
Dauer: 15 Minuten
Material: Klanginstrumente (Klangstäbe, Glöckchen)

Tausend Füße trampeln leise,
wer geht denn bloß auf diese Weise?
Trampeln und/oder die Klangstäbe aneinanderschlagen.

Tausendfuß, der Tausendfüßer!
Der Lärm wird immer größer.
Immer lauter spielen oder trampeln.

Stopp, mach halt, Herr Tausendfuß!
Hast du auf eine Pause Lust?
Stille.

Ruh dich aus, hör auf zu trampeln,
nicht mit tausend Füßen strampeln.
Stille.

Doch was ist das, hört nur mal hin,
ein kleines Füßchen: klingeling?
Trampeln und/oder Glöckchen spielen.

Und noch ein Füßchen kommt dazu?
Wer stört da die schöne Ruh?
Lauter spielen oder trampeln.

Noch mehr Füßchen, kling und klang,
kommen jetzt noch bei uns an.
Sehr laut spielen oder trampeln.

Hundertfuß, der Hundertfüßer!
Der Lärm wird immer größer.
Richtig laut werden.

Stopp, mach Halt, Herr Hundertfuß,
weil jeder einmal ruhen muss.
Stille.

Leg dich hin und komm zur Ruh,
mach deine kleinen Augen zu.
Stille.

Hundert Füßchen halten still,
weil kein Füßchen mehr laufen will.
Flüstern.

Idee: Tina Scherer

Der Frühling ist da!

Lied

Alter: ab 4 Jahren

Dauer: 5 Minuten

1 Der Frühling, der Frühling, der Frühling ist da,
es leuchtet die Sonne wieder hell, fallera.
Dass Bäume wieder sprießen, das wollen wir genießen.
Der Frühling, der Frühling, der Frühling ist da.

2 Der Frühling, der Frühling, der Frühling ist da,
die Tiere erwachen aus dem Schlaf, fallera.
Dass Bienen wieder fliegen, lässt gute Laune siegen.
Der Frühling, der Frühling, der Frühling ist da.

3 Der Frühling, der Frühling, der Frühling ist da,
die Blumen erfreuen uns mit Duft, fallera.
Dass Kinder draußen lachen, lässt die Natur erwachen.
Der Frühling, der Frühling, der Frühling ist da.

4 Der Frühling, der Frühling, der Frühling ist da,
die Wiesen erblühen wieder bunt, fallera.
Und Frühlingsblumen strahlen, so schön, man könnt' es malen!
Der Frühling, der Frühling, der Frühling ist da.

(Melodie: Im Frühtau zu Berge)

Idee: Margot Lindner

Die Reise des Wichtels durch die Elemente

Klanggeschichte

Alter: ab 5 Jahren

Dauer: 15 Minuten

Es war einmal ein kleiner **Wichtel**. Er war nicht sehr groß, ungefähr so hoch wie ein Puppenhaus. Der Wichtel hatte sich auf die Reise gemacht, um alle Elemente kennenzulernen. Er wollte Feuer, Wasser, Luft und Erde besuchen. Und weil der Wichtel sehr abenteuerlustig war und niemals Angst hatte, **klatschte** er vor Freude in die Hände und **kicherte**.

Als Erstes besuchte er die **Erde**. Seine Freundin, die **Wühlmaus**, begrüßte ihn an ihrem Mauseloch. Und – schwupps! – rutschten der Wichtel und die Maus wie auf einer Rutschbahn hinunter in die tiefe Erde. Dunkel war es hier und ganz still. Man hörte nichts als das Geräusch der Wichtel- und Mäusefüße, die sich durch die Gänge bewegten. Hört mal genau hin! Was hört ihr? Genau, gar nichts. Die Erde schluckt alle Geräusche.

Das war dem Wichtel etwas langweilig. Er kletterte und kroch durch die Gänge der Wühlmaus immer nach oben, bis er das Tageslicht sah. Gut, dass er endlich wieder über der **Erde** war!

Aber was war das? Irgendetwas kam von oben, schnappte den Wichtel an seiner Jacke und – hui! – ging es hoch in die **Luft** und weit hinauf in den Himmel. Der **Wind** pfiff nur so um den Wichtel herum.

Ach, das war sein Freund, der **Vogel**, der ihn geschnappt hatte und ihn nun durch die Lüfte trug. Der Wichtel hielt sich gut am Vogelbein fest. Wuuuuusch ging es durch die Luft, über den Wichtelwald hinweg. Die Luft war kalt und rauschte dem Wichtel unter die Jacke. Aber es war herrlich, so zu fliegen und sich ganz frei zu fühlen.

Kaum hatte der Wichtel das gedacht, da landete er – **platsch**! – in einem See. Das **Wasser** rauschte und gluckerte um ihn herum. Gut, dass Wichtel unter Wasser atmen können. Der Wichtel schwamm bis ganz auf den Grund des Sees. Alles hier gluckerte und schwappte. Das gefiel dem Wichtel gut. Er winkte einem großen **Fisch**, der an ihm vorbeischwamm. Und eine **Seeschnecke** betrachtete ihn ganz erstaunt.

Aber was war das? Ein riesiger **Wels** kam angeschwommen. Welse fressen für ihr Leben gern andere Fische – oder auch Wichtel. Der Wichtel paddelte und schwamm so schnell er konnte nach oben und dann weiter Richtung Ufer.

Dort warteten die anderen **Wichtel** auf ihn. Wie gut, dass sie da waren. Sie hatten ein **Feuer** angezündet, damit der Wichtel sich wärmen und seine nassen Kleider trocknen konnte. Das Feuer knackte und zischte lustig und die Flammen tanzten fröhlich auf dem Holz. Und während der Wichtel dem Feuer zusah und sich wärmte und eine heiße Suppe schlemmte, die seine Freunde für ihn gekocht hatten, erzählte er ihnen von seinen Abenteuern.

UND SO GEHT'S:

- **Wichtel:** Holzblocktrommel oder Klangstäbe
- **Wühlmaus:** Kratzen auf Papier
- **Vogel:** Pfeife
- **Fisch:** Triangel
- **Wels:** Schellenband
- **Seeschnecke:** Ratsche oder Rassel
- **Erde:** Trommel
- **Luft und Wind:** Flöte oder Windklangspiel
- **Wasser:** Metallo- oder Xylofon
- **Feuer:** Knistern mit Backpapier

Idee: Tina Scherer

Die klitzekleine Spinne

Lied

Alter: ab 3 Jahren

Dauer: 5 Minuten

Die klitzekleine Spinne kroch in die Regenrinne.
Dann kam der Regen und spült sie wieder raus.
Da kam die Sonne und trocknet alles auf.
Und die klitzekleine Spinne kroch wieder hinauf.

Die klitzekleine Spinne kroch in die Regenrinne.
Dann kam der Wind und pustet sie heraus.
Da kam die Sonne und scheucht den Wind davon.
Und die klitzekleine Spinne kroch wieder hinauf.

Die klitzekleine Spinne kroch in die Regenrinne.
Dann kam die Sonne und heizt die Rinne auf.
Da kam der Regen und spült die Spinne aus.
Und die klitzekleine Spinne geht für heut nach Haus.

ENGLISCHE VERSION:
The iltsy bitsy spider went up the waterspout.
Down came the rain and washed the spider out.
Out came the sun and dried up all the rain.
The itsy bitsy spider went up the spout again.

Idee: Margot Lindner

Ich klatsche in die Hand

Klatschspiel im Kreis

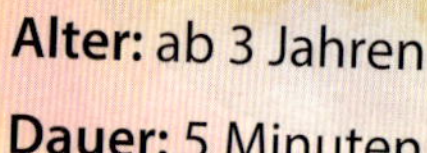

Alter: ab 3 Jahren

Dauer: 5 Minuten

Ich klatsche in die Hand,

Einmal klatschen.

ich bin ein Elefant.

Eine Hand an die Nase, den anderen Arm zwischen Arm und Gesicht durchschieben.

Ich klatsche auf mein Bein,

Auf ein Bein schlagen.

will heut ein Vogel sein.

Arme ausbreiten.

Ich klatsche auf den Bauch

Auf den eigenen Bauch klatschen.

und rufe laut „Du auch!“

Laut „Du auch“ schreien.

Ich klatsche meinen Fuß

An den eigenen Fuß klatschen.

und winke dir zum Gruß

In die Runde winken.

Ich klatsche nur noch leise,

Ganz leise die Hände aufeinanderschlagen.

und springe dann im Kreise.

Im Kreis hüpfen.

Dann ist die Klatscherei – vorbei.

Einmal klatschen und laut „vorbei“ rufen.

Idee: Marion Bischoff

Apfelfrühstück bei Familie Igel

Klanggeschichte

Alter: ab 4 Jahren
Dauer: 15 Minuten
Material: Handtrommel, Xylofon, Laub, Pappröhren

Die Igelfamilie Stachelfein flitzt am frühen Morgen fröstelnd über die feuchte Wiese: Tippel, tappel, tippel, tappel!
Kurze, schnelle Schrittgeräusche mit der Handtrommel machen.

Dicke Nebelschwaden hängen in der Luft und alle spüren es ganz genau: Es ist Herbst!
Überall Feuchtigkeit und Nässe: Plitsch, platsch! Plitsch, platsch!
Tropfgeräusche mit dem Xylofon machen.

Unter dem großen Busch am Spielplatz haben sich die Stachelfeins mit Familie Maus zum Frühstück verabredet. Die Igel freuen sich schon auf den Apfel, den sie gestern dort versteckt haben, also nichts wie hin: Tippel, tappel, tippel, tappel!
Kurze, schnelle Schrittgeräusche mit der Handtrommel machen.

Unter dem Busch ist es schön trocken. Das Herbstlaub raschelt: Raschel, raschel, raschel!
In den trockenen Blättern wühlen.

Plötzlich zieht Wind auf: wuhuuu!
In die Pappröhren pusten.

Und nun beginnt es auch noch zu regnen: Plitsch, platsch! Plitsch, platsch! Plitsch, platsch!
Schneller und lauter werdende Tropfgeräusche mit dem Xylofon machen.

Die Igel kuscheln sich zusammen. Ah, da liegt ja der leckere Apfel! Hoffentlich kommen die Mäuse bald, denn die Stachelfeins haben Hunger. Sie warten und lauschen.
Der Wind ist stärker geworden und fegt in Böen über den Spielplatz: wuhuhuhu!
Kräftig in die Pappröhren pusten.

Plötzlich sind flinke Schritte zu hören: Tippel, tappel, tippel, tappel!
Kurze, schnelle Schrittgeräusche mit der Handtrommel machen.

Das Herbstlaub raschelt: Raschel, raschel, raschel!
In den trockenen Blättern wühlen.

Idee: Karin Schäufler

Da sind sie ja endlich! Völlig durchnässt und zerzaust erscheinen Herr und Frau Maus mit ihren fünf Kindern. „Was für ein Schmuddelwetter!", klagt Frau Maus und alle nicken.
Tropfgeräusche mit dem Xylofon machen, dazu keuchen und im Laub rascheln.

„Das finde ich nicht!", ertönt da ein feines Stimmchen draußen vor dem Busch. „Ich als Schnecke liebe Nässe und Feuchtigkeit! Ich komme dann ganz wunderbar vorwärts und viel, viel schneller voran!" Neugierig streckt die Schnecke ihre Fühler unter den Busch und schaut sich um: „Oh, ein leckerer Herbstapfel! Da könnte ich bestimmt auch ein Stückchen abbekommen?" Draußen wird es ruhiger. Der Wind legt sich: Schsch, schsch, schsch!
Bedächtig und langsam in die Pappröhren pusten.

Auch der Regen lässt nach: Plitsch, platsch! Plitsch, platsch!
Langsame, leiser werdende Tropfgeräusche mit dem Xylofon machen.

„Das wird heute doch noch ein schöner Herbsttag!", freut sich Frau Stachelfein. „Aber jetzt erst einmal ein gutes Frühstück!", brummt Herr Maus mit knurrendem Magen. Endlich machen sich die Stachelfeins, Familie Maus und die Schnecke über den großen, süßen, herrlich leckeren Herbstapfel her. Mmh, wie das schmeckt!

Wir freun uns auf den Winter

Lied

Alter: ab 3 Jahren

Dauer: 5 Minuten

Wir Kinder, wir Kinder, wir freun uns auf den Winter.
Und im Winterwald wird es richtig kalt.
Doch das macht uns nichts, denn wir spielen halt.

Wir Kinder, wir Kinder, wir freun uns auf den Winter.
Wenn der Schnee dann fällt, wird sie weiß die Welt.
Und wir baun einen Schneemann, der ewig hält.

Wir Kinder, wir Kinder, wir freun uns auf den Winter.
Wenn der See zufriert und das Eis dann klirrt,
füttern wir den Vogel, der in den Garten schwirrt.

(Melodie: Laterne, Laterne)

Idee: Marion Bischoff

Gespenstergesang

Mitmachlied

Alter: ab 4 Jahren

Dauer: 10 Minuten

Wir rasseln mit den Ketten, wir geben keine Ruh,
drum hört doch den lauten Gespenstern mal zu.
Wir rasseln, wir rasseln, wir rasseln die ganze Nacht.
Wir rasseln, wir rasseln, wir rasseln die ganze Nacht.

Die Kinder schütteln ihre Arme.

Wir stampfen mit den Beinen, wir geben keine Ruh,
drum hört doch den lauten Gespenstern mal zu.
Wir stampfen, wir stampfen, wir stampfen die ganze Nacht.
Wir stampfen, wir stampfen, wir stampfen die ganze Nacht.

Die Kinder stampfen mit den Beinen.

Wir tanzen auf der Stelle …

Die Kinder tanzen auf der Stelle.

Wir drehen uns im Kreise …

Die Kinder drehen sich.

Wir schweben auf und nieder …

Die Kinder gehen mehrmals in die Hocke und wieder in den Stand.

(Melodie: Zeigt her eure Füße)

Idee: Margot Lindner

Die Tiere freuen sich

Tanz- und Singspiel

Alter: ab 3 Jahren

Dauer: 20 Minuten

Material: leere Körbchen, Nikolausmütze, Sack

**Der Nikolaus, der Nikolaus,
macht heut Besuch bei uns zu Haus.**

Die Kinder singen die erste Strophe und klatschen dazu mit.

**Wir rufen laut: „Herein, herein!",
er wird heut der Beschenkte sein.**

Die Kinder singen und klatschen, der Nikolaus öffnet die Tür und kommt in die Kreismitte.

**Jeder hat dir was gebracht,
was Tiere satt und glücklich macht.**

Die Kinder deuten auf ihre Körbchen.

**Getreide, Heu und viele Kern,
das fressen Maus und Vogel gern.**

Die Kinder leeren ihr Körbchen in den Nikolaussack.

**Kastanien, Eicheln, trocknes Laub,
für Rehe ist das auch erlaubt.**

Wie oben.

**Erd- und Hasel-, Walnuss auch,
die wandern in den Hörnchenbauch.**

Wie oben.

**Nüsse, Apfel, Birne auch,
das picken Krähen gerne auf.**

Wie oben.

**Der Nikolaus, der freut sich sehr,
die Tiere freun sich noch viel mehr.**

Der Nikolaus verbeugt sich und hebt seinen Sack auf den Rücken.

**Nun geht der Nik'laus, Wiederseh'n,
den Tieren wird's jetzt besser geh'n.**

Der Nikolaus geht winkend zur Tür, die Kinder winken ihm nach.

(Melodie: Vogelhochzeit)

UND SO GEHT'S:
Jedes Kind bekommt ein Körbchen. Sie können die Körbchen mit dem im Lied vorkommenden Futter füllen oder pantomimisch mitspielen. Ein Kind, das durch einen Abzählreim oder durch Auslosen bestimmt wird, ist der Nikolaus. Es setzt die Mütze auf, schnappt sich den Nikolaussack und wartet vor der Tür, bis es hereingerufen wird. Die anderen Kinder stimmen mit Ihnen das Lied an.

Idee: Margot Lindner

Hallo, Herr Nikolaus

Lied

Alter: ab 3 Jahren
Dauer: 5 Minuten

Herr Nikolaus, Herr Nikolaus, du siehst so wie ein Bischof aus.
Trägst eine Mitra auf dem Haar,
dein Bischofsstab glänzt gold und klar.
Herr Nikolaus, Herr Nikolaus, du siehst so wie ein Bischof aus.

Herr Nikolaus, Herr Nikolaus, dein weißer Bart, der ist ganz kraus.
Du hast nen langen Mantel an,
darauf zieht man die Stola an.
Herr Nikolaus, Herr Nikolaus, dein weißer Bart, der ist ganz kraus.

Herr Nikolaus, Herr Nikolaus, leer bitte deinen Sack hier aus.
Hast du in den Geschenkesack
für uns ein Päckchen eingepackt.
Herr Nikolaus, Herr Nikolaus, leer bitte deinen Sack hier aus.

Herr Nikolaus, Herr Nikolaus, wir sagen dir auf Wiedersehn.
Hab Dank für die Geschenke hier,
wir bringen dich noch bis zur Tür.
Herr Nikolaus, Herr Nikolaus, wir sagen dir auf Wiedersehn.

(Melodie: O Tannenbaum)

Idee: Marion Bischoff

Wir gehen in den Zoo, Zoo, Zoo

Klatschspiel für zwei

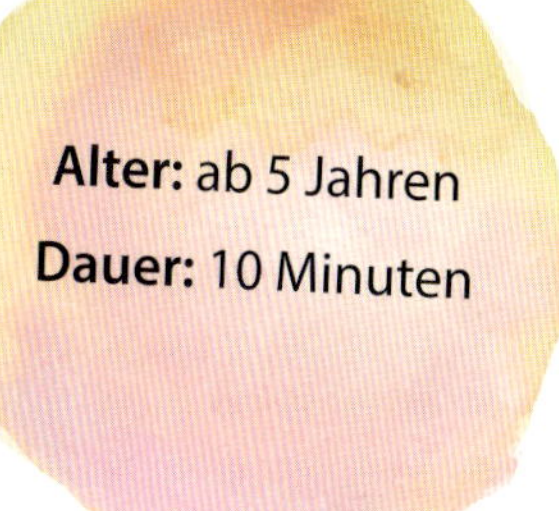

Heut bin ich richtig froh, froh, froh,
wir gehen in den Zoo, Zoo, Zoo.

Da lebt ein Elefant, fant, fant,
der ist uns schon bekannt, kannt, kannt.
Er ist ganz dick und grau, grau, grau,
wohnt hier mit seiner Frau, Frau, Frau.
Die beiden tröten laut, laut, laut,
bis jeder rüberschaut, schaut, schaut.

Jetzt wolln wir weitergehn, gehn, gehn,
um Erdmännchen zu sehn, sehn, sehn.
Sie schaun ganz müde her, her, her,
und putzig sind sie sehr, sehr, sehr.
Die Höhle ist ihr Haus, Haus, Haus.
Sie schlafen erst mal aus, aus, aus.

Der Löwe ist auch faul, faul, faul,
er hat ein großes Maul, Maul, Maul.
Das reißt er ganz weit auf, auf, auf,
und beißt aufs Fleischstück drauf, drauf, drauf.
Er ist ein wildes Tier, Tier, Tier,
der König ist er hier, hier, hier.

Was kann ich als Nächstes sehn, sehn, sehn,
Flamingos vor mir stehn, stehn, stehn.
Und zwar auf einem Bein, Bein, Bein,
wie kann denn das nur sein, sein, sein?
Beim Rennen sind sie flink, flink, flink,
ihr Gefieder leuchtet pink, pink, pink.

Dem Eisbär ist es heiß, heiß, heiß,
vielleicht mag er ein Eis, Eis, Eis.
Er springt ins Wasser rein, rein, rein,
da scheint es kühl zu sein, sein, sein.
Dafür bekommt er frisch, frisch, frisch,
’nen Eimer voller Fisch, Fisch, Fisch.

Die Affen nebenan, an, an,
die sind als Nächstes dran, dran, dran.
Der eine ist zerzaust, zaust, zaust,
ein andrer ihn grad laust, laust, laust.
Jetzt juckt es auch schon mich, mich, mich,
ich bleibe hier gar nicht, nicht, nicht.

Es ist jetzt auch so weit, weit, weit,
zum Heimgehn ist es Zeit, Zeit, Zeit.
Es war ein schöner Tag, Tag, Tag,
weil ich den Zoo so mag, mag, mag.
Bald komm ich wieder her, her, her,
komm doch mit, es ist nicht schwer, schwer, schwer.

UND SO GEHT’S:
Zwei Kinder stellen sich gegenüber auf. Im Rhythmus des Gedichtes klatschen sie die einzelnen Silben mit:
Bei der ersten Silbe klatscht jeder seine eigenen Hände zusammen. Danach klatschen beide Kinder ihre rechten Handflächen ab. Bei der dritten Silbe klatscht wieder jeder in seine eigenen Hände. Als Nächstes klatschen beide ihre linken Handflächen ab. Beim nächsten Mal klatscht wieder jeder seine eigenen Hände zusammen. Danach klatschen beide Kinder dreimal hintereinander sich gegenseitig mit beiden Händen ab.
Dann geht das Ganze wieder von vorne los.

Idee: Leah Schäfer

Wie die kleine Maus (doch noch) Hilfe bekam

Klanggeschichte

Alter: ab 4 Jahren

Dauer: 15 Minuten

Material: Klanginstrumente

Die kleine **Maus**, sie sitzt und friert,
oh weh, wenn sie den Mut verliert!
Sie hat schlimmen Hunger und kalt ist ihr auch,
braucht dringend ein Essen im Mäusebauch.

Ein **Hase** kommt vorbei, er friert im Wind,
läuft vorbei an der Maus, geschwind, geschwind.
„Ach, lieber **Hase**, mir ist schrecklich kalt,
den Mut verliere ich sicher bald.
Ich habe kein Heim und auch nichts zu essen,
gibt du mir was ab von deinem Fressen?"
Doch der **Hase** will schnell heim und aus der Kält',
so kalt ist der Winter auf dieser Welt.

Ein **Fuchs** kommt vorbei, er friert im Wind,
läuft vorbei an der Maus, geschwind, geschwind.
„Ach, lieber **Fuchs**, mir ist schrecklich kalt,
den Mut verliere ich sicher bald.
Ich habe kein Heim und auch nichts zu essen,
gibt du mir was ab von deinem Fressen?"
Doch der **Fuchs** will schnell heim und aus der Kält',
so kalt ist der Winter auf dieser Welt.

Ein **Hamster** kommt vorbei, er friert im Wind,
stoppt vor der Maus, geschwind, geschwind.
„Na, liebe Maus, was frierst du allein,
willst du nicht lieber im Warmen sein?"
„Ach, lieber **Hamster**, mir ist schrecklich kalt,
den Mut verliere ich sicher bald.
Ich habe kein Heim und auch nichts zu essen,
gibt du mir was ab von deinem Fressen?"
„Na klar", sagt der **Hamster**, „ich lade dich ein,
den Winter bei mir zu Gast zu sein."
Zusammen wohnen **Hamster** und **Maus**
im unterirdischen Hamsterhaus.

UND SO GEHT'S:
Die Kinder begleiten die Geschichte mit Klanginstrumenten: für jedes Tier ein anderes Instrument. Überlegen Sie gemeinsam, welche Instrumente zu den Tieren passen.

Idee: Tina Scherer

1, 2, 3, der Sommer ist vorbei!

Lied

Alter: ab 3 Jahren
Dauer: 10 Minuten

1, 2, 3, der Sommer ist vorbei!
Doch wir können's kaum erwarten,
Herbstwind weht durch unsren Garten.
1, 2, 3, der Sommer ist vorbei!

1, 2, 3, der Sommer ist vorbei!
Alle Blätter werden bunter,
fallen von den Bäumen runter.
1, 2, 3, der Sommer ist vorbei!

1, 2, 3, der Sommer ist vorbei!
Drachensteigen, Pfützenspringen,
nachts Laternenlieder singen.
1, 2, 3, der Sommer ist vorbei!

(Melodie: Summ, summ, summ)

Idee: Leah Schäfer

Winterzauber

Klanggeschichte

Alter: ab 4 Jahren

Dauer: 20 Minuten

Material: Xylofon, Klangstäbe, Triangel, Glöckchen, Holzblocktrommel, Zeitungspapier

„Ich habe keine Lust rauszugehen!" Annalena stand vor dem Fenster und schaute hinaus. Es hatte die ganze Nacht geschneit und eine weiße Decke hatte sich überall ausgebreitet. Ihre beste Freundin Carolina war heute bei Annalena zu Besuch und wollte gern mit ihr nach draußen gehen.
Carolina liebte den Winter. „Komm mit, ich zeige dir, wie wunderschön der Winter sein kann."
Nachdem beide ihre Jacken, Schuhe, Schals und Mützen angezogen hatten, liefen sie, so schnell sie konnten, los.
Klangstäbe mehrmals anschlagen.

„Schau mal nach oben", sagte Carolina. Annalena musste staunen. Tausende und abertausende Schneeflocken rieselten zu ihnen herunter. Wie wunderschön das aussah.
Triangel mehrmals anschlagen.

Die beiden Freundinnen liefen weiter. „Schau mal, was ich hier habe", sagte Carolina. „Meinen Schlitten. Komm lass uns damit den Hügel runtersausen."
Mit dem Glöckchen klingeln.

Sie zogen den Schlitten den Hügel hinauf. Das war ganz schön anstrengend!
Auf dem Xylofon die Tonfolge langsam aufwärts spielen, dabei die Töne einzeln anschlagen. Mit dem Glöckchen klingeln.

Oben angekommen, machten sich Annalena und Carolina bereit und setzten sich auf den Schlitten.
„3, 2, 1 und los!"
Dreimal auf die Holzblocktrommel schlagen.

Schnell wie der Wind sausten die beiden auf ihrem Schlitten den Hügel hinunter. Das machte Spaß!
Auf dem Xylofon die Tonfolge langsam abwärts spielen, dabei die Töne streichen. Mit dem Glöckchen klingeln.

Den ganzen Nachmittag fuhren sie mit ihrem Schlitten. Mittlerweile war es schon fast dunkel. Der Wind wehte und wiegte die kahlen Äste der Bäume hin und her. Den beiden Mädchen wurde auch langsam kalt.
Leicht zerknülltes Zeitungspapier in der Hand reiben. In die Hände pusten und sie reiben.

Annalena und Carolina beschlossen, sich wieder auf den Heimweg zu machen. Zu Hause gab es bestimmt eine Tasse heißen Kakao, mit dem sie sich wieder aufwärmen konnten. Sie stapften durch den mittlerweile tiefen Schnee. Den Schlitten zogen sie hinter sich her. Das war ein schöner Tag!
Die Handtrommel reiben und mit dem Glöckchen klingeln.

Idee: Leah Schäfer

Kapitel 3

Geschichten zum Erzählen und Mitmachen

Das Märchen vom dicken, fetten Pfannkuchen

Geschichtensäckchen

Alter: ab 3 Jahren

Dauer: 20 Minuten

Es waren einmal drei alte Frauen, die wollten gerne Pfannkuchen essen. Sie gaben Eier, Mehl und Milch in eine Schüssel und rührten alles zu einem Teig zusammen. Als sie mit dem Rühren fertig waren, holten sie eine Pfanne, stellten sie auf den Herd, taten Fett hinein und gossen den Teig dazu.

Es duftete herrlich! Den drei Frauen lief das Wasser schon im Mund zusammen. Doch der Pfannkuchen dachte nicht daran, sich von ihnen verspeisen zu lassen. Als er fertig gebacken war, erhob er sich aus der Pfanne, sprang auf den Boden, und rollte *kantapper kantapper* aus dem Haus hinaus.

Die drei Frauen standen vor der leeren Pfanne und schauten dem Pfannkuchen hinterher. „Halt!", kreischte die erste. „Bleibst du wohl stehen!", rief die zweite und streckte ihre Hand nach dem Pfannkuchen aus. Die dritte Frau lief hinter ihm her und versuchte ihn einzufangen. Doch sie war einfach nicht schnell genug.

Der Pfannkuchen rollte aber immer weiter und erfreute sich an dem sonnigen Tag. Da begegnete er einem Häschen. „Guten Tag Pfannkuchen", sagte das Häschen. „Guten Tag Häschen Langohr", sagte der Pfannkuchen. „Dicker fetter Pfannkuchen, bleib doch bitte stehen, damit ich dich fressen kann", sagte das Häschen. Da antwortete der Pfannkuchen: „Das kannst du schön vergessen! Ich bin schon drei alten Frauen weggelaufen. Da sollst du mich auch nicht kriegen." Und er rollte *kantapper kantapper* in den Wald hinein.

Da kam ein Wolf angelaufen. „Guten Tag Pfannkuchen", sagte der Wolf. „Guten Tag Wolf Graupelz", sagte der Pfannkuchen. „Dicker fetter Pfannkuchen, bleib doch bitte stehen, damit ich dich fressen kann", sagte der Wolf. Da antwortete der Pfannkuchen: „Das kannst du schön vergessen! Ich bin schon drei alten Frauen weggelaufen und Häschen Langohr. Da sollst du mich auch nicht kriegen." Und er rollte *kantapper kantapper* aus dem Wald hinaus.

Da kam eine Ziege her gehüpft. „Guten Tag Pfannkuchen", sagte die Ziege. „Guten Tag Ziege Meckerliese", sagte der Pfannkuchen. „Dicker fetter Pfannkuchen, bleib

doch bitte stehen, damit ich dich fressen kann", sagte die Ziege. Da antwortete der Pfannkuchen: „Das kannst du schön vergessen! Ich bin schon drei alten Frauen weggelaufen, Häschen Langohr und Wolf Graupelz. Da sollst du mich auch nicht kriegen." Und er rollte *kantapper kantapper* davon.

Da traf er ein Schwein. „Guten Tag Pfannkuchen", sagte das Schwein. „Guten Tag Schwein Ringelschwanz", sagte der Pfannkuchen. „Dicker fetter Pfannkuchen, bleib doch bitte stehen, damit ich dich fressen kann", sagte das Schwein. Da antwortete der Pfannkuchen: „Das kannst du schön vergessen! Ich bin schon drei alten Frauen weggelaufen, Häschen Langohr, Wolf Graupelz und Ziege Meckerliese. Da sollst du mich auch nicht kriegen." Und er rollte *kantapper kantapper* den Weg entlang.

Da kam ein Pferd angaloppiert. „Guten Tag Pfannkuchen", sagte das Pferd. „Guten Tag Pferd Plattfuß", sagte der Pfannkuchen. „Dicker fetter Pfannkuchen, bleib doch bitte stehen, damit ich dich fressen kann", sagte das Pferd. Da antwortete der Pfannkuchen: „Das kannst du schön vergessen! Ich bin schon drei alten Frauen weggelaufen, Häschen Langohr, Wolf Graupelz, Ziege Meckerliese und Schwein Ringelschwanz. Da sollst du mich auch nicht kriegen." Und er rollte *kantapper kantapper* über die Wiese davon.

Langsam wurde es Abend. Der Pfannkuchen rollte so vor sich hin, als auf einmal drei Kinder auf ihn zukamen. Sie waren ganz allein, denn sie hatten keinen Vater und keine Mutter mehr. „Ach, lieber guter Pfannkuchen. Bleib doch bitte stehen. Wir haben den ganzen Tag noch nichts gegessen und sind so hungrig", sagten sie traurig. Da freute sich der Pfannkuchen, dass er helfen konnte, sprang den Kindern in den Korb hinein und ließ sich von ihnen restlos aufessen.

Idee: Leah Schäfer

UND SO GEHT'S:

Material: 1 Säckchen, 1 kleine Scheibe als Pfannkuchen (z. B. aus Pappe), 1 Hase, 1 Wolf, 1 Ziege, 1 Schwein, 1 Pferd, 3 Frauen, 3 Kinder

Lesen Sie die Geschichte vor und spielen Sie dabei die Handlung mit den Gegenständen aus dem Säckchen nach. Das Gesehene wird mit dem Gehörten verknüpft und den Kindern fällt es leichter, sich die Geschichte zu merken. Lassen Sie die Mädchen und Jungen die Figuren im Anschluss anfassen und die Geschichte selbst nachspielen. So ist es für die Kinder leichter, sich an die Handlung zu erinnern.

Die traurige kleine Eule

Alter: ab 4 Jahren
Dauer: 15 Minuten

Klanggeschichte

Im Märchenwald leben viele Märchenwesen und Tiere. Manche davon sind immer fröhlich, wie die **Waldmäuse**, die mit den **Feen** Fangen spielen. Könnt ihr sie im Laub rascheln hören?

Und könnt ihr auch die **Feen** hören, wie sie kichern? Feengelächter ist zart und hell, aber man kann es nur hören, wenn man ganz, ganz leise ist.

Die **Feen** und die **Mäuse** sind also ziemlich lustig und immer fröhlich. Aber es gibt auch eine **Eule**, die immer traurig ist. Nachts sitzt sie in einer hohen Eiche, in der der **Wind** spielt, und ruft in die Nacht. Das kommt davon, dass die **Eule** ganz allein ist, weil nachts die meisten anderen Tiere schlafen, oder?

Nein, das stimmt nicht. Da gibt es zum Beispiel die **Wildschweinfamilie**, die nachts ihre Schlammbäder am Flussufer nimmt. Das ist ein Gegrunze und Gematsche! Schon allein bei diesem Anblick müsste die traurige Eule eigentlich einmal lachen.

Das kleinste **Wildschwein** ist gerade mit dem Kopf in einen großen Matschhaufen gerannt. Es schüttelt sich, dass die Matschklumpen fliegen. Klatsch und flatsch!

Das findet die Eule nun doch ziemlich lustig. Ein kleines bisschen lachen muss sie jetzt schon. Habt ihr schon einmal eine **Eule** lachen hören? Nicht? Das kommt davon, dass man **Eulen** so selten lachen hört, weil sie immer traurig sind.

Die **Feen** freuen sich, dass die **Eule** einmal lacht. Ein paar **Grashüpfer** freuen sich ebenfalls und klatschen laut Applaus. Und ein **Fuchs**, der auf die Jagd in der Dunkelheit geht, bellt mit. „Schön, dass du mal lachst, Eule!", ruft der **Fuchs**. „Und wie gut, dass die **Wildschweine** so eine Matscherei machen!" Auch der **Wind** freut sich und rauscht ordentlich in der alten Eiche. Und auch die anderen Tiere freuen sich mit der **Eule**. Sie klatschen und lachen und der **Wind** rauscht. Das ist ein Lärm im Märchenwald!

UND SO GEHT'S:

- **Feen:** Triangel
- **Eule:** Becken oder Schellenring
- **Waldmäuse:** Metallofon
- **Wildschweine:** Trommel oder Pauke
- **kleines Wildschwein:** hellere Trommel
- **Grashüpfer:** Glöckchen oder Zimbeln, falls vorrätig Mundgeige
- **Wind:** Rasseln oder Maracas
- **Fuchs:** Ratsche

Idee: Tina Scherer

So war mein Tag

Plaudern mit dem Erzählpüppchen

Alter: ab 3 Jahren
Dauer: 5 Minuten
Material: Fingerhüte, Wollreste, Scheren, Wackelaugen, Karton

EIN ERZÄHLPÜPPCHEN FÜR JEDEN

Aus Karton fertigen Sie die Vorlagen, die von den Kindern mit Wolle umwickelt werden sollen. Dafür schneiden sie Kreise mit einem Durchmesser von ca. 5 bis 7 cm aus. In der Mitte schneiden Sie ein Loch von ca. 3 cm Durchmesser hinein.

Die Wolle wird verknotet und nun in vielen Lagen um den Kartonkreis gewickelt. Wenn die Kinder fertig sind, schneiden Sie vorsichtig am äußeren Kreisrand entlang die Wollfäden durch. Legen Sie einen Faden um die Wollkugel und knoten Sie diese fest zusammen. Nun wird in die Mitte der Wollkugel ein Fingerhut geklebt.

Die Kinder verzieren ihre Erzählpüppchen mit Wackelaugen, Kartonmund etc. und stecken sie dann auf ihre Finger.

ERZÄHL MIR WAS

Jedes Kind darf nun mit seinem Erzählpüppchen im Kreis etwas erzählen. Dafür kann es eine Geschichte erfinden oder ein Erlebnis wiedergeben.

Suchen Sie einen Platz für die Erzählpüppchen oder sammeln sie die Figuren aller Kinder in einem Stoffbeutel. Bei jedem Morgenkreis ziehen Sie eine oder zwei Figuren und die Kinder, die sie gebastelt haben, sind in dieser Erzählrunde an der Reihe.

Tipp: Damit wirklich alle Kinder erzählen können, legen Sie die Püppchen zur Seite, bis der Beutel leer ist und alle wieder zurück in den Beutel gepackt werden.

Idee: Marion Bischoff

Igor Igel hat ausgeschlafen

Mitmachgeschichte zum Suchen

Alter: ab 4 Jahren
Dauer: 15 Minuten

VORBEREITUNG:
Verstecken Sie im Vorfeld Bildkarten (oder zum Beispiel Figuren, echte Blumen …) von Krokus, Schneeglöckchen, Biene, Sonne, Baum, Vogel und Schmetterling im Gruppen- oder Bewegungsraum oder draußen. Die Kinder suchen die Karten oder Figuren im Laufe der Geschichte und laufen dorthin.

Igor, der kleine Igel, streckte sich. Er gähnte. „Uuuaaaahhhh, habe ich lange geschlafen! Es ist ja schon Frühling! Jetzt habe ich genug. Ich will hinausgehen."
Strecken und ganz lang machen.

Er schob ein paar der Blätter vor seinem Nest zur Seite, steckte seine Nase durch die Öffnung und schnupperte.
Mit beiden Händen Blätter wegschieben, Nase in die Luft strecken und schnuppern.

„Wonach riecht es denn hier? Die Luft ist ganz frisch und es duftet so wunderbar. Was kann das denn sein?" – „Jetzt weiß ich es. Es ist ein Krokus. Mal sehen, ob ich ihn finde."
Die Kinder suchen den Krokus (Bildkarte, Figur).

Der kleine Igel schnupperte noch einmal. „Hier riecht noch etwas ganz toll. Da ist noch eine Blume. Ich glaube, das ist ein Schneeglöckchen."
Schnuppern und das Schneeglöckchen suchen.

Igor lief weiter. Plötzlich summte etwas in seinen Ohren. Er drehte sich nach links und er drehte sich nach rechts, doch da war nichts. Dann schaute er nach oben und sah eine fleißige Biene, die durch die Luft flog.
Nach links und rechts drehen, nach oben schauen. Die Kinder suchen die Biene.

„Hallo, kleine Biene", rief der Igel. „Wohin fliegst du denn? Ich komme mit dir." Igor lief der Biene mit kleinen Schritten hinterher.
Auf der Stelle gehen.

„Puh, ist das warm", stöhnte Igor nach einer Weile. Er schaute zum Himmel und sah die Sonne, die auf die Erde schien.
Den Schweiß von der Stirn wischen und die Sonne suchen.

Der kleine Igel schaute sich um. Er sah einen großen Baum mit wunderschönen Blüten.
Die Kinder suchen den Baum.

Aus dem Baum kam ein leises Geräusch. Igor war ganz still und hörte noch einmal hin. War das ein Zwitschern? Er schaute ganz genau. Ja, richtig. Da saß ein kleiner Vogel und zwitscherte.
Die Hand ans Ohr halten und hören. Dann die Hand an die Stirn legen und nach etwas Ausschau halten. Die Kinder suchen den Vogel.

Plötzlich flatterte wieder etwas um ihn herum. „Wer bist denn du? Du siehst aber toll aus. Du hast wunderschöne bunte Flügel." „Ich bin ein Schmetterling", rief das Tier und flog davon.
Die Kinder suchen den Schmetterling.

Der kleine Igel hörte ein Brummen. Doch woher kam das Geräusch? Er schaute an sich herunter. „Das kommt ja aus meinem Bauch. Ich habe so lange geschlafen und nichts gegessen. Mein Bauch ist schon ganz dünn. Ich suche mir jetzt erst einmal etwas zu essen.
Die Hand ans Ohr halten. Danach an sich herunterschauen und mit der Hand über den Bauch streichen.

Idee: Leah Schäfer

Das kleine Gespenst hat Husten

Schaurige Vorlesegeschichte

Alter: ab 4 Jahren
Dauer: 10 Minuten

Kennt ihr schon das kleine Gespenst Schwebfuß? Dieses kleine Gespenst ist noch sehr jung, höchstens 423 Jahre alt, und es lebt in einer sehr alten Burg, sehr weit weg in einem sehr tiefen Wald.

Die Zeit um Halloween ist natürlich für alle Gespenster am schönsten, denn dann feiern sie lustige Feste mit Gespenstermusik, Spinnwebtänzen und es gibt ein riesiges Büfett mit allem, was Gespenster und ihre Freunde so lieben, also leckere Spinnenbeinspaghetti, Froschaugenaufläufe, Schleimpudding und natürlich Fischschwanzspießchen.

Die Gespenster aus der alten Burg in dem tiefen Wald laden an Halloween ihre Freunde ein: die Vampire aus der Nachbarburg, einige Hexen aus dem tiefen Wald, die Kobolde vom Berg neben der Burg und manchmal kommen auch einige Elfen, Feen und Wichtel dazu, wenn sie sich trauen. Eine Gespensterkapelle spielt dann laute und lustige Musik und jeder Gast bekommt als Willkommensgruß einen Partydrink aus Waldpfützenwasser. Ein toller Spaß also.

Unser kleines Gespenst namens Schwebfuß freute sich in diesem Jahr allerdings überhaupt nicht auf Halloween. Es war nämlich krank.
„Oh je, ich werd bestimmt nicht gesund bis Halloween. Ich hab nämlich …" – und hier musste das kleine Gespenst aufhören zu sprechen, weil es schlimm husten musste – „… fürchterlichen Husten."

„Ach, nur ein bisschen Husten?", fragte Schauerliese, die beste Freundin von Schwebfuß. Da gerade musste Schwebfuß niesen. „Und auch Schnupfen. Und Halsweh. Und richtig heulen und singen kann ich auch nicht, ich bin nämlich auch noch heiser." Und Schwebfuß machte Schauerliese vor, wie es heulte. Und das hörte sich ganz leise an und gar nicht gruselig. Kein Wunder bei der Heiserkeit.

„In diesem alten Gemäuer ist es einfach immer kalt und nass. Ich hab zwei Paar Unterhosen an und trotzdem erkälte ich mich immer im Herbst", erklärte Schwebfuß und nieste noch einmal. Da war guter Rat teuer.

Schauerliese probierte zuerst ihre beste Medizin, einen Hustensaft aus zerkleinertem Froschlaich, Waldmausurin und etwas Giftbeerensaft. Grunzwurm, ein guter Freund von Schauerliese und Schwebfuß, brachte einen heißen Tee aus Giftlattichblättern und Eichenrinde. Aber nichts half.

Als Halloween herankam und das Fest begann, lag Schwebfuß traurig und allein in seinem Gespensterbett in seinem Zimmer. Aus der großen Festhalle drang nur ganz leise das Gelächter der anderen Gruselgestalten zu ihm herauf. Beinahe hätte Schwebfuß angefangen zu weinen, aber Schwebfuß war ein besonders tapferes Gespenst – und außerdem tat ihm das Weinen im Hals weh.

Da ging die Tür auf und Schauerliese und Grunzwurm kamen herein. Sie brachten ein Heizöfchen mit, dazu drei Becher mit heißer Gespensterbowle, viele lustige Kürbislichter und einen kleinen Kuchen aus Erdkrötenfüßen, garniert mit Giftpilzmarmelade. Lecker! Schnell war ein kleiner Tisch aufgebaut und die drei Freunde ließen sich ihr Mahl schmecken. Sie stießen mit der Bowle an und heulten zu den Gespensterliedern, die aus der Halle heraufdrangen, mit.

Nach und nach kamen noch mehr Freunde dazu, setzten sich zu Schwebfuß ans Bett, brachten noch mehr Leckereien mit und dachten sich lustige Spiele aus. Das war das schönste Halloweenfest, das Schwebfuß je erlebt hatte. Und ob es nun die Gespensterbowle, das Heizöfchen oder die lustige Gesellschaft war, – ob ihr es glaubt oder nicht –, am nächsten Morgen war Schwebfuß wieder gesund.

Idee: Tina Scherer

Kater Karlo und das Waldabenteuer

Fortsetzungsgeschichte

Alter: ab 3 Jahren
Dauer: 20 Minuten

Der kleine Kater Karlo lag auf einer Bank in der Sonne. „Mir ist ja so langweilig", dachte er, „ich will endlich einmal etwas erleben." Und so machte er sich auf den Weg. Er marschierte zum Hof hinaus, überquerte vorsichtig die Straße und lief den Feldweg entlang, bis er am Wald angekommen war. Karlo ging ein Stück in den Wald hinein. Die Bäume wurden immer dichter und er musste aufpassen, dass er nicht über eine Baumwurzel stolperte. Da hörte er ein Knacken. Er drehte sich um und sah …

WIE KÖNNTE ES WEITERGEHEN?

- Der Kater freundet sich mit einem Waldbewohner an und sie spielen miteinander.
- Der Kater trifft auf ein Tier in Not und hilft ihm.
- Der Kater und ein neuer Freund helfen einem anderen Tier oder erleben ein gemeinsames Abenteuer.

UND SO GEHT'S:

Erzählen Sie den Kindern den Anfang einer Geschichte. Danach ist das erste Kind an der Reihe und darf die Geschichte weitererzählen. Wenn es seinen Teil erzählt hat, ist das nächste Kind dran. So geht es immer weiter, bis die Geschichte ein Ende findet.

Tipp: Führen Sie einen Erzählstein ein. Immer derjenige, der mit Erzählen dran ist, bekommt den Stein in die Hand. Er gibt Sicherheit und signalisiert den anderen, dass sie jetzt gerade zuhören sollen.

Idee: Leah Schäfer

Die Froschwäsche

Mitmachgeschichte für die Zunge

Alter: ab 4 Jahren

Dauer: 10 Minuten

Material: Zahnstocher, Fruchtgummifrösche

Es ist gerade Mittagsruhe am See. Die Frösche liegen unter den feuchten Blättern der Blumen am Ufer und ruhen sich von ihrem Morgenkonzert aus.

Nur Fridolin Froschkind badet in der Schlammpfütze von gestern und freut sich seines Lebens. Als Mama Frosch ihn sieht, muss er sofort nach Hause kommen. „Wie siehst du denn aus!?", ruft sie wütend und droht ihm eine gründliche Froschwäsche im großen See an. „So, und nun kommst du mit, damit wir dich wieder sauber kriegen!"

Zuerst streift sie ihm mit ihrer langen Zunge den Schlamm aus den Augen *(lange Zunge machen und vorsichtig über die Augen lecken)* und wäscht ihm das Gesicht. Nach den Augen kommt die Nase *(mit der Zungenspitze kreisen)*, der Mund *(die ganze Zunge nach rechts und links bewegen)*, die Ohren *(sehr kleine Kreise mit der Zunge machen)* und danach sein ganzer Kopf *(Zunge wild durcheinander bewegen)*. „So und nun deine Hände und Arme her!", ruft sie und dann beginnt die Wäsche der Finger *(Zunge von oben nach unten bewegen)*, der rechten und linken Hand und der Arme *(Zunge breit machen und von unten nach oben bewegen)*. Danach kommen die Zehen *(Zunge spitz machen und vorwärts/rückwärts bewegen)*, die Füße *(Zunge spitz machen und von oben nach unten bewegen)* und die Beine *(Zunge breit machen, hoch und runter bewegen)* dran.

Fridolin Froschkind findet das nicht schön, aber „Was sein muss, muss sein!", sagt seine Mutter immer. Und so taucht sie ihn noch einmal ganz unter Wasser *(Gummifrosch ganz in den Mund nehmen und auf der Zunge ablegen)*. Nachdem er wieder ganz sauber ist, darf er auch wieder zu seiner Familie unter die Blätter kommen.

UND SO GEHT'S:

Spießen Sie für jedes Kind einen Fruchtgummifrosch auf einen Zahnstocher auf. Wie in der Geschichte beschrieben, darf jedes Kind seinen Frosch mit der Zunge „waschen" und ihn am Ende der Geschichte genüsslich verspeisen.

Idee: Heike König

Lass uns brüllen, Löwe

Geschichte über Freundschaft

Alter: ab 4 Jahren

Dauer: 15 Minuten

„Aua! Das hast du mit Absicht gemacht!" Der kleine Löwe reibt sich an seiner Vorderpfote und knurrt den kleinen Tiger an. Der Tiger geht einen Schritt auf den kleinen Löwen zu. „Nein. Ich wollte doch nur den Stein anschubsen."

„Von wegen!" Mürrisch dreht sich der kleine Löwe um. Ohne sich noch einmal nach seinem Freund umzusehen, eilt er davon. Traurig sieht ihm der kleine Tiger nach. „Ich wollte doch wirklich nur den Stein schießen", murmelt er.

Dann überlegt er eine Weile. Da fällt ihm ein, wie es gestern war, als der kleine Löwe ihm das letzte Stück Fleisch weggefressen hat. So schnell er kann, rennt er zum kleinen Löwen: „Ich sage dir jetzt mal was: Gestern hast du mich geärgert. Du hast mein Fleisch gefressen, ohne mich zu fragen."

Die Augen des kleinen Tigers blitzen den kleinen Löwen zornig an. „Ich glaube, du willst gar nicht mein Freund sein." Kaum hat er das ausgesprochen, schlägt sich der kleine Tiger die Pfote vor sein Maul. „Du willst wohl auch nicht mein Freund sein. Sieh dir nur die Beule an meinem Bein an. Das warst du mit dem blöden Stein."

Der kleine Löwe deutet auf sein Vorderbein, an dem sich unter dem Fell wirklich eine dicke Beule abzeichnet. „Das war ich?" Erschrocken reißt der kleine Tiger die Augen auf. Der kleine Löwe nickt. Lange sieht er seinen Freund an. „Wir sind echt doof."

Jetzt nickt auch der Tiger. „Da hast du recht. Wir sollten uns nicht streiten." Sie setzen sich nebeneinander ins Gras und schauen in den Sonnenuntergang. Auf einmal springt der kleine Tiger hoch. „Weißt du was, Löwe? Wenn wir wieder streiten, sagt einer von uns beiden nur: *Lass uns brüllen, Löwe*."

„Au ja!" Begeistert springt auch der kleine Löwe auf. „Dann brüllen wir beide, so laut wir können. Und danach spielen wir wieder miteinander."

Wenn du einmal in Afrika bist und durch die Savanne gehst und einen Löwen ganz laut brüllen hörst, hat er sich bestimmt gerade mit seinem Freund gestritten – und wieder vertragen …

Idee: Marion Bischoff

Impulsfragen zur Geschichte:

- Wie war es, als du neu in den Kindergarten gekommen bist? Kannst du dich erinnern?
- Kanntest du schon ein Kind?
- Was kannst du tun, wenn du gern einen Freund haben möchtest?
- Wenn du ein Kind kennenlernst und mit ihm spielst, ist es dann dein Freund? Was ist ein Freund?
- Was machen Freunde?
- Wie fühlt es sich an, ein Freund zu sein?
- Du hast einen Freund und lernst ein neues Kind kennen, das du sehr gern magst. Es ist nun auch dein Freund. Was passiert mit dem anderen Freund? Könnt ihr zu dritt spielen? Oder spielst du einmal mit dem einen Kind und ein anderes Mal mit dem anderen?
- Wie kannst du einem Kind helfen, sich in der Gruppe wohlzufühlen?
- Wie wünschst du dir deinen besten Freund?
- Können Mädchen und Jungen Freunde sein?
- Wie viele Freunde kannst du haben?
- Können Erwachsene auch Freunde sein?

Das kleine Feuerwehrauto

Geschichte über das Wichtigsein

Alter: ab 3 Jahren
Dauer: 15 Minuten

In der Garage der Feuerwache standen viele Feuerwehrautos. Da gab es welche, die hatten eine Drehleiter, andere hatten einen riesigen Wassertank und wieder andere hatten große Werkzeuge. Manchmal fuhr nur ein Fahrzeug zum Einsatz, manchmal auch mehrere. Das kam immer darauf an, welches Feuerwehrauto gerade gebraucht wurde.

Die Feuerwehrautos waren immer sehr stolz, wenn sie zu einem Einsatz gerufen wurden und gaben mächtig mit ihren Taten an.

Doch ganz hinten, in der hintersten Ecke der Garage, stand ein kleines Feuerwehrauto. Bislang wurde es noch nie zu einem Einsatz gerufen. Die anderen Feuerwehrautos lachten es immer aus: „He Kleiner, du musst wohl ein bisschen mehr frühstücken, sonst wirst du nie groß und stark." Darüber war das kleine Feuerwehrauto sehr traurig. Es würde so gern zu einem Einsatz fahren.

Eines Tages kam in der Leitstelle ein Notruf an. „Alle Feuerwehrautos zum Einsatz. „Au prima", dachte das kleine Feuerwehrauto. „Alle heißt, dass ich damit auch gemeint bin." Es schaltete sein Blaulicht und sein Martinshorn an und fuhr hinter den anderen Feuerwehrautos aus der Garage hinaus.

Doch es war kaum auf dem Hof der Feuerwache angekommen, da stellte sich ihm der große, dicke Feuerwehrkommandant in den Weg. „Was willst du denn hier draußen, Kleiner?", brummte er mit seiner tiefen Stimme. „Du bist viel zu klein. Du kannst uns nicht helfen. Fahre wieder in die Garage und stelle dich zurück in deine Ecke!"

Das kleine Feuerwehrauto wollte gerade sagen, dass es schon richtig gut löschen konnte, doch der Feuerwehrkommandant schaute so grimmig. Da verlor es den Mut und fuhr mit hängendem Führerhäuschen wieder zurück in die Garage.

Die anderen Feuerwehrautos hielten sich die Wassertanks vor Lachen. Mit quietschenden Reifen fuhren sie zu ihrem Einsatz und das kleine Feuerwehrauto blieb traurig und einsam zurück.

„So geht es nicht weiter", dachte das kleine Feuerwehrauto bei sich. „Ich habe keine Lust mehr, immer nur in der Garage zu stehen und ausgelacht zu werden. Ich muss etwas unternehmen."
Und so nahm das kleine Feuerwehrauto all seinen Mut zusammen und fuhr einfach los.

Es kam an einer Wiese vorbei, auf der ein Baum stand. Daneben war eine Frau, die das Feuerwehrauto zu sich herwinkte. „Was ist denn passiert?", fragte es. „Ach, meine Katze sitzt auf dem Baum und kommt nicht mehr herunter. Kannst du mir helfen? Die großen Feuerwehrautos sind einfach vorbeigefahren und sagten, sie hätten Wichtigeres zu tun, als eine Katze vom Baum zu holen."

Das Feuerwehrauto strahlte vor Freude. Endlich hatte es seinen ersten Einsatz. Langsam fuhr es die Drehleiter aus und legte sie vorsichtig an den Baum. Die Katze kletterte auf die Leiter und das Feuerwehrauto zog ganz behutsam die Leiter ein, sodass die Frau ihre Katze in die Arme schließen konnte. „Vielen Dank, kleines Feuerwehrauto", sagte sie und das Feuerwehrauto fuhr glücklich weiter.

Kurze Zeit später kam es bei einem Kindergeburtstag vorbei. Die Kinder waren ganz aufgeregt, denn die Kerzen auf dem Kuchen waren schon ganz heruntergebrannt. Sie ließen sich einfach nicht auspusten. Da rollte das kleine Feuerwehrauto seinen Schlauch aus und löschte die Kerzen mit einem dicken Wasserstrahl. Die Kinder jubelten vor Freude. „Hab vielen Dank für deine Hilfe, kleines Feuerwehrauto", sagten die Kinder. „Die großen Feuerwehrautos sind einfach vorbeigefahren und sagten, sie hätten Wichtigeres zu tun, als brennende Kerzen zu löschen."

Das kleine Feuerwehrauto war aber nun sehr müde. Langsam fuhr es wieder zurück in die Garage der Feuerwache, wo die anderen Feuerwehrautos bereits warteten. „Na, du traust dich ja was!", sagte eines der großen Feuerwehrautos. „Einfach wegfahren – das gibt bestimmt eine Menge Ärger."

Da kam auch schon der Feuerwehrkommandant in die Garage. Er machte ein grimmiges Gesicht. Die großen Feuerwehrautos grinsten und warteten darauf, dass er mit dem kleinen Feuerwehrauto schimpfen würde.

„Ich bin unglaublich wütend!", polterte der Kommandant los, „und zwar auf euch großen Feuerwehrautos. Wie könnt ihr denn sagen, ihr hättet Wichtigeres zu tun, wenn jemand eure Hilfe braucht? Ihr solltet euch wirklich schämen!" Die großen Feuerwehrautos blickten beschämt zu Boden. „Und dich, kleines Feuerwehrauto, muss ich sehr loben. Du hast deine Sache großartig gemacht und darfst von nun an zu jedem Einsatz mitfahren. Vielleicht brauchen wir dort ja deine Hilfe."

Und von diesem Zeitpunkt an hatte das kleine Feuerwehrauto fast täglich mehrere Einsätze und die großen Feuerwehrautos bewunderten es und haben es nie wieder ausgelacht.

Idee: Leah Schäfer

Prinzessin Pia und ihr Pony

Fortsetzungsgeschichte

Alter: ab 5 Jahren

Dauer: 15 Minuten

Es war einmal eine kleine Prinzessin. Ihr Name war Pia und sie lebte in einem großen Schloss. Sie liebte es, zu malen, zu singen oder mit ihren Freunden zu spielen. Doch am allerliebsten war Prinzessin Pia im Pferdestall bei ihrem Pony Paulchen. An einem sonnigen Frühlingstag beschloss sie, mit Paulchen auszureiten und ihre Cousine, Prinzessin Charlotte, zu besuchen. Sie sattelte Paulchen und ritt los. Unterwegs bemerkte sie ...

WIE KÖNNTE ES WEITERGEHEN?

– Pia verirrt sich und wird gerettet.
– Pia besucht Charlotte und sie machen einen Ausflug mit Übernachtung im Wald.
– Paulchen verliert ein Hufeisen und Pia muss eine Lösung finden.

UND SO GEHT'S:

Erzählen Sie den Kindern den Anfang einer Geschichte. Danach ist das erste Kind an der Reihe und darf die Geschichte weitererzählen. Wenn es seinen Teil erzählt hat, ist das nächste Kind dran. So geht es immer weiter, bis die Geschichte ein Ende findet.

Tipp: Führen Sie einen Erzählstein ein. Immer derjenige, der mit Erzählen dran ist, be-kommt den Stein in die Hand. Er gibt Sicherheit und signalisiert den anderen, dass sie jetzt gerade zuhören sollen.

Idee: Leah Schäfer

Blaukäppchen und der böse Löwe

Alter: ab 4 Jahren
Dauer: 10 Minuten

Quatschgeschichte

Es war einmal ein kleiner Junge, dem schenkte sein Großvater ein blaues Käppchen. *(Halt!)* Und weil der Junge dieses blaue Käppchen immer und überall aufsetzte, hieß er bald Blaukäppchen. *(Halt!)* Der Großvater aber wohnte ganz allein im Wald. Einmal wurde er krank. Da kochte Blaukäppchens Mutter eine Suppe. *(Halt!)* Dann rief sie Blaukäppchen und sagte: „Bring die Suppe zum Großvater! Aber trödle lange herum und lauf ruhig auch abseits des Weges!“ *(Halt!)* Blaukäppchen versprach es und ging gleich los. Im Wald traf er den bösen Löwen. *(Halt!)* Aber weil der sehr freundlich tat, hatte Blaukäppchen keine Angst. *(Halt!)* Er erzählte dem Löwen gleich, was er vorhatte. „Suche deinem Großvater doch dort auf der Wiese noch ein paar Regenwürmer zum Angeln“, sagte der Löwe. *(Halt!)* Da vergaß Blaukäppchen, was er seiner Mutter versprochen hatte, und lief auf die Wiese. Der Löwe aber rannte ganz rasch zum Haus des Großvaters und fraß ihn auf. Dann setzte er die Nachthaube des Großvaters auf, legte sich in sein Bett und deckte sich fast bis oben hin zu. Nach einer Weile kam Blaukäppchen mit seinen Regenwürmern und setzte sich zu ihm auf das Bett. „Großvater“, sagte Blaukäppchen, „du siehst heute ganz anders aus. Warum hast du denn so große Ohren? Und warum hast du so einen großen Mund? Kommt das, weil du krank bist?“ „Nein“, rief der Löwe, „das kommt, weil ich dich fressen will!“ Und dann packte er den armen Knaben und verschlang ihn mit einem Happs. Dann war er satt, legte sich wieder hin und schlief ein. Kurze Zeit später kam der Fischer vorbei und hörte den bösen Löwen laut schnarchen. *(Halt!)* Er wunderte sich und trat leise ins Haus. Als er den Löwen sah, nahm er einen Löffel und schnitt ihm den Bauch auf. *(Halt!)* Was für ein Glück! Blaukäppchen und der Großvater lebten noch! Der Fischer half den beiden heraus. Gemeinsam häkelten die drei dem Löwen den Bauch wieder zu – aber erst, nachdem sie viele Edelsteine hineingepackt hatten. *(Halt!)* Als der Löwe aufstehen wollte, fiel er zu Boden und war tot. Blaukäppchen, Großvater und der Fischer aber freuten sich sehr.

UND SO GEHT'S:
Im Text sind immer wieder Fehler eingebaut. Sobald die Kinder einen Fehler bemerken, springen sie auf und rufen laut: Halt! Wer kennt das Märchen von Rotkäppchen schon und weiß wie es richtig geht?

Idee: Ute Langhammer

Teilen macht Spaß

Geschichte mit Gedicht

Alter: ab 4 Jahren
Dauer: 15 Minuten

Carlotta strahlt vor Freude. Ihre Mama hat gestern Waffeln gebacken und es sind noch welche übrig. Und ausnahmsweise darf sie diese heute mit in den Kindergarten nehmen. Mama hat gestern extra noch Petra, die Erzieherin, gefragt. Und Petra war einverstanden. Carlotta freut sich schon sehr auf die Frühstückspause und kann es kaum erwarten.

Als es dann endlich so weit ist, rennt sie zu ihrer Kindergartentasche und holt ihre Brotdose mit den Waffeln heraus. Die anderen Kinder holen ebenfalls ihr Essen.

Da hören sie plötzlich, wie jemand weint. Lukas steht im Gruppenraum und hat seine Tasche in der Hand. „Leer", schluchzt er. „Ich habe mein Essen zu Hause vergessen." Lukas ist ganz traurig.

Da hat Petra eine Idee. „Wie wäre es denn, wenn wir heute mal etwas anderes machen. Wir veranstalten ein Büfett. Das heißt: Jeder legt sein Essen in die Mitte und wir teilen alles. Dann hat jeder etwas zu essen und außerdem macht Teilen Spaß."

Alle Kinder sind einverstanden – alle, bis auf Carlotta. Sie hatte sich doch so auf ihre Waffeln gefreut. Und jetzt sollte sie sie weggeben? Carlotta hält ihre Dose fest an sich geklammert. Das bemerken auch die anderen. Aber Petra sagt, dass das schon in Ordnung ist, wenn Carlotta nicht mitmachen möchte. Die anderen Kinder legen ihr Essen in die Mitte: Lili hat einen Apfel dabei, Valentin ein Käsebrötchen, Ali ein paar Trauben, Selma ein Butterbrot und Linnea eine Banane. Petra schneidet alles in kleine Stücke und dann kann es schon losgehen. Jedes Kind darf sich aus der Mitte nehmen, worauf es Appetit hat.

Bald darauf hört man ein zufriedenes Schmatzen. „Mmh, dein Apfel ist sehr lecker", sagt Valentin. „Das stimmt", erwidert Ali, „aber hast du schon von dem Käsebrötchen probiert? Das schmeckt auch ganz toll." Die Kinder tauschen ihr Essen und unterhalten sich darüber. Nur Carlotta sagt nichts. Und ihre Waffeln schmecken ihr plötzlich auch nicht mehr. Traurig sitzt sie am Tisch. Dicke Tränen kullern ihr übers Gesicht.

„Was ist denn mit dir los?", fragt Petra. „Ich will auch mitmachen", schluchzt Carlotta und schiebt ihren Waffelteller in die Mitte. Petra nimmt ihre Waffeln und schneidet sie in kleine Stücke. Ein größeres Stück lässt sie auf Carlottas Teller, die anderen Stücke legt sie in die Mitte. „Darf ich mir denn auch eine Traube nehmen?", fragt Carlotta vorsichtig. „Na klar", sagt Ali. „Und du musst unbedingt noch von dem Butterbrot probieren", ruft Selma.

Carlotta ist zufrieden. Teilen macht richtig Spaß. Und zum Schluss beschließen alle, dass sie so ein Büfett bald wieder einmal machen wollen.

Idee: Leah Schäfer

Teilen macht Spaß

Reimgedicht

Carlotta kann es kaum erwarten,
sie will in den _______________ (Kindergarten).

Denn heute darf sie Waffeln essen,
doch Lukas hat sein Brot _______________ (vergessen).

Die Kinder wollen sich beeilen
und mit ihm ihr Essen _____________ (teilen).

Nur Carlotta will das nicht
und macht ein trauriges _______________ (Gesicht).

Den Kindern macht es großen Spaß,
zu essen gibt's für jeden _______________ (was).

Carlotta fühlt sich ganz allein,
sie will auch ein Teil der Gruppe _______________ (sein).

Jetzt teilen alle - das ist toll
und machen ihre Teller ______________ (voll).

Astronaut Freddy und seine Rakete

Mitmachgeschichte auf dem Mond

Alter: ab 3 Jahren

Dauer: 15 Minuten

Astronaut Freddy ist gerade aufgewacht. Er ist noch ein bisschen müde, gähnt ganz laut und streckt sich erst einmal.
Gähnen und sich strecken. Dabei die Arme ganz weit nach oben dehnen.

Doch plötzlich hat er es ganz eilig, denn ihm ist gerade etwas ganz Wichtiges eingefallen. Er darf heute mit seiner Rakete zum Mond fliegen. Schnell geht er ins Bad zum Zähneputzen. Denn auch ein Astronaut braucht blitzeblanke Zähne. Er schraubt seine Zahnpasta auf, gibt sie auf die Zahnbürste und los geht es.
Zahnpastatube aufdrehen, Zahnpasta auf die Bürste geben, Zahnpastatube wieder zudrehen und Zahnputzbewegungen ausführen.

Zum Frühstücken ist er jetzt viel zu aufgeregt. Er zieht sich seinen Raumanzug an – erst ein Bein, dann das nächste. Danach die Arme und anschließend den Reißverschluss noch schließen. Zum Schluss muss noch der Helm aufgesetzt werden.
Die Anziehbewegungen ausführen.

Freddy nimmt seinen Astronautenrucksack und setzt ihn auf. Gestern Abend hat er sich schon eine Flasche Wasser, ein Käsebrot und ein paar Kekse eingepackt, falls er doch noch Hunger bekommt. Er läuft zu seiner Garage. Freddy hat eine ganz besondere Garage. Sie ist ganz hoch und oben auf dem Dach befindet sich ein großes Tor, das man aufklappen kann. Und darin steht seine Rakete Frieda.
Den Rucksack aufsetzen und Gehbewegungen machen.

„Guten Morgen, liebe Frieda!", begrüßt der Astronaut die Rakete. „Jetzt geht es gleich los. Nur noch schnell tanken." Freddy schraubt Friedas Tankdeckel auf, nimmt den großen Kanister aus der Ecke und füllt die Rakete randvoll mit Treibstoff.
Den Tankdeckel aufschrauben, die Rakete betanken und zuschrauben.

Freddy klettert die Leiter rauf und setzt sich in die Rakete. Er schnallt sich an und gibt in sein Raketen-Navi „Mond" ein.
Eine imaginäre Leiter hinaufsteigen, sich anschnallen und Knöpfe am Computer drücken.

Dann geht der Countdown los: 10, 9, 8, 7, 6, 5, 4, 3, 2, 1, Start! Die Rakete setzt sich in Bewegung. Freddy wird ganz schön durchgeschüttelt.
Gemeinsam laut mitzählen und bei „Start" in die Luft springen. Danach wild zappeln.

Freddy schaut aus dem Fenster. Alles wird kleiner – zuerst die Tiere und Menschen, dann die Häuser in den Städten. Er fliegt immer höher und höher. Mittlerweile ist er schon so hoch, dass er bereits den Weltraum sehen kann. Überall funkeln Millionen Sterne. Und ganz klein unter sich kann Freddy jetzt auch die Erde erkennen.
Die Hand über die Augen halten und so tun, als würde man etwas genau betrachten.

Da meldet sich das Raketen-Navi und sagt, dass sie jetzt gleich auf dem Mond landen werden. Freddy freut sich. Jetzt ist es endlich so weit!
Die Arme in die Luft strecken und jubeln.

Die Rakete landet auf dem Mond und Freddy klettert die Leiter hinunter.
Eine imaginäre Leiter hinunterklettern.

Vorsichtig tastet er mit seinem Bein nach dem Boden. Ob er vielleicht einsinkt? Nein, alles gut. Freddy kann beruhigt losgehen.
Sich mit beiden Händen an der Leiter festhalten, dabei mit einem Bein vorsichtig den Boden ertasten.

„Schau mal, Frieda, wie toll es hier ist", ruft er seiner Rakete zu. Freddy hüpft voller Freude über die weite Fläche des Mondes.
Auf der Stelle hüpfen.

Er bückt sich und hebt ein paar Steine auf, die er in seine Tasche packt. „Die nehme ich mit nach Hause. Dann kann ich mich immer an diesen tollen Ausflug erinnern.
In die Hocke gehen, Steine einsammeln und in eine Tasche packen. Danach die Tasche umhängen und aufstehen.

Zum Schluss macht er noch ein Bild von seiner Rakete Frieda, wie sie da so auf dem Mond steht.
Ein Foto machen.

Dann klettert er wieder seine Leiter hoch, setzt sich auf seinen Platz und schnallt sich an. Diesmal gibt er in sein Raketen-Navi „Zu Hause" ein.
Eine imaginäre Leiter hinaufsteigen, sich anschnallen und Knöpfe am Computer drücken.

Dann beginnt der Countdown: 10, 9, 8, 7, 6, 5, 4, 3, 2, 1, Start! Die Rakete setzt sich in Bewegung. Freddy wird wieder ganz schön durchgeschüttelt.
Gemeinsam laut mitzählen und bei „Start" in die Luft springen. Danach wild zappeln.

Freddy schaut aus dem Fenster und sieht den Mond immer kleiner werden. Zufrieden lehnt er sich zurück und sagt: „Das war ein schöner Tag!"

Idee: Leah Schäfer

Mäuseadvent in der alten Villa

Aufpassgeschichte

Alter: ab 4 Jahren

Dauer: 10 Minuten

Material: 3 Nüsse für jedes Kind, Plätzchen

In der **Alten** Gasse unten in der **Altstadt** wohnen Oma Dorle und Opa Rudi in einer **alten** Villa – und in ihrer Küche lebt schon seit vielen Jahren die Maus Alf unter dem **alten** Küchenschrank. Immer morgens, wenn Oma Dorle an der **alten** Spüle das Geschirr abwäscht und Opa Rudi zum Holzschnitzen im Schuppen verschwindet, huscht Alf unter den **alten** Küchentisch. Dort sucht er nämlich heimlich nach heruntergefallenen Krümeln.

Alf kann es kaum erwarten, denn Oma Dorle und Opa Rudi frühstücken heute nicht nur knusprige Brötchen mit hausgemachter Kirschmarmelade, sondern sie haben auch die Keksdose mit den selbst gebackenen Adventsplätzchen geöffnet. Hm, wie die Plätzchen duften! Der ganze Raum riecht ganz wunderbar nach Anis, Nelken und Zimt, nach Kardamom, Muskat und Vanille. Am Adventskranz brennen Kerzen und auch Tannengrün verströmt einen angenehmen Duft.

Alfs Schnurrbarthaare zittern aufgeregt und ihm läuft das Wasser im Mund zusammen. Als Oma Dorle das Geschirr hinüber zur **alten** Spüle trägt, flitzt Alf aus seinem Versteck. Aber plötzlich bremst er ab: Huch! Was ist denn da los? Unter dem **alten** Küchentisch sitzt ja schon jemand! Eine fremde Maus knuspert in aller Seelenruhe an einem Stückchen Zimtstern!

Vorsichtig tappt Alf näher, während Oma Dorle klappernd die **alten** Teller und Tassen in den **alten** Küchenschrank einräumt. „Was machst du hier?“, fragt Alf die fremde Maus. „Ich frühstücke! Das siehst du doch!“ „Warum frühstückst du denn hier?“, möchte Alf wissen. „Weil ich Hunger habe! Das kannst du dir doch denken!“, antwortet die andere Maus. „Aber warum frühstückst du bei uns in der **alten** Villa?“ „Warum denn nicht? Du bist ja auch hier!“ „Ich wohne aber schon ewig unter dem **alten** Küchenschrank!“, erklärt Alf. „Jetzt wohne ich eben auch hier!“, antwortet die andere Maus. „Wo es so herrlich nach Advent duftet, da bleibe ich gern!“

Die fremde Maus hat kaum zu Ende gesprochen, da beginnt Oma Dorle mit dem **alten** Besen unter dem **alten** Küchentisch zu kehren. Mit einem kräftigen Schwung erfasst der Besen die beiden Mäuse und fegt sie unter den **alten** Küchenschrank. Sie purzeln bis vors Mauseloch, rappeln sich auf und klopfen sich erst einmal Krümel und Staub aus dem Fell.

„Schön hast du's hier! Sehr gemütlich!", meint die fremde Maus und verschwindet im Wandloch. „Ich zieh bei dir ein!", ruft sie von drinnen. „Ich wollte schon immer mal in einer **alten** Villa unter einem **alten** Küchenschrank wohnen! Außerdem können wir nun gemeinsam Advent und Weihnachten feiern! Ist das nicht herrlich?"

Alf denkt nach: Warum eigentlich nicht? Ein bisschen Gesellschaft kann nicht schaden. Krümel gibt es hier jede Menge und in der **alten** Villa ist schließlich genug Platz.

Oma Dorle hat sich unterdessen an den **alten** Küchentisch gesetzt und kichert leise vor sich hin. „Das hat ja gut geklappt!", murmelt sie. Sie beobachtet die flackernden Adventskerzen, beißt zufrieden in eine Kokosmakrone und lässt mit Absicht ein Stückchen auf den Fußboden fallen. Oma Dorle und Opa Rudi wissen nämlich schon lange, dass die Maus Alf unter ihrem **alten** Küchenschrank wohnt. Und damit er immer satt wird, versorgen sie ihn tagtäglich unauffällig mit Krümeln – morgens, mittags und abends. Ja, und damit Alf nicht mehr allein ist, hat Opa Rudi eine andere Maus aus dem Schuppen in die **alte** Villa mitgebracht. Außerdem denken die beiden **Alten** auch an sich, denn ein bisschen Gesellschaft kann ihnen nicht schaden.

UND SO GEHT'S:

Jedes Kind erhält als Spieleinsatz 3 Nüsse. Lesen Sie die Geschichte vor. Die Kinder hören aufmerksam zu, denn immer dann, wenn das Wort oder die Silbe **alt** fällt, erheben sich alle kurz von ihren Plätzen und setzen sich wieder hin. Steht ein Kind an der falschen Textstelle auf, muss es eine Nuss abgeben. Ziel ist es, möglichst alle Nüsse zu behalten, weil sie nach Spielende von den Kindern gegen die gleiche Anzahl Adventsplätzchen eingetauscht werden.

Gut, dass die Kinder die Nüsse untereinander teilen können und somit jedes Kind Plätzchen bekommt.

Idee: Karin Schäufler

Kati, Ben und der Zoobesuch

Quatschgeschichte

Alter: ab 3 Jahren
Dauer: 15 Minuten

Kati und Ben machen heute einen Ausflug in den Zoo. Es geht schon früh los. Doch zuerst müssen sie frühstücken und die Zähne putzen. Ben gibt die Marmelade auf seine Zahnbürste. *(Halt!)*

Danach setzen sie sich an den Frühstückstisch und Kati streicht sich Zahnpasta auf ihr Brötchen. *(Halt!)*

Jetzt müssen sie sich schnell anziehen. Sie setzen ihre Schuhe auf und binden ihre Mützen zu. *(Halt!)*

Sie fahren mit dem Auto. Mama setzt sich in den Kindersitz und Ben setzt sich ans Steuer. *(Halt!)* Mama, Ben und Kati fahren durch die Stadt. Dort gibt es viele Ampeln. Immer wenn die Ampeln rot sind, darf Mama weiterfahren. *(Halt!)*

Im Zoo angekommen, gehen sie zuerst zu den Eisbären. Ihr Fell ist ganz grün. *(Halt!)* Ein Eisbär spielt mit einem großen Ball. Er stupst ihn mit seiner Schnauze an und läuft dann hinterher.

Im Gehege nebenan sind die Elefanten. Sie sind groß und grau und haben kleine Stupsnasen im Gesicht. *(Halt!)* Einer der Elefanten taucht seinen Rüssel in einen Eimer Wasser und versucht, die Kinder nass zu spritzen. Igitt – nichts wie weg hier.

Kati zieht Ben mit sich. „Komm, lass uns in das Streichelgehege gehen. Dort sind Ziegen, Schafe, Kaninchen und Meerschweinchen." „Au ja." Ben ist begeistert. „Dann können wir wieder auf den Meerschweinchen reiten." *(Halt!)*

Nachdem sie alle Tiere gestreichelt haben, gehen sie erst einmal zu den Seelöwen. Da ist gerade Fütterungszeit. Sie bekommen gerade ihr Futter: Schnitzel mit Pommes und Salat. *(Halt!)*

Kati, Ben und Mama haben langsam auch Hunger. Aber zum Glück haben sie ihre Rucksäcke mit ihren Brotdosen und Trinkflaschen dabei. Schnell suchen sie eine Bank, auf der sie schlafen können. *(Halt!)*

Ben öffnet seine Brotdose und nimmt einen Schluck Wasser daraus. *(Halt!)*
Kati beißt in ihr Brötchen. Das schmeckt lecker. Zum Schluss werfen sie die Rucksäcke in den Mülleimer und packen den Abfall wieder ein. *(Halt!)*

Frisch gestärkt wollen die drei jetzt zu den Löwen gehen. „Schau mal, Mama", sagt Kati, „der Löwe hat aber tolle Streifen." *(Halt!)*
„Ja", sagt Mama, „und das Weibchen hat eine große buschige Mähne." *(Halt!)*

Bevor sie das nächste Gehege erreichen, kommen sie an einem Eisstand vorbei. Dort gibt es die leckersten Eissorten: Vanille, Schokolade, Erdbeere, Zitrone, Stinkesocken, Himbeere. *(Halt!)*

Mama und Ben nehmen ihr Eis in einer Waffel. Kati hat lieber einen Becher. Dann tropft es nicht so und sie kann es mit Messer und Gabel essen. *(Halt!)*

Nachdem das Eis gegessen ist, gehen die drei jetzt zu den Flamingos. Sie sind quietschgelb und stehen gern auf drei Beinen. *(Halt!)*

Langsam wird es Zeit, nach Hause zu gehen. Doch bevor sie den Zoo verlassen, will Ben unbedingt noch zu den Giraffen. Er mag sie sehr gern, denn Giraffen haben sehr lange Ohren. *(Halt!)*

Ben, Kati und Mama gehen zum Parkplatz. Dort steht ihr Flugzeug. *(Halt!)*
Sie steigen ein und fliegen los. *(Halt!)*

Zu Hause angekommen, ziehen sie noch ihr Abendessen aus und essen ihre Kleider. *(Halt!)*

Kati und Ben dürfen noch das Sandmännchen putzen und schauen sich anschließend die Zähne an. *(Halt!)*

Jetzt geht es schnell ins Bett. Es war ein langer Tag. Ben legt sich auf seine Decke und deckt sich mit seiner Matratze zu. *(Halt!)*

Kati schaut sich noch schnell eine Nachttischlampe an. Dann macht auch sie das Bilderbuch aus. *(Halt!)*

Gute Nacht, ihr beiden!

UND SO GEHT'S:
Im Text sind immer wieder Fehler eingebaut. Sobald die Kinder einen Fehler bemerken, springen sie auf und rufen laut: Halt! Danach sagen die Mädchen und Jungen, wie es richtig heißen muss.

Idee: Leah Schäfer

Das Gespenst und Ritter Roland

Fortsetzungsgeschichte

Alter: ab 5 Jahren

Dauer: 10 Minuten

Das kleine Gespenst spukte um Mitternacht durch die Burg. „Immer diese Spukerei", maulte es vor sich hin. „Ich will nachts auch mal schlafen. Hier ist ja um diese Uhrzeit überhaupt nichts los." Durch das Geschimpfe des kleinen Gespensts wurde der junge Ritter Roland wach. Er stand auf, schlüpfte in seine Hausschuhe und schaute nach, woher dieser Lärm kam …

WIE KÖNNTE ES WEITERGEHEN?

- Roland und das Gespenst erschrecken sich fürchterlich voreinander und freunden sich an.
- Sie helfen sich gegenseitig: Roland leistet dem Gespenst beim Spuken Gesellschaft und das kleine Gespenst begleitet den jungen Ritter tagsüber.
- Sie finden eine Schatzkarte und gehen auf Schatzsuche.

UND SO GEHT'S:

Erzählen Sie den Kindern den Anfang einer Geschichte. Danach ist das erste Kind an der Reihe und darf die Geschichte weitererzählen. Wenn es seinen Teil erzählt hat, ist das nächste Kind dran. So geht es immer weiter, bis die Geschichte ein Ende findet.

Tipp: Führen Sie einen Erzählstein ein. Immer derjenige, der mit Erzählen dran ist, bekommt den Stein in die Hand. Er gibt Sicherheit und signalisiert den anderen, dass sie jetzt gerade zuhören sollen.

Idee: Leah Schäfer

Kapitel 4

Reime & Rätsel

Muh macht die Kuh

Einfache Reime

Alter: ab 3 Jahren
Dauer: ca. 5 Minuten

Die Maus ist im ____ (Haus).

Die Kuh macht ____ (Muh).

Der Hase hat 'ne kurze ____ (Nase).

Der Igel sieht sich nie im ____ (Spiegel).

Der Wolf fährt gerne ___ (Golf).

Durch die Rinne kommt 'ne ____ (Spinne).

Die Hand steckt im ___ (Sand).

Den süßen Kuchen muss man ___ (suchen.)

Idee: Marion Bischoff

Zum Fasching geh ich als ...

Rätselreime

Alter: ab 4 Jahren
Dauer: 5 Minuten

1 Zum Fasching geht Frieda als
Pirat und fährt auf hoher See,
und Paula hat 'nen Zauberstab,
denn sie ist eine ______ (Fee).

2 Zum Fasching geht Max als Dompteur,
mit Peitsche und mit Hut,
und Emil kommt als Hexer rein: das steht
ihm richtig ______ (gut).

3 Zum Fasching geht Jan als Pilot
und macht sich fein und schick,
und Timo wird ein Hummelchen, schön
weich und rund und ______ (dick).

4 Zum Fasching geht Karla als Vampir
und sieht ganz gruslig aus,
und Anne hat 'nen langen Schwanz, denn
sie ist eine ______ (Maus).

Idee: Karin Schäufler

Ich fühle mich mal so, mal so

Reimrätselgedicht zu Gefühlen

Alter: ab 5 Jahren

Dauer: 10 Minuten

Ich fühle mich nicht immer gut,
bin manchmal gar nicht heiter,
bin traurig und zutiefst betrübt,
doch ich mach' trotzdem ______ (weiter).

Ich fühle mich oft voller Kraft,
bin glücklich, mutig, froh,
freu' mich an vielen Dingen sehr
und mach' auch weiter ______ (so).

Ich fühle mich manchmal ganz krank,
dann geht es mir nicht gut,
bin schwach und lustlos stundenlang,
doch ich schöpf' wieder ______ (Mut).

Mal auf, mal ab. Mal so, mal so:
Es wird noch vieles geben!
Doch ich bin ich und freue mich
auf dieses tolle ______ (Leben).

Idee: Karin Schäufler

Wer bin ich?

Tierische Rätsel

Alter: ab 3 Jahren
Dauer: 5 Minuten

1 Ich bin klein, seh' niedlich aus,
ich bin nicht schnell und trag' mein Haus!
(Schnecke)

2 Ich habe Schuppen, schwimme gern,
an Land zu gehen liegt mir fern!
(Fisch)

3 Ich bin bunt, hab' zarte Flügel,
schwebe sanft dort übern Hügel!
(Schmetterling)

4 Ich wache über Haus und Hof,
ich belle laut und bin nicht doof!
(Hund)

5 Ich bin verschmust, kann sehr gut schauen,
bin manchmal frech und kann miauen!
(Katze)

6 Ich hab' Punkte, bin sehr klein,
bin Rot und Schwarz, wer kann ich sein?
(Marienkäfer)

Idee: Karin Schäufler

Alle zu Tisch!

Rätselreime rund ums Essen

Alter: ab 3 Jahren
Dauer: 5 Minuten

Ich ess' nicht mit dem Schnabel,
drum nehm' ich eine _____ (Gabel).

Ich geb' auch meiner Puppe
mit einem Löffel _____ (Suppe).

Ich schneide mit dem Messer,
zerkleinern geht so _____ (besser).

Essen, trinken, lachen
sind alles feine _____ (Sachen).

Sehen, riechen, schmecken
heißt: Leckeres ent_____ (-decken).

Gemüse, Fleisch, auch Kuchen
kannst du gern ver_____ (-suchen).

Eier, Brot und Wurst,
ein Wasser gegen _____ (Durst).

Nudeln, Bulgur, Reis
servieren wir nur _____ (heiß).

Kartoffeln, Mus und Brei,
die wünsch' ich mir her _____ (-bei).

Gelee und Marmelade,
die schmecken niemals _____ (fade).

Eiscreme, Pudding, Milch,
die mag doch jeder _____ (Knilch).

Idee: Karin Schäufler

Wo sitzt der Floh?

Reimspiel mit Bewegungen

Alter: ab 4 Jahren

Dauer: 5 Minuten

Oh, oh, oh, wo sitzt der Floh?
Es juckt mich ______ (so).

Hand an den Kopf legen, um Ausschau zu halten. Sich selbst leicht kratzen.

Ist es vielleicht der kleine Wicht,
der immer mich hier zwickt und __________ (sticht)?

Mit zwei Fingern einen klitzekleinen Punkt anzeigen, dann mit dem Zeigefinger auf den Körper tippen.

Oder ist es der riesengroße
mit der kunterbunten _________ (Hose)?

Mit beiden Armen etwas ganz Großes darstellen, dann von oben nach unten über die Hose streichen.

Ist es der, der die Nase rümpft
und alle andern Flöhe _________ (schimpft)?

Die Nase rümpfen, mit erhobenem Zeigefinger auf die anderen Kinder zugehen.

Es ist der mit den Segelohren,
er hat sich gegen mich _________ (verschworen).

Große Ohren andeuten, Augen aufreißen.

Doch dann kommt er angeflogen.
Es war alles nur ____________ (gelogen).

Arme ausbreiten und durch den Raum fliegen.

Jetzt muss ich mich nur richtig waschen,
dann kommt kein Floh mehr her zum _________ (Naschen).

Waschbewegungen andeuten und winken.

Idee: Marion Bischoff

Nüsse, Pflaumen, Mais

Rätselreime zur Erntezeit

Alter: ab 3 Jahren
Dauer: 5 Minuten

1 Bohnensuppe ess ich gern,
drum ernte ich heut Bohnen!
Bohnen ernten dort am Strauch,
das könnte sich heut ______ (lohnen).

2 Erbsen schmecken süß und fein,
drum ernte ich heut Erbsen!
Doch roh soll man sie nicht verzehr'n,
damit ist nicht zu ______ (scherzen).

3 Mais ist schmackhaft, superlecker,
drum ernte ich heut Mais!
Auch Popcorn wird aus Mais gemacht,
wie jeder von uns ______ (weiß).

4 Pflaumen ess ich gerne frisch,
drum ernte ich heut Pflaumen!
Die sind so saftig und so süß,
Genuss für meinen ______ (Gaumen).

5 Nüsse knacken – das macht Spaß!
Drum ernte ich heut Nüsse!
Und weil ihr toll geraten habt,
bekommt ihr Schoko- ______ (Küsse).

Idee: Karin Schäufler

Tatütata, die Feuerwehr

Abzählreime

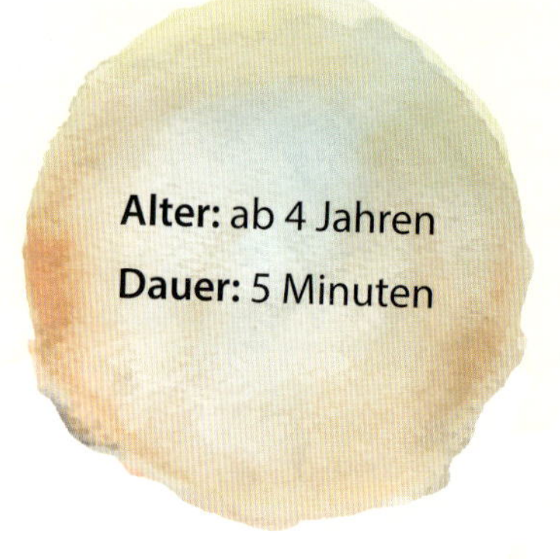

1 Tatütata, die Feuerwehr
kommt mit Martinshorn daher.
Braust mit Blaulicht durch das Land,
ist blitzschnell bei jedem Brand.
Schlauch ausrollen, Wasser an,
Feuer löschen – du bist dran.

2 5 kleine Mäuse wollen sich verstecken,
rennen durch die Scheune, bis in alle Ecken.
Ecken gibt's nur vier,
du kleine Maus bleibst hier.

3 Es war einmal ein Elefant,
der trötete durchs ganze Land.
Trötet hier und trötet dort,
trötet an so manchem Ort.
Trötet auch vor deinem Haus,
es ist zu laut und du bist raus.

4 1, 2, 3, 4, 5, 6, 7,
ich will mit dem Flugzeug fliegen.
Bis nach Spanien an das Meer,
am Sandstrand spielen mag ich sehr.
Dann spring ich in die Wellen rein
und du musst sein.

5 Es war einmal ein kleiner Zwerg,
der wohnte hinter einem Berg.
Sein Haus stand neben einer Wiese,
darauf lag ein großer Riese.
Doch der Riese schlief ganz tief,
schnarchte, bis das Haus stand schief.
Der Zwerg sprang auf den Riesen drauf,
kitzelt ihn und weckt ihn auf.
Der Riese geht jetzt auch nach Haus,
1, 2, 3 – und du bist raus.

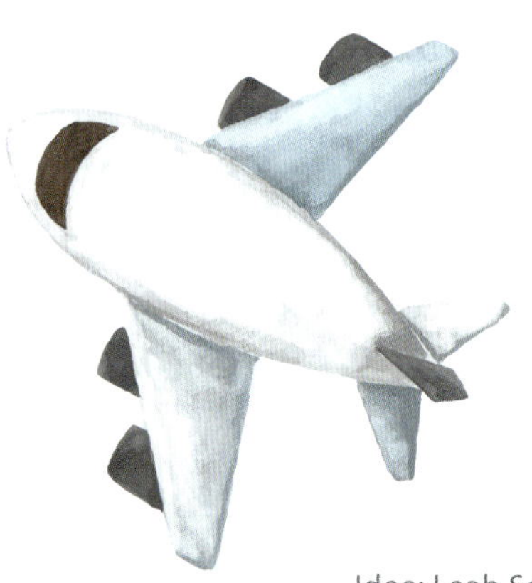

Idee: Leah Schäfer

Der Nikolaus hat Schnupfen

Reimrätselgedicht

Alter: ab 3 Jahren

Dauer: 10 Minuten

Der Nikolaus hat Schnupfen,
drum niest er in der Nacht.
Da sind ganz viele Kinder
vom Niesen _____ (aufgewacht).

Der Nikolaus erschreckt sich
und hat sich schnell versteckt.
So kann ihn keiner sehen,
so wird er nicht _____ (entdeckt).

Da täuscht er sich, der Weißbart,
denn Kinder, die sind schlau!
Sie laufen auf die Straße
und suchen ganz _____ (genau).

Da hinterm Schneemann kniet er,
der gute Nikolaus!
Er bibbert in der Kälte,
sieht ganz verfroren _____ (aus).

Die Kinder woll'n ihm helfen
und schnappen sich den Sack,
verteilen die Geschenke:
Puh, das war ganz schön _____
(knapp).

Der Nikolaus hat Schnupfen
und ruht sich erst mal aus,
trinkt heißen Tee, isst Kuchen,
dort hinten in dem _____ (Haus).

Am Morgen sind die Teller
und Stiefel prall und voll.
Der Nikolaus ist dankbar:
„Ihr Kinder, ihr seid _____ (toll)!"

Idee: Karin Schäufler

Hokuspokus 1, 2, 3

Zaubersprüche

Alter: ab 4 Jahren
Dauer: 5 Minuten

1 Hokuspokus 1, 2, 3,
alles jetzt verzaubert sei.
Ene mene Bärentatze,
du bist eine kleine Katze.

2 Hokuspokus 1, 2, 3,
alles jetzt verzaubert sei.
Ene mene grüner Klee,
Letizia ist jetzt eine Fee.

3 Hokuspokus 1, 2, 3,
alles jetzt verzaubert sei.
Ene mene Urlaubsreise,
alle Kinder sind ganz leise.

4 Hokuspokus 1, 2, 3,
alles jetzt verzaubert sei.
Ene mene Sauerkraut,
alle Kinder sind jetzt laut.

5 Hokuspokus 1, 2, 3,
alles jetzt verzaubert sei.
Ene mene Kuschelteddy,
vor mir stehen jetzt Spaghetti.

6 Hokuspokus 1, 2, 3,
alles jetzt verzaubert sei.
Ene mene Düsenflieger,
Jonas ist ein wilder Tiger.

7 Hokuspokus 1, 2, 3,
alles jetzt verzaubert sei.
Ene mene hohe Wand,
der Paul ist jetzt ein Elefant.

Idee: Leah Schäfer

Mmh, lecker!

Rätselreime zu Obst & Gemüse

Alter: ab 4 Jahren
Dauer: 5 Minuten

WELCHES GEMÜSE IST GEMEINT?

Schmecken wirklich wunderbar:
Tomate, Gurke, ________ (Paprika).

Diese Sorten kennt ihr auch:
Kürbis, Rotkohl, Mangold, _______ (Lauch).

Kohlrabi, Erbsen und Salat,
Kartoffeln, Gurke und _________ (Spinat).

FRUCHTIGE QUATSCHREIME

Süß wie Zucker sind Zitronen
und klein wie Nüsse sind ______ (Melonen).

Zum Mittag gibt es Traubenkerne,
mit Senf mag ich's besonders _______ (gerne).

Bananenschalen, Pflaumenstein
machen Müsli frisch und _________ (fein).

Idee: Karin Schäufler

Printed in December 1995 by Leva spa
for Edizioni Charta, Milan